MT 2023

D1565480

# HITLER'S
# EXECUTIONER

# HITLER'S EXECUTIONER

## JUDGE, JURY AND MASS MURDERER FOR THE NAZIS

## HELMUT ORTNER TRANSLATED BY SUSAN HAYNES-HUBER

FRONTLINE
BOOKS
LONDON

HITLER'S EXECUTIONER
Judge, Jury and Mass Murderer for the Nazis

This English edition published in 2018 by Frontline Books,
an imprint of Pen & Sword Books Ltd, Yorkshire - Philadelphia

Copyright © Helmut Ortner, 2018
ISBN: 978-1-47388-939-2

The right of Helmut Ortner to be identified as Author of this work has been
asserted by him in accordance with the Copyright, Designs and Patents Act 1988.
A CIP catalogue record for this book is available from the British Library
All rights reserved.

No part of this book may be reproduced or transmitted in any form or by any
means, electronic or mechanical including photocopying, recording or by any
information storage and retrieval system, without permission from the
Publisher in writing.

Printed and bound by TJ International Ltd, Padstow, Cornwall

Pen & Sword Books Ltd incorporates the imprints of Pen & Sword Archaeology,
Air World Books, Atlas, Aviation, Battleground, Discovery, Family History, History,
Maritime, Military, Naval, Politics, Social History, Transport, True Crime, Claymore
Press, Frontline Books, Praetorian Press, Seaforth Publishing and White Owl

For a complete list of Pen & Sword titles please contact:

PEN & SWORD BOOKS LTD
47 Church Street, Barnsley, South Yorkshire, S70 2AS, UK.
E-mail: enquiries@pen-and-sword.co.uk
Website: www.pen-and-sword.co.uk

Or

PEN AND SWORD BOOKS,
1950 Lawrence Road, Havertown, PA 19083, USA
E-mail: Uspen-and-sword@casematepublishers.com
Website: www.penandswordbooks.com

'The German perpetrator was not a special kind of German.
What we have to say about his convictions applies not only to him,
but to Germany as a whole.'

*Raul Hilberg*


'No, what happened in the past is not absent from the present simply
because it is past.'

*Alfred Grosser*

# Contents

# List of Plates

Roland Freisler, the President of the Volksgerichtshof, photographed on 1 September 1942. (Bundesarchiv, Bild 183-J03238/CC-BY-SA 3.0)

Roland Freisler, the laywer, with one of his clients, Otto Strasser, in 1930. (Author)

The inaugural gathering of Prussian law clerks at a camp in Jüterbog, north-eastern Germany, in 1933. (Bundesarchiv, Bild 183-H26606/CC-BY-SA 3.0)

The inauguration of the newly-appointed Attorney General, Heinrich Lautz, at the District Court in Berlin, on 31 August 1936. (Bundesarchiv, Bild 183-H25930/CC-BY-SA 3.0)

The four men who imposed Nazi ideology on the German legal system. (Bundesarchiv, Bild 183-J03166/CC-BY-SA 3.0)

The Reich Minister of Justice, Otto Georg Thierack (on the right), greets the new President of the People's Court, Roland Freisler, in his office at the end of August 1942. (Bundesarchiv, Bild 183-J03230/CC-BY-SA 3.0)

The opening of a session of the Volksgerichtshof, for the trials of those involved in the 20 July 1944 assassination attempt on Adolf Hitler. (Bundesarchiv, Bild 151-39-23/CC-BY-SA 3.0)

Roland Freisler during the 20 July 1944 trials. (Bundesarchiv, Bild 151-17-15 and Bild 151-29-35/CC-BY-SA 3.0)

Dr Carl Friedrich Goerdeler, the former Mayor of Leipzig, speaking during his trial for his involvement in the 20 July plot. (Bundesarchiv, Bild 151-58-16/CC-BY-SA 3.0)

Roland Freisler faces a witness as the latter gives the Nazi salute on entering the Volksgerichtshof during the trial of the 20 July plotters. (Bundesarchiv, Bild 151-10-11/CC-BY-SA 3.0)

Another of the accused in the 20 July trials, Carl Wentzel, appears before Roland Freisler. (Bundesarchiv, Bild 151-53-30A/CC-BY-SA 3.0)

Ferdinand Freiherr von Lüninck appearing before the Volksgerichtshof for his part in the 20 July plot. (Bundesarchiv, Bild 151-52-31A/CC-BY-SA 3.0)

Roland Freisler discussing plans of the *Wolfsschanze* complex during the trials after the 20 July plot. (Author)

The ruins of the Volksgerichtshof, photographed in 1951. (Bundesarchiv, B145 Bild-P054489/CC-BY-SA 3.0)

A memorial plaque on the site of the Volksgerichtshof.

Foreword

# The Presence of the Past

While I was working on this book, people often asked me whether it still made sense to talk about our National Socialist past today. Some of these people were acquaintances who think that our history now really is history. Others were friends who argue that we have to close the book sometime, even on such a horrific past as ours.

I pointed out that most Germans – and I am not talking about the older generation here – still refuse to believe what their fathers and grandfathers did and what they allowed to happen between 1933 and 1945. I used examples to illustrate the collective and individual attempts which have been made to escape this dark past. The reaction I received was frequently doubt, incomprehension, sometimes even protest. Not everyone was a Nazi, they said, not everyone committed crimes, and the Germans were not the only ones who had committed atrocities. To me, this stank of justification, the repression of guilt.

One thing is certain: on Day One after Hitler, many people in Germany were filled with shame and grief over what had happened in the preceding years. However, it is a sad fact that there were far more who, hardly had the nightmare ended, were already repressing what they had seen and experienced instead of accepting it into their consciousness as their own history. An entire people was trying to escape its past. That was then – and now?

Is the post-war generation, the generation to which I belong and which, to put it in the words of former German chancellor Helmut Kohl, enjoyed 'the mercy of late birth', now eager to draw a line under a dark but not too distant past? Is this politically and morally innocent generation now finally released from its obligation to face the Hitler regime and its inheritance? Or: does the responsibility of the members of this generation not begin with the question of where they stand with regard to the guilt of their grandparents and parents? With the question of whether they want to remember?

This book is about guilt and atonement, failure and cowardice. It is about courage, uprightness and resistance. It is a book about perpetrators and victims, repression and denial – and about remembering.

The main subject of this book is one particularly monstrous Nazi institution, one which could not have existed without the willing support and active compliance of legal professionals – the Volksgerichtshof (People's Court). It has received extensive historical, political, legal and journalistic coverage – as has the legal system in the Third Reich in general. Interested readers can trace the fatal course of jurisprudence in Hitler's Germany from its euphoric beginnings to its destructive end. Yet, despite the many works written by historians about the creation, structure, function and everyday workings of the Volksgerichtshof, there is very little literature on the life and work of Roland Freisler. It is with his name that the cruellest era of this tribune of terror is associated.

From 1942 to 1945, Freisler was President of the Volksgerichtshof. As early as 1934, however, he was already an untiring mastermind of National Socialist law. This book traces his career, his influence and his death. How did a grammar-school boy from a bourgeois, conservative background become such a ruthless dispenser of death sentences? How did his fanatical mind develop? What was his rigorous legal standpoint based on?

It is of course obvious that a mere personal biography is hardly going to produce new and surprising insights. History must not be reduced to persons alone, to public and private lives. In the past, Freisler has been portrayed as a demonic monster who stood for the German legal system under the Nazis, frequently in an attempt to relativise the evil deeds of thousands of his fellow Nazi judges by doing so. The fact is, Freisler was no demon in a red robe. He was simply a particularly consistent executor of the National Socialists' interpretation of the law.

This is why I decided to start with Freisler the man and proceed from there to the structures of National Socialist law, describing the correlation between them. The story of Roland Freisler's life is told in the context of his age and illustrated by numerous documents, especially in view of the fact that his role was by no means limited to that of President of the Volksgerichtshof.

As a lawyer, government official, publicist and judge under the Nazis, Freisler, completely free of opportunism, did not even need to bend the law. He simply interpreted and applied it ruthlessly in accordance with the wishes of the National Socialist regime. Any defendant appearing before him – especially in the last years of the War – could expect to receive a death sentence. This book is therefore also about the victims, their life stories and their fate. An extensive chapter documents their death sentences – court verdicts bearing mute testimony to a merciless legal system.

While researching this book, I spoke to many – perhaps the last – contemporary witnesses, to people who themselves were brought before the Volksgerichtshof and sentenced to death and who only survived because the War ended before the date scheduled for their execution. I also spoke with judges whose job it was to apply Nazi law and whose judgement often meant death for the accused. The impression I gained was that some of them seem to have no problem living with this heavy burden. They view themselves as unjustly accused, their belief in the Vaterland abused by the politicians. Hardly any admit personal responsibility. Not a trace of remorse or shame. On the contrary, many of them see themselves as victims of a 'fateful era'. During my interviews with former Nazi judges and prosecutors, I saw few signs of doubt on their part that their actions had been justified. They exhibited an almost sickening self-complacency.

In the 1970s, Hans Filbinger, prime minister of the federal state of Baden-Württemberg, hit the headlines when it was revealed that he had been responsible for death sentences as a wartime judge in the navy. Eventually, this led to his resignation – which was not entirely voluntary and not exactly typical for post-war Germany. At the time, author and playwright Rolf Hochhuth coined the term 'furchtbarer Jurist' (dreadful lawyer), and even today, these dreadful lawyers still maintain that the sentences they pronounced were legitimate.

The shameful justification put forward by these Nazi judges – 'What was legal then cannot be unlawful today' – had been used by many of them before Filbinger. It is the excuse so frequently heard after the War, with those involved claiming to have been bound by the law. The truth, however, is that between 1933 and 1945, with opportunistic and at times fanatical cold-bloodedness, German judges brought formally-applicable law to bear with an organized brutality and lack of scruples which rendered the Weimar Constitution no more than a worthless scrap of paper.

No-one forced them to do this. They were acting of their own free will, the legal minions and executors of the National Socialist regime. A few of these men still survive, old men now, and well provided for by state pensions. And most of them are still convinced that at the time, they were only doing their duty. Roland Freisler was no demon from the pit of hell; he was a typical representative of the German people. His career was a *German career*. He was the merciless agent of a merciless judiciary, a consistent accomplice to a murderous system, an exemplary murderer in judge's robes – and it was the Germans who made his deeds, his influence and his career possible.

The fact that this book, after having been translated into numerous languages, is now once again appearing in a new edition demonstrates that the desire of subsequent generations to understand *how it could happen* is unbroken. TV documentaries on Freisler such as the much-acclaimed MDR production entitled *Hitler's Williger Vollstrecker* ('Hitler's Willing Executioner'), which was broadcast by German TV channel ARD in many regions, have done their part.

This book speaks out against the dangers of forgetting the lessons of the past. Because it is not forgetting, but remembering, that sets us free.

*Helmut Ortner*
*Frankfurt am Main, August 2018*

Prologue

# A Death Sentence, or The Second Career of Roland Freisler

Friday, 17 November 1944. Shortly before 10 a.m., a closed van takes 21-year-old Margot von Schade across Berlin from the detention centre in Moabit to Bellevuestrasse – to the Volksgerichtshof. In silence, she sits opposite two other women: 23-year-old Barbara Sensfuss and 40-year-old Käthe Törber. All three women are charged with 'Wehrkraftzersetzung' (hindering the war effort). The trial is due to begin in just a few hours. What are they planning to do with the women? What can they expect?

Margot and the other two women had only been notified that morning that the trial would take place today. And now, as they drive through the streets of Berlin, only glimpsed through the windscreen over the driver's shoulder, she is despondent. And alone. She thinks of her family: her mother, her stepfather, her sister. Where are they now? She is gripped with fear.

An hour later: a vast chamber with chalk-white walls. Three chairs in front of the judge's bench – they are for the defendants. In rows to the left and right of them stand uniformed guards. They look intimidating: 'There is no escape', their faces seem to say. At the front end of the chamber, impossible to overlook as it hangs from the ceiling to the floor, a blood-red swastika flag. In front of it, on a slender pedestal, a bust of Hitler. Margot von Schade stares as if hypnotized at the huge red flag. It appears threatening. She risks a hurried glance at the public gallery, which is an anonymous mass of brown and black uniforms. She can hear the muted murmur of voices. It all seems so hazy and unreal.

One of the guards barked 'All stand!', and the order echoes through the chamber. Suddenly, there is silence. The door to the side of the judge's bench opens. The members of the court enter. Red robes, red caps, grey and black uniforms – the associate judges. And striding in front of them is the President: Roland Freisler. She looks into his face. For a second, their eyes meet. Then Freisler glances at his wristwatch. The trial begins . . .

Margot von Schade follows the proceedings of the tribunal as if in a trance. Later – she has no idea how much time has passed – she is suddenly shocked out of her daze: 'Defendant Schade! Stand!' Freisler's piercing voice is impossible to ignore. He reads out the bill of indictment out, item by item. But this is more than mere reading aloud – it is a tirade of accusations. He proclaims with pathos and theatrical gestures that the accused made subversive remarks in public following the 'cowardly and craven attack on our Führer on 20 July'. After a special radio bulletin reporting 'the Führer's miraculous escape', he continues, the accused stated in a derogatory tone: 'Bad luck'. And as if that were not enough, the accused actually commented in public that the 'criminal officers who carried out the attack' were 'not cowardly, but had in fact demonstrated great courage'.

A buzz of indignation spreads through the audience in the public gallery, rising in pitch as Freisler, his voice dripping with outrage, quotes from the indictment a word which must have seemed to every upright National Socialist the ultimate depravity: this degenerate girl had actually called the Führer a 'Scheissgefreiter' (damned private) – 'unbelievable!'

By now, Freisler has worked himself into a rage, and his fanatical gaze is fixed on Margot von Schade. She looks down at the floor. What can she say in answer to this venomous monologue? How can she make herself heard? How can she defend herself? Even if she does succeed in interrupting Freisler's tirade for a moment, he barks out a reprimand before she has managed to say more than a few sentences. Will no-one in the room help her? Where is her defence counsel? Margot von Schade feels powerless, completely at the mercy of this angry man and completely alone.

When they called the other two women to give evidence a short time before, the two women who were her fellow defendants but turned out to be witnesses for the prosecution, there was so much she had wanted to say. She had wanted to tell the court what really happened after that radio announcement on 20 July, but Freisler had not permitted her to speak.

And there, sitting just a few steps away from her, are the two women who were once her friends and are now shifting all the blame to her. They are only trying to save their own skins. And Margot von Schade senses that this tribunal welcomes every denunciation. A lesson that teaches the onlookers in the courtroom exactly what happens to anyone who places themselves outside the 'Volksgemeinschaft' (national community). It's like a mediaeval witch-hunt, she thinks. And I am the witch, ready for burning.

Later, tired and no longer able to follow this macabre drama, she hears the monotonous voice of her defence counsel. Her summing-up sounds rehearsed, indifferent. But is this woman really 'her' counsel? No, Margot does not trust her. And why should she? They have only spoken once before today, in the detention centre, and just for a few minutes. The lawyer knows nothing about her, nor is she interested in getting to know her. To her, Margot is just a 'case', a number, and nothing more. The court has appointed her to 'defend' Margot, and she is simply doing what is expected of her.

Now, as the tribunal draws to a close, Margot von Schade senses how perilous her position is. In the past few hours, she has seen how the court treated her co-defendants as women who, though they had been 'misled', were 'at heart' honest and upright citizens. She heard their counsels present arguments in their defence, and even Freisler had expressed understanding for their behaviour.

Not so in her case. From the outset, Freisler's manner towards her was irritable and hostile. But why? Is it because she comes from an aristocratic family? After 20 July, is anyone with a 'von' before their surname suspected of having conspired with Stauffenberg? Is Freisler so hard to her because she does not answer with the penitence and remorse he expects of her?

These are the thoughts running through her head. Wasn't there a cynical tone in Freisler's voice just now when he said: 'This is the family, the environment the accused comes from . . .' Hadn't he growled, with feigned indignation, 'Tell me who you associate with and I'll tell you who you are . . .'? Every small detail was used against her, even the letter her sister Gisela sent her while she was in prison. The guards had of course opened it, and it was produced as incriminating evidence. In the letter, Gisela had described a pleasant evening out, dancing and singing with friends. Freisler saw this as further proof of her decadent family background.

This Margot von Schade, this rebellious, spoilt brat, had dared to 'insult the Führer most shamefully in public' and with her subversive comments, even expressed regret that the assassination attempt had failed. He, Freisler, was determined to make an example of this treacherous young woman as a warning to others.

The court retires to consider its verdict. But is that verdict not a foregone conclusion? Margot von Schade sits depressed and uneasy on her chair. Time appears to stand still. She feels as if she were in a vacuum.

She has completely lost her sense of time when the president and the associate judges re-enter the courtroom to pronounce sentence. Once again, Freisler's piercing voice rings out:

'Defendant Sensfuss – stand!'

Not guilty!

'Defendant Törber – stand!'

Not guilty!

Margot sees a glimmer of hope. If the other two were acquitted, I might get away with only a prison sentence . . .

'Defendant von Schade – stand!'

Margot's gaze is fixed straight ahead. Red robe, red flag . . .. the bust of the Führer. . .

'For hindering the war effort, aiding and abetting the enemy, defeatist comments and treason, I sentence you . . . to death!'

The death sentence? For me? That can't be true . . . I'm not a criminal or a murderer . . . Death sentence? While Freisler reads out the reasons for the judgement, she tries to process the unbelievable implications of the sentence. Death penalty? Is her life to be over so soon? Just because of a few flippant remarks while out with friends? The other two women were there as well. They laughed and cracked jokes. Why were they acquitted? Why do I have to die?

A death sentence for this? It can't be true!

Her eyes search the crowd, looking for the face of her stepfather, who she knows is in the public gallery. Is it true? Are they going to kill her? Does she have to die? Will today, the 17 November, really be the day when her fate is signed? Is all life has left in store for her the guillotine?

Margot von Schade, now Margot Diestel, survived. The premature end of the 'Thousand-Year Reich' saved her life. The advance of the Russian forces prevented her execution. She survived the air raids in her cell, then the tortuous transfer from Berlin to the prison in Stolpen in Saxony. And it was here that in the last days of the War, a courageous guard defied orders to shoot all prisoners before the arrival of the Soviet troops. Instead – the Red Army was at the gates of the city – he issued discharge papers: 'Margot von Schade is herewith discharged'. Stamped, signed, dated. It was 3 May 1945.

Four days later, in Reims in the west of France, General Jodl signed the German capitulation. The War was over.

Twenty-four years later, Margot von Schade – one of the few survivors – began to write down her life story: her youth, the denunciation, her arrest, the death sentence from the Volksgerichtshof, her gruelling ordeal in various prisons, the constant fear of death. The record was actually only intended for her grandchildren. She wanted them to know what had happened in Germany. But almost by coincidence, the story became a moving historical document. Her memories of the Nazi reign of terror – written down by her husband, Arnold Diestel – found a publisher. The book is set to open the eyes of the young generation.

'We must not allow this to happen again.'

Looking back, Margot Diestel does not see herself in any way as a member of the resistance. However, even as a young girl, she already recognized what the reign of the Nazis was doing to Germany and the world: 'As a 21-year-old in the quiet and peaceful town of Demmin, I knew some things and suspected many others. The criminal regime filled me with disgust, and I was lippy. I would loudly voice my opinions to anyone, as if we were living in peacetime, as if there were no Gestapo and no concentration camps', she remembers. Her nonchalance almost cost her life – in the name of the German people. The statement of the reasons for the judgement is included in her book. It documents an era of legally-sanctioned terror.

### In the name of the German people

In the criminal proceedings against
horse trainer Margot von Schade from Demmin, born 27 March 1923 in Burg Zievrich (district Bergheim a.d. Erft)
for subversion of the war effort
First Senate of the Volksgericht, in response to the charges brought by the Oberreichsanwalt (senior Reich prosecutor), in the main hearing on 17 November 1944, involving:

as judges:
President of the Volksgerichtshof
Dr Freisler, Chairman
Landgerichtsdirektor (regional court director) Dr Schlemann,
SA Brigadeführer Hauer,
NSKK-Obergruppenführer
Regierungsdirektor Offermann
Deputy Gauleiter Simon,
as representative of the Oberreichsanwalt:
Landgerichtsrat (regional court judge) von Zeschau,

First Senate of the Volksgerichtshof ruled as follows:
Margot von Schade glorified the would-be assassins of 20 July, expressed regret that the attempt on the life of our Führer had failed, attempted to vilify our Führer and in shameless self-abasement, engaged in 'political' discourse with a Russian.

Forever dishonoured, she is therefore sentenced to death.

Reasons:

The defendant admits to commenting 'Bad luck!' on the attempted assassination.

The bad luck being that the attempt was not successful!!!

This alone strikes her from our midst. We want absolutely nothing to do with an individual who expresses solidarity with traitors to our people, the Führer and the Reich, traitors whose despicable plan, if it had succeeded, would have plunged us into disgrace and death.

Moreover, however, Margot von Schade, and this may serve to reveal the full extent of her depravity, made these base comments on the basis of a fundamentally traitorous and dishonourable attitude . . .

It is hardly surprising that, as she herself admits, she announced that she and her female friends were going to the reception for the Führer's speech with the words 'Herr Hitler is speaking!' It is enough to fill anyone with anger and shame to hear a German woman speak in such a way in the year 1944 . . .

Any German who abases themselves so far as to engage in such discourse with a Bolshevik, who glorifies such cowardly acts of treason against our history, who attempts to vilify the Führer in such a way, also besmirches the honour of our entire nation. In the interests of maintaining our purity, we want nothing more to do with an individual who has completely abandoned their loyalty, their honour and their whole personality in this way, forever destroying them. Persons who spread subversion (§ 5 KSSVO), who make themselves the minions of our enemies of our people in their attempts to uncover potential weaknesses (§ 91 b StGB) must pay with their lives, because we are bound to protect the moral stance of our homeland and indeed that of our people, which is fighting for its life, at all costs.

As a convicted criminal, Margot von Schade must bear the costs.

Signed Dr Freisler Dr Schlemann

Forty-six years later, Steinhorst near Hamburg. Sitting opposite me is the same woman who was condemned to death by Freisler in Berlin.

How does she feel today when she reads her death sentence? Is she angry, does she want revenge? 'No', she says, shaking her head, 'I just feel paralysed and let down. Almost every judge in the Volksgerichtshof was restored to office after the War. None of them was called to take responsibility for their deeds or convicted, and that is disappointing.'

Life has been good to the vivacious girl of those days and the upright woman of today. Later, but not too late, she at least received compensation of a private nature. She could not expect state compensation in this country. She was a victim, not a perpetrator. And in Germany, the state tended to take more care of the latter.

Several months before this, I was already 'searching for clues' in a very quiet, elegant residential area of Munich, close to the Nymphenburg Canal. A modern apartment building with eleven apartments: on the door of the ground-floor flat on the left, a plain cardboard sign reads: Russegger. None of the neighbours has any idea that the old lady who lives among them is actually Marion Freisler, the widow of former President of the Volksgerichtshof Roland Freisler. 'She lives a very quiet life and hardly speaks to anyone', one of the building's residents tells me. And Frau Russegger has no wish to speak to me, either. Weeks before, I had sent a letter asking to interview her. There were so many questions I wanted to ask her; for example, what she thinks today of her husband's professional dealings and what she told her sons about their father. She did not answer my letter. I decided to travel to Munich. One last attempt, although it failed.

During my research, I came across newspaper articles from the year 1958. A Berlin Spruchkammer (de-nazification tribunal) – the last in Germany – had imposed an atonement fine of 100,000 marks on Freisler's estate. This sum corresponded to the value of two properties in Berlin which had been under the management of trustees since the end of the War and which Freisler's widow claimed were hers. For years, she had fought to regain ownership of the buildings on the grounds that they had been purchased with her dowry. However, the Spruchkammer ruled that they had been purchased by Freisler for his wife and paid for with his earnings. The tribunal based its decision on the fact that the instalments paid for the properties coincided with the dates when Freisler received his salary and the various stages of his career. Further investigation had also revealed that Frau Freisler was without financial means of her own.

After a hearing that lasted four-and-a-half hours, and which Freisler's widow, alias Frau Russegger, who was living in Frankfurt at the time, had not attended because 'it would just be too distressing for her', the tribunal rejected her appeal. The fine to the same amount, which had been imposed by the Berlin tribunal on 29 January 1958, corresponded to the value of the two properties, which were now seized by the court in place of the atonement fine.

Almost thirty years later, in February 1985, the widow, or rather her pension, made the headlines again. This time it was not at her own prompting. An SPD member of the Bavarian Landtag (state parliament), Günther Wirth, had made it public that after the War, Frau Rossegger received not only the usual widow's pension for her husband, who died in an air raid in Berlin, but also, since 1974, a so-called Schadensausgleichsrente (compensation pension) granted by the pension office in Munich on the grounds that if he had survived the War, Freisler 'would have been employed as a lawyer or senior civil servant'.

At the time, it was above all the ludicrous argumentation that created a stir. 'For constitutional reasons', the Bavarian welfare officers could not maintain that Freisler, if he had survived, 'would have been sentenced to death or at least to lifelong imprisonment.' Instead, it seemed to them 'equally probable' that the highest-ranking Nazi judge 'would have continued to work in the profession for which he was trained or another profession, particularly as the possibility of an amnesty or a ban on practising law for a limited period' would also have had to be considered.

The *Süddeutsche Zeitung* commented at the time that whoever 'contrived, formulated and approved' such a notification 'must have the soul of a butcher's dog'. The 'Münchner Rentenfall' (Munich pension case) triggered strong reactions in almost all the big German newspapers. 'How can someone who wanted, encouraged and prolonged the War be a victim of war?' asked Franz-Josef Müller, a Munich social democrat who had appeared before Freisler in 1943 at the age of 18 as a member of the 'White Rose' resistance group and had been sentenced to five years in prison by him.

Forty years after Freisler perished with the Third Reich, the question of his pension polarized opinions on how Germany was dealing with its Nazi past. A reader's letter to the *Süddeutsche Zeitung* said it was a disgrace 'that there are people who have nothing better to do than dig around in old pension records forty years after the end of the War'. And this was not an isolated voice.

Robert M.W. Kempner, American prosecuting counsel during the Nuremberg War Trials, also commented in the same newspaper: 'In addition to the war victims' compensation and her compensation pension, the widow also receives a widow's pension from social insurance', he wrote, and his detailed letter to the editor revealed further controversial points. 'Freisler', he continued, 'had never paid social insurance contributions, because he had his generous judge's salary. And Freisler's widow was not entitled to a widow's pension, because no pension was paid if a civil servant was guilty of inhumane behaviour. This is specified in Article 131 of the Grundgesetz (German constitution). In such cases, a pension is only granted if the employer, that is the state, makes up the missing amount. This means that the state must have paid a significant amount, as the widow receives social security.' At the end of his letter, Kempner criticised the fact that in considering the issue of his widow's pension, Freisler was classified as a president of the court and wrote that in his opinion, 'as [Freisler was] the gravedigger sounding the death knell of the Germany judicial system, the calculation should have been based on the standard wage of a gravedigger working in a public cemetery'.

Alarmed by the intense public reaction, the Bavarian Minister for Labour and Social Affairs at the time, Franz Neubauer (Christian Social Union), instructed his civil servants to correct the decision on the pension. However, he stated at a later press conference that 'for legal reasons, it was no longer possible' to withdraw the dubious document. Instead, the minister ruled that the war victim's pension should be excluded from pension increases until such time as the amount of the disputed compensation for damages was reached.

Despite headlines, letters to the editor and heated debate – the case of pension payments such as those to Freisler's widow were in no way uncommon.

To many, it may seem grotesque, even cynical, that the surviving relatives of leading Nazis claimed benefits and compensation, but in fact, the Bundesversorgungsgesetz (federal law on war pensions) contained a handy niche for just such cases. In the 1950s, those profiting from it included Lena Heydrich, widow of Reinhard Heydrich, SS-Obergruppenführer and architect of Hitler's 'Final Solution' to 'the Jewish problem', the daughters of Hermann Göring and Heinrich Himmler and the widow of the Gauleiter of Franconia, Julius Streicher, who after the War had her husband insured for his freelance work as publisher of the Nazi propaganda magazine Der Stürmer – and was awarded pension benefits of DM 46,000.

Dr Ernst Lautz, Oberreichsanwalt at the Volksgerichtshof and responsible for innumerable death sentences, received a supplementary pension payment of DM 125,000 after the War, and Dr Curt Rothenberger, state secretary in Hitler's Ministry of Justice and sentenced to seven years' imprisonment at the Nuremberg Trials, even received the sum of DM 190,726 on top of his generous monthly pension of over DM 2,000.

However, what was new about the Freisler case was that not only was the widow claiming benefits as a 'victim of war' and payment for her husband's previous 'achievements', but the calculation was based on the artificial projection of the theoretical professional career of a Nazi criminal up to the age of retirement. The arguments may have been absurd, and yet: there is every indication that the Munich civil servants had made a legally correct decision. It is an undisputed fact that Freisler was one of the most prolific mass murderers in the Nazi regime. Under his presidency – from 1942 to 1945 – and in part with he himself presiding as judge, the Volksgerichtshof passed an average of ten death sentences every day. But as Freisler did not fall into the Allies' hands after the War and was therefore not among the war criminals tried in Nuremberg, no judgement was ever passed on him.

Even at the Nuremberg Judges' Trial, the sentences passed were moderate prison terms which none of the accused served in full due to the generous granting of pardons. And there was little hope that judges in the newly-proclaimed Federal Republic of Germany would exact expiatory justice by sentencing their former colleagues. In the 1950s, in a questionable judgement, the Bundesgerichtshof (Federal Court of Justice) had drawn a line under the past by granting all Nazi-era judges a double 'Rechtsbeugungs-Prinzip', the right to pervert the course of justice: this meant that a judge could only be convicted of murder or other serious crimes if he was at the same time found guilty of perverting the course of justice. In the case of the Nazi jurists, this meant furnishing proof of 'direct intent' – an almost impossible task. It had to be established without doubt that the accused had knowingly or intentionally violated laws valid at the time. An absurd reasoning. Almost all judges in the Third Reich, and particularly the red-robed murderers in the Volksgerichtshof, were acting in complete harmony with the laws introduced by the Nazi regime of terror. And it would have been even more difficult to prove Freisler guilty of intention to pervert the course of justice than in the case of any of the other Nazi judges who survived the end of the War and, as a rule, continued their career on the bench in Chancellor Adenauer's new Germany.

Statistics from the Berlin justice department on surviving members of the Volksgerichtshof who are still alive speak for themselves. The jurists who were still alive in 1984, when the data were gathered, and who served on the bench after the War included two county court judges, one chief judge of a county court, two associate judges in regional courts, four chief judges in regional courts, four associate judges in higher regional courts, six public prosecutors, three senior public prosecutors and even two senate presidents. Volkgerichtshof judges who were not employed by the Federal Republic after the end of the Second World War remained the exception. So indeed, why not assume that Freisler would have escaped prosecution and gone on to launch a second successful career? In other words, the argumentation of the Munich social bureaucrats did have a certain logic. Freisler – a German career.

Margot Diesler, one of the few among Freisler's victims who survived, received a one-off compensation payment of DM 920 for what she had suffered. Yet the same state granted the widow of her tormentor a generous pension. It is not the fact that Freisler's widow was granted a pension in itself that is scandalous, but the justification that was offered. And even more distressing is the thought that Freisler could have continued as a judge under the new Republic like so many of his brown-shirted colleagues, that he might have continued to serve as an 'upholder of the law'.

There was to be no second career for Freisler. But what about his first career? How did an ambitious grammar-school boy and officer cadet become the National Socialist jurist and fanatical 'hanging judge' Roland Freisler? How did he become head of one of the most feared terror institutions in Nazi Germany – the People's Court?

Who was this Roland Freisler?

# Chapter 1

# The Ceremony

On the morning of 14 July 1934, a select group of prominent jurists and National Socialist Party members gathered in Berlin at Prinz-Albrecht-Strasse 2. There, in the building that had formerly housed the now disbanded Landtag (state parliament) of Prussia, everything had been meticulously prepared for the dramatic first appearance of the newly-formed Volksgerichtshof. At the front of the assembly hall, two huge swastika flags hung from the gallery to the floor. Between them stood a row of Nazi standard-bearers wearing highly-polished boots and forbidding expressions. Ornamental bushes and flower boxes were arranged in front of the speaker's podium, lending an austere freshness to the scene.

The rows of chairs facing the podium filled the whole chamber. Seated on them were the distinguished guests, wearing suits or uniforms, in the seats of honour Reichsführer-SS (Commander of the SS) Heinrich Himmler and beside him, Minister of Justice Franz Gürtner, who had held office for two years, and Reich Justice Commissioner Hans Frank. The president of the Reichsgericht, the supreme civil and criminal court, Erwin Bumke, and Oberreichsanwalt (senior Reich prosecutor) Karl Werner had arrived from Leipzig, where the court was based. Behind them sat representatives of the SA and SS, the Wehrmacht and judicial administration departments. And finally, in the last two rows, sat the thirty-two judges and associate judges of the new Volksgerichtshof, waiting to take the oath of office in their new place of work.

Originally, the ceremony was to have taken place twelve days earlier, but the Nazi leaders were otherwise engaged at the time. They were busy directing the extrajudicial executions of the 'conspirators' of the 'Röhm Putsch' (The Night of the Long Knives). Shortly after the Nazis seized power in 1933, the leader of the SA, Ernst Röhm, had already boldly expressed ambitions to take control of inner-political developments in Germany. Röhm supported the idea of a 'second revolution' which would have given the army of Brownshirts wide access to government offices, increasing their power and influence. Hitler saw this as a threat to the inner homogeneity of Nazi organizations and called Röhm a 'rootless revolutionary'. Together with the other leaders of the NSDAP, he decided to liquidate Röhm and his followers. In a cloak-and-dagger operation, Röhm and a series of other high-ranking SA men, including Gregor Strasser, were murdered. Even politicians and military personnel with no direct connection to Röhm fell victim to the rigorous purge that took place between 30 June and 2 July. Without a trial and often without even questioning them, Hitler's death squads murdered members of the SA and SA sympathizers, including his predecessor as Chancellor, General Kurt von Schleicher, and his wife. This bloodbath, in the course of which Hitler rid himself of former comrades-in-arms who had fallen out of favour, claimed more than 200 lives. And so there had been no time for a grand opening of the Volksgerichtshof. Now, the massacre over, there was time to celebrate.

In his opening speech, before the members of the new Volksgerichtshof were sworn in, Justice Minister Gürtner referred to the events of 30 June. He saw the 'putsch' as an illustration of just how critical the danger of 'violence' against the Reich was and how necessary it was to have effective legislation in place. Gürtner's demeanour was theatrical, his words unctuous. And for those in the chamber who may have been so moved that they were unable to follow the justice minister's words, the speech was printed verbatim in the next day's edition of the party newspaper, the *Völkischer Beobachter*:

> In this solemn ceremony to which I have invited you here today, the Volksgerichtshof for the German Reich convenes. Through the confidence placed in you by the Reich Chancellor, you, gentlemen, have been appointed judges at the Volksgerichtshof. As your first act, you will swear a solemn oath to carry out your duties faithfully. Every people, no matter how healthy, every state, no matter how firmly established, must remain in a state of constant vigilance lest it fall victim to an attack such as that of 30 June. Such an attack does not always take the form of imminent violence, which can only be suppressed by means of direct violence. All too often, acts of treason and high treason are preceded by lengthy and widespread preparations which are not always easily recognized and which draw many – both guilty and even completely innocent parties – into their wake.
>
> The sword of the law and the scales of justice will lie in your hands. Together, they symbolize the power of the judge's office, an office which the German people in particular has always held

in deep reverence and on which it has bestowed the independence necessary to follow the conscience.

I know, gentlemen, that you are imbued with the solemn gravity of this office. Exercise your function as independent judges committed solely to the law and accountable only to God and your own conscience.

In this expectation, I now ask you to pledge yourselves to perform your duties faithfully by swearing a solemn oath:

I swear, so help me God!

You will swear by God the omnipotent and omniscient to remain faithful to Volk and Vaterland, to abide by the constitution and laws of the land, to carry out your official duties conscientiously and to faithfully exercise your function as judges of the Volksgerichtshof and dispense judgement in all conscience.

A speech full of pathos and which received lengthy applause from the audience in the chamber. They too, were seized by the 'solemn gravity' of the occasion, and their expressions revealed pride. Were they not witnessing the birth of a new and unique court of justice? This court was endowed by the law of 24 April with all powers formerly held solely by the Reichsgericht, the Imperial Court of Justice, the power to judge such crimes as high treason, treason, attacks on the Reichspräsident, particularly serious damage to military resources and the murder or attempted murder of members of the government of the Reich or state governments. The guests at the opening ceremony fully appreciated that such a court was urgently needed at that moment, in a time of change on a national level, no matter how the international press might rail against it, claiming that it was a summary court. For Gürtner, the outraged protests from the press abroad could only be the result of 'either unfortunate ignorance of the procedural stipulations for the Volksgerichtshof and a lack of understanding of the German sense of justice or malicious intent to stamp on any attempt to create a new Germany'.

In fact – and Gürtner was perfectly aware of this – the new Volksgerichtshof was legally a special tribunal. As the interim President, Gürtner inaugurated the longest-serving of the three senate presidents, Dr Fritz Rehn, as the new Judge-President. As a 'man of the first hour', Rehn was a particularly apt choice for the position. Former chairman of the special court in the district court of Berlin, he had gained adequate experience with Nazi legal practice and had proved that the National Socialists could rely on him. The new regime had already set up the first extraordinary courts on 21 March 1933. In such courts, the accused appeared not before local judges well-versed in specific legal areas, but hand-picked NS jurists. The 'Decree of the Reich Government on the Establishment of Special Courts' made short work of the process of trying defendants: the period of notice was three days and could be reduced to twenty-four hours. Moreover, the decree abolished other cornerstones of the due process of law: it states clearly 'There will be no oral hearing on the warrant of arrest'. This laid the system wide open to arbitrary dispensation of justice, wrongful convictions, and excessive and cruel punishments – even murder in the name of the law. Rehn had performed his tasks to the full satisfaction of the new regime. And now he was being rewarded – for reasons of legal status only on a provisional basis – with the title of President of the highest extraordinary court, a meteoric rise for the ambitious jurist.

Rehn was assisted by Wilhelm Bruner, senate president from Munich – just a few months later, after Rehn's death on 18 September 1934, Bruner took over as executive Volksgerichtshof President and remained in office until 1936 – and Eduard Springmann, senate president from Düsseldorf. They were joined by nine other professional judges. Four of the 'honorary' associate judges, the other five being high-ranking members of the army, came from the Ministry of the Reichswehr. The remaining eleven members of the court represented the various NS organizations. Everyone wanted – and would have – their role to play in this new court.

The day before the opening ceremony, the *Deutsche Allgemeine Zeitung* had informed its readers of the appointment of the judges and the requirements. The author commented approvingly that: 'The judges of the court have been appointed with special regard to the appointment of personages with extensive knowledge of criminal law, with political foresight and vast experience.'

Altogether, the initial staffing list of the court comprised eighty employees. This meant that the Volksgerichtshof was still far smaller than the Reichsgericht, and its organizational structure was by no means ideal from the point of view of its keenest advocates. The new court was separate from the Reichsgericht, but initially, the prosecution counsel still came from a branch office of the Reichsanwaltschaft (Reich prosecutor's office), which was based in Leipzig. The head of this branch office was Reichsanwalt Paul Jorns, a jurist who had worked on cases of high treason during the Weimar Republic and proved himself a loyal servant of the regime as investigator in the case of the murder of Rosa Luxemburg and Karl Liebknecht in 1919. He was assisted by senior prosecutors Wilhelm Eichler and Heinrich Parrisius, who one year before, together with Oberreichsanwalt Karl Werner, had conducted the preliminary investigations against the alleged perpetrators of the Reichstag Fire and who was one of the prosecutors in the subsequent trial.

These were all seasoned lawyers and committed to 'the German cause'. The Nazi leaders expected consistent and harsh dispensation of justice, and these men would ensure that they would get it. In its edition of 15 July 1934, the *Völkischer Beobachter* revealed what could be expected of the 'new German judicature' and the Volksgerichtshof. In bold terms, a commentator anticipated the end of the era of 'liberal criminal law' and enlightened his readers:

> Since Germany achieved political union and eradicated the manifestations of an outdated and diseased age, political crime and political offences must be seen in a different light. We do not need to rethink our idea of criminal law in itself in order to see that a special court is required for the crimes of treason and high treason – new circumstances create new requirements: the political unity of the German people, purchased with the blood of thousands, cries out to be defended. And in the Volksgerichtshof, it has found a defence against the traitor, the saboteur, against negating elements from within.

He continued:

> Anyone who turns against the political unity of the National Socialist state today will be judged by this court. The disastrous trial of the Reichstag arsonists is still fresh in our memory. Despite the blatantly political motivation behind the crime, it dragged on for months, delayed by politically inexperienced judges who, in order to reach an 'objective judgement', again and again called for fresh testimony from experts, questioned countless witnesses and nevertheless produced a miscarriage of justice. This in particular makes the need for politically trained expert judges obvious.
>
> Historically speaking, the Volksgerichtshof, which convenes for the first time today and is intended to be a permanent institution, therefore represents something completely new within the German legal system. It marks the end of an inglorious chapter in the history of German justice, an era in which politically and criminologically insensitive German legal authorities were so intent on objectivity and loyalty to the constitution that they were unable or unwilling to see what was happening around them.

And the opinion of this commentator in the official Nazi Party newspaper was not only shared by staunch supporters of the NSDAP. Judges of a nationalist-conservative persuasion, still convinced of their 'judicial independence', could also identify with it. Were the objectives not the rebirth of the German nation and to ward off danger to the people, the Fatherland and the Führer? And had the arson attack on the Reichstag building not clearly shown that the Communist threat had by no means been averted? And the protracted trial of the arsonists had surely demonstrated the need for a court with the power to take more decisive and consistent action against the enemies of the people and their puppet masters?

Indeed, the National Socialist rulers had been infuriated by the course and outcome of the Reichstag Fire trial. In the end, four of the five defendants were pronounced not guilty, though to the Nazis, they were no less than Communist subversives. Not merely a defeat for the German legal system, but a scandal . . .

In the late evening of 27 February 1933, fire broke out in the building of the German Reichstag. For the National Socialists, who had come to power just a few days previously, this was proof that the Communists were in no way willing to accept the new political situation. The Nazis were convinced that it was the work of arsonists and a signal that a revolution was imminent. Would there now be an armed Communist uprising?

That same night, a Dutch travelling journeyman was arrested at the scene of the fire. His name: Marinus van der Lubbe. But had he been acting alone? Was he a lone arsonist with no accomplices and not following anyone's orders? For the Nazis, there could be no doubt: this was the work of the Communists . . .

On 30 January, the very day on which the Nazis seized power, not only Minister for Trade and Industry Alfred Hugenberg but also Minister of the Interior Wilhelm Frick and Hermann Göring had pushed for a ban on the Communist Party (KPD). Hitler, however, was against it – for the time being. He was afraid that a ban would provoke serious inner-political conflict and strikes, which would not have served his purposes in view of the upcoming election.

Now, however, after the Reichstag Fire, he was forced to take action. Just one day after the fire, on 28 February 1933, Hitler had signed two emergency decrees: the 'Decree of the Reich President for the Protection of the People and State' and the 'Decree of the Reich President against Treason against the German People and Actions of High Treason'. Their most controversial content: the introduction of 'Schutzhaft' (protective custody) and the suspension of basic rights granted under the Weimar

Constitution. Thousands were arrested soon after – mostly KPD party functionaries, but also social democrats and trade unionists. Hitler now had the legal basis for dealing with his political opponents once and for all.

Meanwhile, the investigations into the Reichstag Fire were in full swing. The Nazis seized the psychologically opportune moment to throw their propaganda machine into action, conjuring up the image of a Communist threat everywhere. As one individual acting alone, van der Lubbe did not fit their scenario. The puppet masters, the real perpetrators behind the arson attack – the 'agents of world communism' – had to be identified and convicted.

And the tireless investigators found what they were looking for: Ernst Torgler, Chairman of the KPD faction in the Reichstag, was arrested after turning himself in to the police in order to prove his innocence when he learned that he was a suspect, having been one of the last persons to leave the building before the fire was discovered. And three Bulgarian emigrants – Georgi Dimitrov, Blagoy Popov and Vassil Tanev – were also arrested after witnesses reported seeing them at the scene of the fire.

On 24 April 1933, following the preliminary examination, Oberreichsanwalt Werner indicted the three Bulgarians, van der Lubbe and Torgler on charges of high treason and arson. Not long before, on 29 March 1933, the Nazis had hurriedly pushed through the 'Law on the Imposition and Execution of Capital Punishment', already presaged in the 'Decree of the Reich President for the Protection of the People and State', authorizing the imposition of the death sentence with retroactive effect for certain serious crimes committed between 1 January 1933 and 28 February 1933. This made it possible to demand the death sentence for the defendants in the Reichstag Fire case.

The trial against the five defendants opened on 21 September 1933 before the Reichsgericht. Only one of the accused, Ernst Torgler, chose a defence counsel, Berlin lawyer Alfons Sack, who is said to have sympathized with the NSDAP. The others had to place their trust in court-appointed counsel. The main hearing lasted several months. However, the evidence presented produced no new insights into a possible Communist conspiracy. Not even the reward of 20,000 Reichsmarks, offered by the police shortly before the beginning of the trial, brought any results.

Instead, as German citizens became disillusioned with the course of the eagerly-anticipated trial, a rumour that the Nazis had set the fire in the Reichstag themselves for propaganda purposes began to gain ground.

At last, shortly before Christmas, on 23 December 1933, the court finally reached a verdict. Van der Lubbe was sentenced to death and to 'perpetual loss of honour for high treason, seditious arson and attempted common arson'. Surprisingly, the other four defendants were pronounced not guilty.

In summing up the grounds for the decision, the court stated that van der Lubbe's death sentence was justified because the Reichstag Fire had been a political act. The court also stated that in the spring of 1933, the German people faced the threat of world Communism and stood on the brink of chaos. The arson attack, it said, was the work of the Communists, whose perfidious plans van der Lubbe had carried out. In giving the reasons for its decision, the criminal division also made mention of defamatory claims that the National Socialists had laid the fire in the Reichstag themselves. These absurd and malicious allegations had been spread by 'expatriated rogues' and their lies had been completely refuted in the course of the trial, the chairman stated in a piercing voice.

And yet: the National Socialists, who had accompanied the trial with clamorous propaganda and had high hopes of its outcome, were indignant and angered by the verdict.

The journal *Deutsches Recht*, the central organ of the Bund Nationalsozialistischer Deutscher Juristen (BNSDJ – Association of National Socialist German Legal Professionals) commented that the verdict was a 'blatant miscarriage of justice'. Later, during a dinner, Hitler himself called it 'ridiculous' and the judges 'senile'. It followed that it was high time to think about establishing a special court. In a cabinet meeting held on 23 March 1934 and attended by Hitler, Göring, Röhm and Minister of Justice Gürtner, it was decided that trials for treason and high treason would be handed over to a special tribunal. Just one month later, on 24 April 1934, the Volksgerichtshof was officially founded. The deputy editor-in-chief of the *Völkischer Beobachter*, Wilhelm Weiss, later described this historic moment:

> . . . . it is with good reason, therefore, that the National Socialist state, after the seizure of power, has created a special court for the trial of the most serious crimes existing in the field of politics. Anyone familiar with the sentencing policy of German courts before the NSDAP came to power will fully appreciate the necessity for such a court. Any objection that before 30 January 1933, the highest court in the country, the Reichsgericht in Leipzig, already tried and adjudicated on cases of treason and high treason, must be deemed invalid. The cases brought and dealt with by this court

could not lead to a satisfactory solution in the National Socialist sense, because in its work and tendency, the Reichsgericht was dominated by the general fundamental political and spiritual attitude which prevailed in the democratic state of Weimar. As a rule, any trial for high treason in Leipzig was an affair which immediately led to confrontations in the Reichstag and shameless agitation by the gutter press against anyone who made even a modest attempt to at least protect the Reich from the most blatant acts of treason . . . In this sense, then, the Volksgerichtshof is an organic creation of the National Socialist state, being a form of expression of basic National Socialist concepts in the field of the administration of justice.

Hitler was satisfied. Here, at last, was a tribunal such as that already envisaged in *Mein Kampf* in 1924: 'One day, a German national tribunal will judge and sentence tens of thousands of the organizers responsible for the criminal November betrayal and for the consequences that followed.'

And six years later – in the Reichstag election, the NSDAP had just achieved its national breakthrough, increasing the number of its parliamentary seats from 12 to 107 on 25 September 1930 – giving evidence before the Leipzig supreme court in a case of high treason brought against three young officers, Hitler left no doubt as to his intentions of creating a national constitutional court. Asked by the judge to explain a remark attributed to him that 'heads would roll' when the National Socialists came to power. Hitler stated 'May I assure you that when our movement in the course of a legal struggle comes to power, a German state court will come, November 1918 will find its revenge and then heads will roll.' The judge then asked him how he imagined the establishment of the Third Reich. 'The National Socialist movement will endeavour to achieve its aims by constitutional means. The constitution prescribes for us the methods, but not the goal.' Hitler had thus clearly stated his objectives before the highest court in Germany: to achieve office by constitutional means and then, once in power, to transform the entire state according to his National Socialist Weltanschauung.

And the passing of the Ermächtigungsgesetz (Enabling Bill) on 23 March 1933 – quite legally, with the majority of the votes of the Reichstag members – laid the foundations for this. The establishment of a People's Court was thus just one link in a whole chain of National Socialist policy.

Hitler can therefore not be said to have duped anybody, including the judiciary. His plans for a Volksgerichtshof already existed. And now, in

April 1934, they became reality. The National Socialist regime now had a tribunal which would put an end to any leniency towards 'traitors and enemies of the people'. Hitler was satisfied. One Volk, one Reich, one judiciary – one Führer . . .

He had turned 45 just four days before the establishment of the Volksgerichtshof, and everywhere in the Reich, the Führer's birthday had been duly celebrated. In particular in the capital, Berlin:

> The love and veneration of the German people for its Führer and Volkskanzler was particularly evident on this, his 45th birthday. The entire capital city of the Reich is a sea of flags. There is not one house which is not hung with the flag of the National Socialist revolution to mark the significance of this day. Every building of the Reich, the state and the municipal administration, every private residence and factory is displaying the flag. The decorations in the windows of many stores in the inner city are particularly impressive, with portraits and sculptures of the Führer, framed with flowers and fresh greenery.

Collective celebrations such as that described here with such enthusiasm by a reporter of the *Düsseldorfer Nachrichten* in its evening edition of 20 April 1934 were staged all over Germany, not just in Berlin, with the help of the Party organizations which had already established themselves in every district and every village as the spearhead of the new face of Germany. And the Party definitely had no cause to complain of a lack of support from the people.

The euphoric atmosphere of national change was also apparent at the festive event taking place on the morning of Saturday, 14 July 1934. When the official part was over, the guests mingled in the spacious foyer, shaking hands, exchanging comments on the dignified and fitting solemnity of the opening ceremony and expressions of mutual respect. They were united by a feeling that they were witnesses to an important, even momentous occasion in the history of the German judiciary.

Among the guests in the foyer was a tall, lean man with a narrow face who seemed particularly sought-out by the Party bigwigs and legal dignitaries: Roland Freisler, undersecretary in the Ministry of Justice. It was in part due to his immense personal efforts that the Volksgerichtshof had come into being. In numerous articles and speeches, he had persistently emphasized the necessity for a new National Socialist judiciary with clearly delineated areas of responsibility and competence, self-confidently proclaiming that a fundamental reform of German law was required. As a National Socialist of the first hour, this was a great day for him. Germany now had its Volksgerichtshof – a tribunal against the enemies of the people, the Party, the state and the Führer. The German legal system could now apply the laws passed previously by the NS regime.

Now was the hour of the enforcers – and Roland Freisler was an enforcer par excellence.

# Chapter 2

# The Lawyer from Kassel

October 30th 1893 was a happy day for Julius Freisler and his wife Charlotte. It was the day their son was born. They had already chosen a name far in advance of the big event: if it was a boy, the baby would be christened Roland. And it was a boy. His father, engineer Julius Freisler, was particularly proud. Just a few years before, he had moved into the Reich from Klantendorf in Moravia and settled in Celle near Hamburg, where he met and fell in love with the graceful, shy Charlotte Auguste Schwerdtfeger – and promptly married her.

Secretly, he had wished for a son. Julius Freisler was a proud and happy man. Wasn't little Roland the spitting image of him? Shortly after Roland was born, the young family moved to Hamelin, where Charlotte Freisler gave birth to her second child, also a boy, on 28 December 1895. They named him Oswald. Just one month later, Julius Freisler was offered a job he could not refuse: a top position in the Duisburg port engineering authority. Even though it pained him to be separated from his family, Julius Freisler had to think of his career prospects. And so his wife and the two children remained in Lower Saxony for the time being, later joining him in Aachen, where the ambitious engineer had moved after being offered a professorship at the Königliche Baugewerbeschule (Royal Academy of the Building Trades).

This position not only boosted Julius Freisler's status, but gave him and his young family a secure income. At first, the two boys attended primary school. Then, in 1903, 10-year-old Roland moved to the Kaiser-Wilhelm-Gymnasium (grammar school), where he was a keen and ambitious student. Ambition was still one of his outstanding characteristics as a 15-year-old secondary school student in Kassel, where the Freisler family moved in 1908 and where he participated with particular enthusiasm in political debates. Four years later, he passed his Abitur (German university entrance qualification) as the best in his class.

He then enrolled at the University of Jena and began to study law. However, when the 'Great Patriotic War' broke out, he left the city, and in August 1914 joined the 167th Infantry Regiment in Kassel as a Fahnenjunker (probationary officer cadet). Like all young men of his generation, he considered it his patriotic duty to enlist and to fight for the Reich, for Germany and for victory. After a brief period of training, the young recruit was first posted to Flanders, where he was wounded a short time later and had to be sent to a military hospital in Germany. Following his recovery, he was sent with his regiment to the Eastern Front. There, he carried out his duties in such an exemplary manner that he was promoted: as the leader of a reconnaissance patrol, he was made a Leutnant. The young lieutenant exhibited such bravery in the field that he was awarded the Iron Cross. But this military honour did not protect him or his comrades against defeat and imprisonment. Like thousands of other German soldiers, Roland Freisler spent the rest of the War as a PoW in an officers' camp near Moscow.

After the October Revolution and the Treaty of Brest-Litovsk, the Russians handed over management of the camp to the prisoners and made Freisler one of the camp superintendents, responsible for organizing food supplies. Opinions differ about Freisler's position as a camp superintendent. Some quote contemporary witnesses who allegedly reported that Freisler engaged in in-depth study of Marxism during this time, learned Russian and quickly made a career as a 'Bolshevik'. Others see Freisler's role in the management of the camp merely as further evidence of the fact that he always managed to turn any new situation to his own personal advantage. In later life, Freisler never denied having been a camp superintendent – but he vehemently objected to references to his 'Bolshevik past'.

In July 1920, Roland Freisler returned to Germany, first to Kassel and then to Jena, where he resumed his law studies. He had briefly considered a career as an officer, but in the chaotic post-war years, dominated by constant violent conflict between Communists, Social Democrats, conservative groups and volunteer corps, he found no reliable point of reference. It seemed to him that the most sensible thing to do was to focus on his private career rather than on politics. And so he returned to Jena – paving the way for his career in the judiciary.

Roland Freisler was every bit as diligent and ambitious as a student as he had been as a schoolboy. He graduated with ease, and in 1921, presented his doctoral thesis entitled 'Fundamentals of business organization', which was rated 'summa cum laude' and one year later, was published in the *Schriften des Instituts für Wirtschaftsrecht* of the University of Jena.

The young 'Dr jur'. then went to Berlin, where, in 1923, he passed the major state legal examination and served his term as an Assessor juris (fully-qualified lawyer). On 13 February 1924, he again returned to Kassel, this time to establish a law firm with his brother, who had now also obtained his law degree. The brothers agreed on a clear division of labour. Roland would handle only criminal cases, while Oswald would concentrate on civil lawsuits. The firm soon made a name for itself, and the brothers had no lack of clients.

Roland Freisler quickly earned respect as a lawyer. He had a reputation for being extremely competent in his field and a skilled public speaker. His speeches in court were clear and well thought-out, and he was a master of stalling tactics and the art of the probing question. In non-political proceedings, he was a mild-mannered, almost restrained lawyer, but in political trials, he became an aggressive defence counsel with emphatic gestures and razor-sharp comments who never shied away from a confrontation with the court. From the standpoint of his clients, he was a good lawyer. He demonstrated his legal skills so impressively, especially in difficult appeal proceedings, that the Reichsgericht in Leipzig, under whose third criminal division the provincial high court of Kassel fell, soon became aware of the young lawyer Dr Freisler.

At the same time, he pursued his second – political – career with the same relentless energy. In 1924, Roland Freisler won a seat on the Kassel city council, representing the right-wing nationalist splinter party Völkisch-Sozialer Block (People's Social Block). However, when Hitler was prematurely released from the Landsberg prison on 24 December of that year and immediately began the reorganization of the NSDAP, Freisler, like thousands of others of similar political persuasion, discovered his National-Socialist 'home' and became a member of the larger party, with the NSDAP membership number 9679.

Perhaps the ambitious lawyer Freisler sensed that Hitler would soon unite all right-wing and nationalist splinter groups within the Reich and succeed in seizing political power in Germany. Roland Freisler wanted to play a role in this 'new Germany', and not as part of the anonymous masses, but in the front line.

From then on, Freisler represented the NSDAP on the Kassel city council. Infected by the enthusiasm of the National Socialist movement and driven by his own strong craving for recognition, he became a rigorous proponent of a National Socialist Germany. Whether in court or in the council chambers – he fought to promote the ideas and further the interests of his party. And his own interests. In addition to working in the flourishing law firm which he continued to run with his brother Oswald, he was now pursuing his political ambitions with even greater vigour.

More reticent in his private life, Freisler married Marion Russegger on 23 March 1928. His fellow members of the Party in Kassel celebrated with the couple, although locally, Freisler's Party position was not uncontroversial. As deputy Gauleiter (district leader), he had his sights fixed on the position of Gauleiter for Hesse-Nassau North, presently occupied by Dr Schultz, who was a close confidant of Rudolf Hess. Growing tired of Freisler's numerous intrigues and attacks, Schultz, supported by his influential party colleague, wrote a letter to the party leadership. In it, he confirmed that his deputy was indeed an outstanding speaker and lawyer at a regional level, but stated that he was unsuitable for a position of authority due to his moodiness. And Gauleiter Schultz was not alone in his opinion.

More than once, Freisler's excessive zeal and his hectic and tumultuous way of going about things had cast a shadow over his standing, even within the Party. Some party functionaries also took objection to his 'business acumen', accusing him of mixing political and private interests. On the other hand, he had eloquently defended numerous Party members, often even succeeded in getting them acquitted. And his sharp rhetorical skills rendered the Party impervious to all attacks from the opposition on the city council. Surely this was a man who was fighting openly and with great dedication for the Party and the national cause?

Not even his critics within the Party could deny Freisler's strengths and his success. And they were in the minority. In Northern Hesse, Freisler was considered an invaluable member of the Party. He was one of the local NS celebrities. For this reason, occasional criticism of his grandstanding and vicious attacks on anything he perceived as 'anti-German' had little or no effect.

For example, there was an incident in the Kleines Theater in Kassel, a theatre which had staged a play entitled *Seele über Bord* ('Soul Overboard') by the Hessian author Ernst Glaeser, writer of the very successful autobiographical novel *Born in 1902*. In the third act of the play, a detective, disguised as a priest, approaches a young woman in a Catholic church with obvious intentions. The young woman silently prays to the Saviour for help, but in vain. The press was full of praise for the actors' performance, and not one critic took offence at the content of the play. Nevertheless, word soon spread what a blasphemous piece of work was now being staged in Kassel, despite the fact that the church was treated in a quite different manner in the course of the play and that the script gave no indication, not even a hint, of the dramatist's personal opinion on religion.

A letter to the editor of the local newspaper the *Kasseler Post*, published after the première of the play, and in which an anonymous reader complained in no uncertain terms about this 'sacrilegious drama' mobilized protest against the play. At the next performance, a troop of guardians of national morality, led by lawyer and NSDAP member Roland Freisler, stormed the theatre, interrupted the play and mistreated a member of the audience who dared to speak up in defence of the playwright and the play. There were no legal consequences for the perpetrators of this violent heckling action. No action was taken against them. Instead, the play was banned and the author charged with 'blasphemy'. A charge of 'blasphemy' was also filed against the author Kurt Tucholsky, who had defended the play and described the attack in an article. This took place in 1926, and it was the first time that NSDAP man Freisler had publicly demonstrated his eagerness to quash all 'anti-German activities' – even through the use of violence.

Four years later, on 23 June 1930, the fanatical National Socialist Freisler once again moved against his political opponents – this time, a little more skilfully. In the Kassel city council, he filed for a motion of censure against the police commissioner of the city. The background story: a few days before, Freisler had organized Nazi meetings in four restaurants in Kassel. These meetings had been attended by people wearing uniforms which had been prohibited by the Hessian government in a decree issued on 11 June. The National Socialists ignored the ban. Numerous Party members turned up outside the restaurants wearing their brown shirts and the swastika armband. A provocation, particularly in the eyes of the Communists. On 18 June, the day of the NSDAP meetings, they held public meetings of their own, as did the Social Democratic Reichbanner Schwarz-Rot-Gold, whose members, also unannounced and in full uniform, marched through the streets of Kassel.

This explosive situation led to violent confrontations following one of the Nazi meetings. Fifty policemen had been deployed to ensure that people attending the event were able to enter the meeting hall despite verbal insults and threats, but had then been ordered to stand down by the police chief. Violent brawling then broke out between Communists and National Socialists, and numerous people were injured.

Freisler placed the blame entirely on the police. In his opinion, they had failed in their duty to protect those attending the meeting from the Communists. In a city council meeting, he filed for a motion of censure against the police commissioner. Freisler stated that as the latter, former lawyer Dr Hohenstein, was a Jew, he could not be impartial in matters concerning the National Socialists. And having already talked himself into a rage that evening, Freisler also sharply attacked the officer in charge, Polizeileutnant Schulz, a Social Democrat, claiming that the police alone and not the NSDAP members, who had only tried to defend themselves, were to blame for the incident.

Neither the chief of police nor his lieutenant were willing to take these accusations lying down, and they filed a complaint against Freisler. There was a trial. The Kassel magistrate's court found Freisler not guilty of slandering Schulz, but fined him 300 marks for his slanderous attack on Dr Hohenstein. A minor, but nevertheless painful, defeat for Freisler. His expression as he left the courtroom betrayed his anger. Later, in the company of sympathizers, he spoke of his hopes for the future. He was convinced that time was on their side – on his side, that of the Party and of the National Socialist cause. And when their day came, such scandalous sentences would be a thing of the past.

Although Freisler had no easy task in Hesse, a state ruled by the Social Democrats and in which the administration, the police and the judiciary opposed the increasingly vehement attacks of the Nazis with greater determination than elsewhere in the Republic, he made strong progress in his legal and political career. Together with Hans Frank – the man who founded the BNSDJ in 1928, who became the leader of the NSDAP's national legal division in 1930, was later Reichsminister without portfolio and finally, from 1940 onwards, would be governor-general in Poland – Freisler now enjoyed a reputation as an outstanding jurist in the NSDAP. Freisler was seen as a loyal member of the Party who could be relied upon to make quick and unequivocal decisions. In short, he was a man who pursued all his ambitions systematically and with the single-mindedness and lack of scruples required in order to advance his career.

Yet despite his excellent standing as a lawyer, access to the inner leadership circles of the Party still remained barred. Although he proved himself as an outstanding Party lawyer and as an NSDAP representative in the Prussian regional parliament, where he held a seat from 1932 onwards and where he repeatedly drew attention through vicious verbal attacks during legal debates, the door to the centre of power within the Party remained closed to Freisler.

Later, historians attributed this to the fact that Freisler was not radical enough at that time in his treatment of the Jews, that in fact he hardly mentioned them. But it may simply have been that Freisler's political sphere of action was geographically too far removed from the Nazi capitals of Berlin and Munich.

It was not long, however, before the new political situation freed the ambitious politician and NSDAP member from the provincial backwaters and took him to Berlin, to the very centre of National Socialist power. There, on 30 January 1933, Hitler had been appointed new Reich Chancellor by the ageing Reichspräsident Hindenburg.

'We've done it', Hitler had declared amidst shouts of jubilation from his followers in the 'Kaiserhof' hotel as he arrived there following the appointment ceremony at Wilhelmstrasse 77, formerly the official residence of Bismarck. Everyone wanted to shake hands with the Führer: Goebbels, Hess, Röhm, Göring – the line of people waiting to congratulate him seemed never-ending. In the evening, the National Socialists organized a gigantic celebration. From seven o'clock in the evening until well past midnight, 25,000 Hitler supporters and steel-helmeted units filed through the Brandenburg Gate carrying torches and to the sound of military marches. Freisler and his fellow Party members in Kassel also celebrated this triumph on 30 January 1933. It was their day, their victory.

Hitler's appointment to the office of Reich Chancellor was not the result of a strategic move by the National Socialists. In fact, the Nazis took power completely legally. Hitler and his nine ministers from the German National People's Party (DVNP) and three National Socialist ministers enjoyed the confidence of the Reichstag, having achieved the simple majority required by the constitution. It was not until 23 March 1933, when Hitler passed the Enabling Act, that the political situation changed completely. Shortly after they seized power, the Nazis had begun the process of 'Gleichschaltung' (enforced coordination or synchronization) throughout the country. A 'Reichsstatthalter' (Reich governor) was appointed for every state, and behind the Reich governors, the NSDAP Gauleiters ensured that every association and institution, every authority and club was 'coordinated' or brought into line with Nazi ideals. The German people appeared to have been waiting for this, and the majority of German citizens seemed perfectly happy to live under the swastika banner.

New elections had been held on 5 March – the Reichstag had been dissolved on 1 February. The results were disappointing for the NSDAP. Hitler and his followers were convinced they would gain the absolute majority, but in fact won a mere 43.9 per cent of the votes. It was only through an alliance with the DVNP that the Nazis were able to form a 'government of national uprising' – a government constitutionally elected by the majority of the German people.

Hitler could now continue to expand his power. And above all, he could at last settle old scores with his opponents. The Enabling Act gave him almost unlimited powers, for a period of four years, in the fight to 'remedy the distress of people and Reich'. Three years previously, Hitler had already announced in a speech to NS party members in Munich, what his enemies could expect if he came to power: 'We National Socialists have never claimed to represent of a democratic standpoint; rather, we have openly declared that we merely make use of democratic means in order to gain power, and that once we have seized power, we will ruthlessly deny to our opponents all those means afforded to us in opposition.'

And that time had now come. On 23 March 1933, Hitler's speech to the Reichstag left no doubt as to the low esteem in which he held it: 'It would be inconsistent with the aim of the national uprising and it would fail to suffice for the intended goal were the government to negotiate with and request the approval of the Reichstag for its measures in each given case.'

Almost threateningly, he ended his speech to the parliamentarians with these words: 'However, the government is just as determined as it is prepared to accept a notice of rejection and thus a declaration of resistance. May you, Gentlemen, now choose for yourselves between peace or war!'

That was clear enough. In an impassioned speech, Social Democratic member of parliament Otto Wels pleaded that the Act would mean the end of parliamentary democracy. However, the majority of the members of the Reichstag refused to follow his call to vote against the Enabling Act. Only his own party voted against the legislation. Even if the Communists who had been arrested before the election had been able to cast their votes, Hitler would still have had a safe two-thirds' majority. And so he was endowed with all powers he needed to overthrow the Weimar Republic. Eighty-two per cent had voted for Hitler and his Enabling Act – in effect digging their own graves.

Later claims – often made by post-war politicians – that the members of the Reichstag had been intimidated and terrorised by the Nazis were nothing more than attempts to create a legend after the fact. Hitler and his henchmen had no need of such ploys. Almost exclusively, the other political parties were concerned with holding on to their own power, and the Republic was only of strategic interest to them. As the historian Hansjoachim Koch very aptly stated: 'Weimar died not because of its enemies, but because it had no true friends, not even among the Socialists.'

Although the Reichstag was in fact not abolished after 23 March 1933, it became little more than an assembly dominated by the National Socialists. Its function consisted in occasionally gathering to listen to the words of its masters and then dutifully applauding Hitler's speeches and shouting 'Heil Hitler'. The path was free for the staging of Nazi power and the ruthless implementation of the 'national awakening'. And to achieve these aims, the Nazis needed reliable men in all areas – men like Roland Freisler.

Shortly after Hitler came to power, Freisler had received a letter from Berlin: his appointment as a head of department in the Prussian Ministry of Justice. At just 40 years old, Freisler had climbed the first really important rung on the career ladder. But that was not enough. Barely four months later, on 1 June 1933, he was appointed Staatssekretär (undersecretary) in the Prussian Ministry of Justice under Minister Dr Hans Kerrl.

In a letter addressed to 'Dr jur. Freisler, in this house', the Minister informed him on 31 May 1933:

> At my suggestion and as stated in the notification received by you on the 29th of this month, the Prussian Ministerpräsident has appointed you to the position of undersecretary in the Prussian Ministry of Justice with the status of a civil servant. You will take up your new office on 1 June 1933. From this date on, you will fall under salary grade 3 and receive a fixed annual salary of 24,000 Reichsmarks and any other salaries to which you may be entitled under Prussian salary law . . .
>
> Kindly make arrangements to have your name removed from the register of lawyers at the district and local court of Kassel with immediate effect . . .

On 19 June, the newly appointed undersecretary notified the president of the Landgericht in Kassel of his promotion and requested that his name be deleted from the list of lawyers:

> Following my appointment to the position of undersecretary in the Prussian Ministry of Justice with the status of a civil servant, I consider my status as a lawyer to have lapsed automatically. I therefore assume that my name has already been removed ex officio from the list of lawyers at the Land- und Amtsgericht Kassel.
>
> Should this assumption be incorrect, I request that my name be deleted from the list . . .
>
> Heil Hitler!

Despite his new career in Berlin, Freisler kept his residence in Kassel. He still made appearances there as a militant NSDAP man. Just a short time before his promotion to undersecretary, he had stormed the Kassel town hall together with local members of the Party and then – encouraged by the success of this mission – had proceeded to the Oberlandesgericht (regional court of appeal) with the intention of seizing this building, too, for the National Socialists. However, the President of the Oberlandesgericht, Dr Anz, succeeded in persuading Freisler and his Party friends that it hardly became a high-ranking official of the judiciary to be attempting to take a court building by force. He managed to convince Freisler to 'desist from vulgar behaviour'. However, the effect of his words was only temporary. Shortly afterwards, cheered on by his followers, Freisler had the swastika flag hoisted above the main entrance to the court building.

Months later – now undersecretary – Freisler invited Dr Anz to take coffee with him in Berlin, where he had now taken up residence. He praised the 'valiant conduct' of the President of the Kassel Oberlandesgericht in opposing him and his men so forcefully. Freisler even attempted to use his newly-found influence to secure a promotion to President of the Berlin Kammergericht (supreme court) for Anz. But Freisler was not yet powerful enough to overcome the misgivings of the Party leaders, who were unwilling to appoint a man who was not a member of the NSDAP as head of the Berlin Kammergericht.

Freisler was a man full of contradictions. On one hand, he was a steadfast believer in the principles of National Socialism. On the other hand, this did not mean that he could not respect a non-partisan stance in others, as long as it was not oppositional. He could be gracious in his private dealings with others but was subject to abrupt mood swings. People perceived him as temperamental, unpredictable and, frequently, intolerably arrogant.

The appointment of the ambitious new undersecretary also brought a change of tone in the offices of the Prussian judiciary. During his first few days in office, Freisler phoned the President of the Berlin regional court, Dr Kirschstein, and demanded. 'Sir, as Landgerichtspräsident, where do you stand on the principles of National Socialism?' When Kirschstein replied: 'I have always followed liberal and democratic principles', Freisler answered sharply: 'Then may I assume that you are not interested in cooperating with us?' Kirschstein: 'You are quite right. I have no interest in collaborating with the NS regime in any way'. Freisler responded by instructing the Landgerichtspräsident to refrain from any official acts with immediate effect. This meant the end of Dr Kirschstein's career. Not long afterwards, the rebellious Landgerichtspräsident retired – it is not known whether under pressure or not.

Freisler's manner in his dealings with subordinates was unambiguous. He was benevolent towards and appreciative of anyone who shared his National Socialist Weltanschauung, while anyone who showed signs of thinking differently or sympathizing with the opposition was treated with hostility and contempt.

Not many jurists were as stout-hearted as the President of the Berlin Landgericht, Dr Kirschstein. Now, after 1933, they quickly and submissively pledged their allegiance to the Nazi regime and diligently set to work to help organize and implement a legal system which met the demands of the National Socialists.

The meteoric rise of the then 40-year-old Dr Roland Freisler in the years leading up to 1933 was in no way surprising. It was quite in keeping with his ambition, his instinct for power, his ruthlessness – and his legal acumen. But above all, he owed his advancement to the new political situation. Freisler's further career would be inextricably linked to the Nazi regime and the moral decline of the judicial system in the years that followed – a judicial system that blithely placed itself in the service of the Hitler regime.

How could this happen? How was such cold functionality and unbelievable brutality possible? How did this unholy alliance between the planners in the NS centres of power and the willing and compliant enforcers in the judicial administration offices and courtrooms come about? Is the picture of a judiciary that was 'bound and gagged', that became enslaved to an evil regime and in the end, was completely at its mercy, an accurate one?

Not long after the Nazis seized power, the Senatspräsident at the Reichsgericht and chairman of the Deutscher Richterbund (German Federation of Judges), Karl Linz, had assured the Führer in the name of all German judges that they were 'unanimously determined to do everything within their power to achieve the aims set by the government'.

And the judges would be true to their word.

# Chapter 3

# One Volk, One Reich,
# One Führer – and One Judiciary

At the beginning of 1933, the chairman of the Deutscher Richterbund (German Federation of Judges), senate president Karl Linz, warned his colleagues in his monthly column for the *Deutsche Richterzeitung*, 'The future hardly looks good for the German judiciary. Instead, there is every indication of fresh attacks and new struggles for the future of the law and an independent administration of justice.'

But such misgivings were quickly forgotten. On 19 March 1933, in a declaration, the executive committee of the Richterbund welcomed 'the will of the new government to end the immense distress . . . of the German people' and offered its full support in the process of 'national reconstruction'. In the *Deutsche Richterzeitung*, German judges could read a statement from their supreme organ on the rebuilding of Germany:

> It is our conviction that the collaboration of all parties striving for the rebuilding of this country will lead to the recovery of our entire public life and thus to the resurgence of Germany.
>
> German law shall apply in German territories! The German judge has always been a nationalist and conscious of his responsibility. He has always been socially committed and has dispensed justice solely on the basis of the law and the dictates of his own conscience. This must continue to be the case!
>
> May this great undertaking, the renewal of our state, soon instil in the German people the awareness of its unconditional unity.

The statement ended with an assurance that the Deutscher Richterbund had 'complete confidence' in the new government.

Other professional associations, unwilling to be outdone, were soon also publicly pledging their loyalty to the new regime. Just one day after the statement from the Richterbund, the Preussischer Richterverein (Prussian Association of Judges) hastened to declare:

> We, the judges and public prosecutors of Prussia, see the awakening of the German people as the correct path to end the immense distress and impoverishment of our people . . . In this process of national renewal in Germany, Prussian judges and public prosecutors vow to collaborate actively in the field of jurisprudence to achieve a renewal of the legal system and the German national community. We, too, see it as our duty to support and promote the honour and dignity of the new state which has come into being through the national revolution.

In the days that followed, both the Deutscher Notarverein (German Association of Notaries Public) and the Deutscher Anwaltsverein (German Association of Lawyers) published statements in which they welcomed 'the strengthening of national thinking and striving' and assured the NS government that it would endeavour in every way to support the 'recovery of the Volk and the Reich'.

What these spokesmen of the legal professions apparently turned a blind eye to was the fact that the new rulers had already begun to subordinate the law to their political and racial convictions alone. Just one day after the Reichstag fire, on 28 February 1933, a 'Decree for the Protection of People and State' had suspended important civil liberties in one fell swoop and given the Nazis the initial legal basis for the persecution of their political opponents.

In addition, the new government had passed a 'Decree on Treason against the German People and Activities of High Treason', which blurred the line between criticism of the regime and treason. Merely suggesting that the Nazis might have set fire to the Reichstag themselves for propaganda reasons, for example, was now interpreted as treason.

And finally, on 24 March, the Reichstag passed Hitler's Enabling Act, which gave him the power to enact legislation deviating from or altering the constitution without the consent of parliament. As briefly mentioned before, the only resistance came from the Social Democrats, the KPD members already having been removed.

And the judiciary? For the majority of judges, the end of the Weimar Republic was not unsettling, but liberating. In the hectic years of the Republic, their basic attitude had not changed. More than ever before, they

24

were right-wing nationalists, their political sentiments anti-republican, anti-parliamentarian – and anti-Semitic. In other words, the German judiciary was highly susceptible to political promises of salvation such as those offered by the National Socialists. They saw the seizure of power by the 'national concentration' of National Socialists and right-wing conservatives as a normal change of government – perfectly legal and highly necessary. Even if some felt a slight sense of unease when Hitler was appointed Reich Chancellor, the majority of judges were optimistic and had great hopes for him.

Not one line of their official publications mentions the erosion of the constitution. On the contrary: Hitler's right-wing statements fell on fertile ground in the judiciary. No matter how blatantly the rights of individuals had been restricted, one thing mattered more than all else to the judges: their idea of 'judicial freedom', which in the eyes of many had been accorded such little respect in the Weimar Republic. Hitler, on the other hand – or so they assumed – would not curb their independence.

But in their eagerness to embrace the cause of the National Socialists, they had failed to notice that, in his speech before the Reichstag, Hitler spoke only of the irremovability, the secure tenure of judges, not of their independence, and that in this context, he stated that in future, jurisprudence should no longer focus on the rights of the individual, but on the rights of the people. Excerpts from Hitler's speech to the Reichstag, 23 March 1933:

> Our legal institutions must above all work to preserve this Volksgemeinschaft. The irremovability of the judges on the one hand must ensure a flexibility in their judgements for the welfare of society on the other. Not the individual, but the Volk as a whole must be the focus of legal concern! . . .
>
> In future, high treason and betrayal of the Volk will be ruthlessly eradicated! . . .
>
> The foundations on which the judiciary is based can be none other than the foundations on which the nation is based. Thus may the judiciary always take into consideration the difficult burden of decision carried by those who bear the responsibility for shaping the life of the nation under the harsh dictates of reality!

The jurists found no cause for concern in Hitler's words. And so, in a plenary session on 29 March, the Reichsgericht adopted a resolution which was forwarded to the Reich Ministry of Justice with a request

25

for it to be forwarded to the Reich Chancellor. In it, the members of the Reichsgericht expressed their gratitude that the Reich Chancellor had prevented interference in the administration of justice:

> The Reichsgericht welcomes the fact that in his government declaration on 23 March 1933, the Reich Chancellor acknowledged the irremovability of judges as the foundation of the legal system. Only the knowledge of his independence can give a judge the inner freedom he requires to carry out his high office. To safeguard the Volksgemeinschaft through his adjudication, with this freedom and subject only to the law, is the true task of the judge. Every German judge must take to heart the Reich Chancellor's admonition that the foundations on which the judiciary is based can be none other than the foundations on which the nation is based and that the burden of decision carried by those who bear the responsibility for shaping the life of the nation under the harsh dictates of reality must always be taken into consideration.

It should be noted that this is not the affirmation of some National Socialist judge from the provinces, but a resolution adopted by the members of the German supreme court. While the new rulers had already begun to dismantle the foundations of an independent legal system, the lawyers of the Reichsgericht invoke an 'inner freedom' and 'independence' of German law of which Hitler himself had made no mention. Not even Hitler's threat that there 'barbaric and ruthless action' would now be taken against the opponents of the 'national revolution' caused them any qualms.

On the contrary: there were many who enthusiastically welcomed the idea of vigorous action against all enemies of the Volk. In the interests of the 'German cause', stated the *Deutsche Richterzeitung*', 'practicality and objectivity, impartiality and independence' could be suspended for a certain time. Professional opportunism or political blindness?

In the current-affairs section of the *Deutsche Richterzeitung*, Chairman Karl Linz repeated the demands formulated by the BNSDJ on 24 March 1933 in Leipzig, stating in no uncertain terms what 'judges with secure tenure' could expect in future: 'All German courts, including the Reichsgericht, must be cleansed of judges and officials of non-Aryan descent . . . All non-Aryan lawyers who have been registered members of Marxist parties, that is, of the SPD and KPD, must be barred from practising law with immediate effect. The same, of course, applies to judges with Marxist leanings.'

Just a short time later, it became clear that these were not merely informally-voiced demands. On 1 April 1933, even before the Law for the Restoration of the Professional Civil Service came into effect on 7 April 1933, the justice ministers of the German states, in anticipatory obedience, had suspended all Jewish judges, state and public prosecutors in a 'defensive anti-Semitic boycott'. There was a marked lack of protest from the judiciary.

All judges of 'non-Aryan descent', and also those who had supported republican parties or professional associations in the past, could now be transferred or forced to take retirement without statement of cause, for 'administrative reasons'. 'Blitzartig', – a favourite word of the Nazis meaning 'with lightning speed' – the legal system was 'cleansed', and was now 'judenfrei' (free of Jews). This had noticeable effects in large cities, where almost 10 per cent of the judges were Jewish. And this was only the beginning of the anti-Semitic purges which were to culminate in the passing of the 'Nuremberg Laws'.

At this early stage, it was already clear that the vast majority of judges remained unmoved by this aggressive action against their colleagues. The Chairman of the Richterbund, Linz, following an audience with Hitler, reassured the few critics among its members, appealing to them to cooperate 'in order to achieve our objectives' and stating that to this end, 'certain measures' were necessary. In the May edition of the *Deutsche Richterzeitung*, Linz gave the following report on his meeting with the Führer:

> The Chairman first thanked the Führer on behalf of the Richterbund for granting the audience and for his pledge before the Reichstag to uphold the irremovability of judges and expressed the wish of the federation that the independence of the judiciary should be upheld. The Chairman gave, for example, the following assurances: In the name of all German judges, he affirmed that they would work unanimously and with all their strength to achieve the aims set by the government, both out of an awareness that the current government was the bulwark of the German people against the Bolshevist threat and out of the deep-seated conviction of every judge that it is their duty to apply all their energies for the benefit and safeguarding of the state . . .
>
> The Reich Chancellor indicated his approval of these statements and declared that he would maintain the independence of the judiciary, even though certain harsh measures were necessary.

Linz ended his report with the following heartening words to his colleagues in the judiciary: 'We can therefore rest assured that the measures introduced under the Law for the Restoration of the Professional Civil Service will be withdrawn as soon as possible.'

As late as December 1932, Linz had stated in the same publication that he feared some measures being introduced 'might damage the standing of the courts and judges'. These earlier misgivings were now completely forgotten. In the course of just a few months, Linz had become a willing and submissive tool of the National Socialist regime. And he was not alone in this. The majority of German judges were in full support of the government, a standpoint the judges' associations had not adopted since 1919.

'Certain measures' were accepted without protest. After all, they were necessary in the interests of the 'national revolution'. And were there not advantages in this 'cleansing' of the judiciary? The 'membership book officials' of the Weimar Republic were finally getting their just deserts, and the banning of the rebellious 'Republican Association of Judges' was also viewed with general satisfaction within the ranks of the 'new' judiciary.

The new Civil Service Restoration Act might not immediately have brought the sweeping success the Nazi government had hoped for, but it at least ensured that just one year after the change of government, the majority of positions as presidents of the regional courts of appeal and the regional courts were occupied by 'reliable national forces'.

The enforced synchronization of the legal system was also progressing rapidly. Despite initial attempts by the executive committee of the Richterbund to maintain its autonomy, the vast majority of the affiliated associations called on their members to 'support the united battle front of Adolf Hitler' and to join the BNSDJ.

In the early summer of 1933, the Nazi government began to break up the German judges' professional associations, and with great success. In a telegram to Reichsjuristenführer (Chief Jurist of the Reich) Hans Frank dated 23 May 1933, the executive board of the Richterbund also declared that 'the and all affiliated associations' was now joining the BNSDJ under the leadership of Reich Chancellor Adolf Hitler.

By 30 May 1933, the amalgamation of the various judge's associations in Germany was complete. Soon, there was only one professional organization, the Deutsche Rechtsfront (German Law Front) under the direction of the BNSDJ. So great was the demand for new membership books for judges – membership rose from about 1,600 in January 1933 to 30,000 by the end of the year – that the association was forced to cease registering new members temporarily.

The Convention of German Jurists in Leipzig in early October 1933 gave the legal professionals their first major opportunity to publicly demonstrate their allegiance to the new order. More than 20,000 legal professionals from all over the Reich attended the convention, which was held under the motto 'German Law to the German People through National Socialism'. The climax of the convention was a demonstration in front of the Reichsgericht. Reichsjurist Frank greeted his colleagues with the words 'German jurists! Heil! Heil!' and delivered a speech on 'Ideas of the National Socialist Revolution and the shaping of German law'. Following his address, he invited the judges to take the 'sacred oath'. In forceful words, he conjured up the inseparable alliance with the Führer:

> German jurists I invite you to join with me in pledging this oath:
> We swear by eternal God, by the spirits of our dead, we swear
> by all those who have become the victims of a legal system
> foreign to the nature of our people, we swear by the soul of the
> German people to follow our Führer as German jurists to the
> end of our days.

This ritualistic mass event ended with a rousing 'Sieg Heil! Sieg Heil! Sieg Heil!' And for those who could not be present in Leipzig, the historic event was pictured on the cover of the October edition of the *Deutsche Richterzeitung* under the heading 'The Rütli oath in front of the Supreme Court'. In the foreground jurists with their right arms extended in the Hitler salute, behind them the steps of the Reichsgericht and the Nazi bigwigs, framed by swastika flags – one people, one Reich, one party, one Führer – and one legal system.

In spite of the Law for the Restoration of the Professional Civil Service, in spite of the undermining of the basic rights guaranteed by the Weimar Constitution, despite discomfort over the fact that the SA had managed, through intimidation and threats, to thwart all attempts by the legal authorities to initiate investigations into the unbridled actions of its fanatical troops, despite the dissolution of their professional associations – almost to a man, the judges supported the National Socialist regime. The enforced synchronization had long become a voluntary self-synchronization. Judges in Germany now took their oath of office with their right arm raised in the Nazi salute. The judges stood behind Hitler.

And once again, the Chairman of the Richterbund, Linz, saw the events of the preceding months in a wholly positive light. In the *Deutsche Richterzeitung*, published as the specialist journal of the 'judges and public prosecutors in the BNSDJ' following the dissolution of the Richterbund, he extolled the new 'feeling of solidarity' among its members.

In his view, German judges were now in an even stronger position than before. In the person of Reichsjuristenführer Frank, they had a leader who 'has the best interests of the judges at heart'. 'The BNSDJ is the right place for us', he assured his colleagues, and concluded his article with the now obligatory oath of loyalty:

> We swear always to revere the Führer of the people: We pledge loyalty to him to the end. We stand at his disposal with all that we have and with all our energies. Our revered Reich Chancellor Adolf Hitler Sieg Heil! Sieg Heil! Sieg Heil!

But it was not only the judiciary, looking to an authoritarian restoration of state and law to redress the social, political and professional slights it had suffered under the Weimar Republic, which hastened to embrace the cause of the National Socialists. The field of jurisprudence, too, discovered its 'true vocation' and placed its research and teaching departments in the service of 'the national reform'. Hair-raising right-wing constructions helped to systematically transform the jurisdiction and administration of justice to conform with National Socialist ideals.

In books, essays, lectures and treatises, German professors of law competed with each other, falling over themselves to discuss new terms such as 'Führertum', 'völkische order' and 'racial equality' and to discover in them new challenges for the world of jurisprudence. The professors, the majority of whom held anti-republican and anti-democratic views, did not hold the accomplishments of a liberal Rechtsstaat (state under the rule of law), such as equal status before the law, guaranteed rights for the individual, the limitation of the power of the state, in very high regard in the first place. Their authoritarian beliefs now became mingled with an authoritarian state ideology.

The professors set about redefining the term 'Rechtsstaat' in line with Nazi ideology. In his speech on the 'Verreichlichung der Justiz' (centralization of the judicial system) before judges, Hermann Göring had once stated self-confidently that 'the state we have created deserves the title of Rechtsstaat', explaining that its rights and laws had their roots in the community of its people.

Carl Schmitt, Professor for Public Law and a leading figure in the National Socialist wing of the Rechtwahrerschaft, a man who from an early date was convinced that 'the whole of German law today must be governed exclusively by the spirit of National Socialism', recommended the use of phrases such as 'the German Rechtsstaat', 'National Socialist Rechtsstaat' or even 'Adolf Hitler's German Rechtsstaat' in order to avoid unwelcome associations with the 'liberal Rechtsstaat'. In his numerous publications, Schmitt went to great lengths to incorporate the 'ethnic element' into the National Socialist concept of law and to inculcate 'racially characteristic legal thinking' into the judiciary. In 1934, he wrote:

> We know, not on the basis of feeling, but as the result of rigorously scientific insight, that any law is always the law of a specific people. It is an epistemological verity that only those who are participants in a racially determined legal community to which they existentially belong are capable of seeing the facts, of hearing statements correctly, understanding words correctly and evaluating impressions of persons and events correctly.
>
> Right down to our deepest, unconscious emotions and to the last fibre of our brain, we are rooted in the reality of our national and racial identity. Not every person who strives to be objective and who is subjectively convinced that he has made sufficient effort to be objective in fact achieves objectivity. No matter how critical his stance or how shrewd his endeavours, no matter how many books he reads or how many books he writes, a person of another race thinks and understands differently because of his very otherness, and in every crucial train of thought, he remains subject to the existential conditions of his own race . . .
>
> We seek a bond that is more reliable, more dynamic and deeper than the deceptive commitment to the easily twisted words of a thousand legal paragraphs. And where else could that bond lie but within ourselves and our own kind? Once again, in view of the inseparable connection between the rule of law, the civil service and judicial independence, all questions and answers point to the exigency of a single ethnic identity without which a total Führerstaat could not exist for even one day.

And the judges understood Carl Schmitt's message: judicial independence, yet total dependence on the political leadership. And they accepted it. The Führer as the supreme judge.

Another excerpt from Schmitt's writings:

> The Führer protects the law against the gravest misuse in as far as, in the hour of danger, he immediately creates law by virtue of his role as Führer and the supreme legal authority . . . The true

31

Führer is always also a judge. His role as a judge springs from his role as Führer. Anyone who separates one from the other or even poses one against the other either turns the judge into a counter-Führer or an instrument in the hand of a counter-Führer and seeks to dismantle the state by means of the judiciary . . . In reality, the Führer's deed was an act of true jurisdiction, a deed not subordinate to justice but itself constituting supreme justice.

Carl Schmitt and numerous other jurists sympathetic to the Nazi cause explained, justified, even perfected the legal terror of the National Socialists. 'What we need', stated Otto Koellreutter, like Schmitt a professor of law, in 1934 in 'The German Führerstaat', 'is only the political, National Socialist man. To educate him in the spirit of the Führer and hereby contribute the blocks that form the foundation of the German Führerstaat seems to me to be today's most urgent task for all German professors. Heil Hitler!'

In their eagerness to ingratiate themselves with the new regime, the professors vied with each other to come up with ever-new terminology, for example to distinguish the National Socialist Rechtsstaat from the 'civil Rechtstaat'. In their opinion, justice should only be dispensed by 'a man whose roots lie within the Volk and who is therefore uniquely able to judge what is beneficial for the people and what is harmful', as Göring once described his ideal judge.

In contrast to the liberal state, there will be no more feeble consideration for the individual. With regard to sentencing and the penal system, lawbreakers, enemies of the state and enemies of the national community can expect only one thing: the full rigour of the law and if necessary, total destruction. We have finally learned that human head shape and other racial characteristics are neither a coincidence nor inconsequential, but the expression of and basis for a person's innermost feelings and intentions.

Fiery statements such as these, from a young faculty assistant at the University of Breslau, were by no means the ramblings of isolated fanatics, but commonplace. And soon they were no longer limited to academic writings and terminology. The discussion on the 'new' vision of the Rechtsstaat was soon to have practical consequences.

Step by step, all fundamental principles ensuring a humane criminal law system were suspended and abolished – not least with legitimation by the experts on legal theory. The focus was no longer on protection of the rights of the individual against the state; the rights of the state now took precedence over those of individuals. Once again, it was 'state philosopher' Carl Schmitt who put it into words: 'In a crucial case, normalization only means a commitment of the Führer to the benefit of the disobedient.'

In other words: protection of the individual and legal certainty were things of the past. The focus was now firmly on the 'protection of the ethnic community'.

This 'right of protection' applied not only to 'antisocial criminals' but above all to political opponents of the system. And an official criminal law commission under the chairmanship of Minister of Justice Gürtner now decided whether the Volksgenosse (racial compatriot) could still be considered a member of the ethnic community or if the application of 'full rigour' or even 'total destruction' was indicated. In addition to the 'right of protection', the Nazi legal scholars also emphasized the importance of the 'völkische Treuepflicht' (the people's duty of allegiance):

> National Socialist criminal law must be based on the 'völkische Treuepflicht': the duty of allegiance is the highest national and thus moral duty for National Socialist and German thinking. In German thinking, moral evaluation, the sense of duty and the sense of justice are in harmony . . . It is the task of the National Socialist state to mete out expiatory punishment to those who fail in this duty of allegiance and have therefore placed themselves outside the national community. Just punishment strengthens, protects and secures the Volksgemeinschaft [national/ethnic community], but also serves the purpose of education and betterment of the perpetrator and the Volksgenosse who is not yet lost.

Henceforth, then, every offence, even petty theft, was viewed as 'Treuebruch', a breach of trust, a betrayal of the Führer and the German people. Numerous experts on criminal law published treatises on the relationship between Volk, state and Führer which went far beyond the borders of jurisprudence. There was hardly a lecture, hardly an essay that was not peppered with terms such as 'loyalty', 'honour' and 'duty', and hardly a field of law, right down to tenancy or commercial law, that was not imbued with National Socialist ideology by the professors of law.

Anyone who violated the law placed themselves outside the community, was guilty of 'betrayal' – and was an enemy of the people. The courts wasted no time considering whether and why the individual had broken the law, but merely examined whether the wrongdoer was still to be considered as part of the Volksgemeinschaft or not. And whether it was worth undertaking to rehabilitate offenders or whether they should be 'weeded out' was based not on the deed itself, but on the 'delinquent personality'. Here, too, the jurists, aided and abetted by their colleagues from the medical faculties, had already provided the necessary instrument: the insidious concept of specific 'criminal types'.

Wherever laws and decrees were drafted – from the Law against Dangerous Habitual Criminals to Protecting the National Community from Juvenile Delinquency, The Ordinance on Antisocial Parasites or the redefinition of murder – the focus was always the 'delinquent personality'. The underlying premise: people do not become criminals; they are born criminal.

In other words, the world of jurisprudence played a major role in the development and establishment of the inhumane Nazi legal system. With commitment, enthusiasm and of their own free will, German professors provided the theoretical foundation for a barbarization of the law.

Critical voices were few and far between. Like the judges, the academics had quickly and without great regret rid themselves of their Jewish and Social Democratic colleagues shortly after the Nazis took power. As a result of the passing of the Law for the Restoration of the Professional Civil Service, almost one-third of the 378 judges were dismissed in April 1933 alone, the majority of them on grounds of race. The positions of these 'non-Aryans' were filled with independent scholars who supported the Nazis, ensuring that in future the legal system would be in the hands of individuals loyal to the 'nationalist cause' and trained in the new National Socialist view of the law.

Like the judiciary and the universities, the new regime had also purged the bar of 'politically undesirable elements and non-Aryans' soon after it took over. Germany had always had a particularly high number of Jewish lawyers. Before 1933, there were 19,500 lawyers admitted to the bar, 4,394 (around 22 per cent) of them of Jewish descent. The percentage was far higher in cities like Frankfurt and Berlin. And there were numerous Jewish lawyers on the board of the Deutscher Anwaltsverein (German Lawyers' Association). All this was to change radically under the National Socialists.

Some 1,500 lawyers, the majority of them Jews, were disbarred under the Law for the Restoration of the Professional Civil Service. The homogenized bar associations announced new codes of ethics and professional conduct. In Berlin, for example, it was made illegal for 'Aryan' and 'non-Aryan' lawyers to found or operate joint legal chambers, and citizens who engaged a 'non-Aryan' lawyer to represent them were publicly denounced. On 28 August 1933, for example, the newspaper *Hessische Volkswacht* published a list of litigants 'who had shamelessly employed Jewish lawyers'. In the spring of 1933, the BNSDJ had declared that it would 'never cease to pursue its demand that all Jews, without exception, must be removed from every legal sphere'. Already by this time, no protest was heard from German lawyers.

They were all dancing to the Nazis' tune. The regional lawyers' associations called on their 'non-Aryan' members to withdraw. And in its new directives, the legal journal *Juristische Wochenschrift* declared that in future, only contributions 'by Aryans' would be published.

In the Deutsche Rechtswahrer front, there was no room for Jews and Republicans, and lawyers now no longer saw themselves as 'free advocates', but as 'servants of the law'. Ignoring their history, they, too, suddenly felt a special duty of loyalty to the state.

Minister of Justice Gürtner stated with satisfaction: 'As defence counsel, the lawyer has been brought closer to the state and the community . . . he has been incorporated into the community of the guardians of the law and has abandoned his former position as a partial representative of the interests of the accused.' It is true that some within the profession still flirted with their 'free' status as lawyers, now defined as the 'exercise of a state function', but the reality was already a different one. Anyone who believed, for example, that they could get away without giving the 'German greeting' (Hitler salute) in the courtroom was officially reprimanded by the lawyers' Ehrengericht (court of honour). However, as the majority of lawyers now felt quite at home under the National Socialist legal system, this professional tribunal seldom had cause to intervene. The Hitler salute had become just as much a part of their identity as the robes they wore.

In other words, Carl Schmitt's call for German law in its entirety to be governed solely by 'the spirit of National Socialism' had become reality, and without notable resistance. Judges, public prosecutors, professors of law and lawyers were now all marching arm in arm – the German 'law guardians' front was mobilized. Enforced homogenisation from above – voluntary self-homogenisation from below.

One people, one Führer, one legal system. A united front against anyone who thought differently, felt differently, lived differently – who was unwilling or unable to conform to the National Socialist Weltbild. Anyone who did not support the 'national revolution' was a 'traitor', an 'enemy of the people'.

The Volksgerichtshof had been created to deal with just such traitors and enemies of the German people, and one warrior was already preparing to do battle in the front line of justice: Roland Freisler.

Chapter 4

# Undersecretary and Publicist

In the Prussian Ministry of Justice, Roland Freisler was considered an extremely talented and industrious man. His superior, Minister of Justice Kerrl, valued not only his absolute loyalty to National Socialist principles but in particular the fact that as undersecretary, Freisler had a talent for recognizing in advance which way the wind was blowing. And so, when it was decided that German criminal law needed comprehensive reform, Kerrl gladly assigned the task to him. Several attempts had been made in the past to revise the criminal code of 1871. So far, however, only fragments had been reviewed. And now, following the seizure of power by the Nazis and the birth of the new Germany, it was important that the principles of the National Socialist state should also be anchored in the criminal code.

In September 1933, the Prussian Ministry of Justice issued a memorandum with the title 'National Socialist Criminal Law', in the drafting of which Freisler had played a leading role. For Kerrl, this was an attempt, with the support of his undersecretary, to put forward his own ideas on important National Socialist principles for inclusion in the criminal code, aware as he was that in Gürtner's Reichsjustizministerium and in the Akademie für deutsches Recht (Academy for German Law) in Munich, recently founded by Hans Frank, they were already hard at work on a draft for a reformed penal code. In entering the race to be at the forefront in the creation of a new legal framework, Kerrl was not only demonstrating his political allegiance, but also defending his reputation. Freisler had similar ambitions, which forged a bond between the two.

All three reform commissions could be sure of support from the majority of judges, as high-ranking jurists had increasingly demanded legal reform over recent years. As the President of the Hamburg Oberlandesgericht (higher regional court of appeal) Rothenberger, voicing an opinion shared by many, put it: 'it is essential to dispel the Party's misgivings about the legal system through a National Socialist jurisprudence and to prevent unjustified attacks on the judiciary by emphasizing the necessity for the proper administration of justice'.

In his memorandum, Freisler expressed the view that the sole purpose of the totalitarian state was to serve the Volksgemeinschaft (national community). As Hitler had already stated in his speech on 23 March 1933: 'Not the individual, but the Volk as a whole must be the focal point of legislative efforts.' This was Freisler's maxim, too. He saw the main functions of the criminal code as 'the destruction of elements which threaten the peace' and the 'expiation of culpable wrong'. It was important, he went on, to stabilize the new system, to increase its external security and maintain its internal security. And the most important function of court sentences, in Freisler's eyes, was 'to protect the national community against those who refuse to bow to the law'.

His remarks culminated in the proposal that every perpetrator should be seen and treated as an enemy of the state, irrespective of whether the offence was of a criminal or a political nature. The state, said Freisler, was waging war against crime, against 'Untermenschen' (sub-humans). His memorandum called for court regulation of almost all areas of life. In order to anchor National Socialist principles in criminal law, he suggested new offences such as 'protection of the race and Volk tradition' or 'the violation of racial honour'. For Freisler, the worst crime of all was treason. Like so many other Germans, he was still influenced by the trauma of defeat in 1918.

His language was that of battle, of war. Carl Schmitt's theories of the totalitarian state, in particular Schmitt's distinction between friend and enemy, were the starting point of his deliberations. Freisler categorically rejected the concept of a differentiated treatment of 'criminals'. A criminal was a criminal and as such an enemy of the state. The criminal code, he declared, was the embodiment of the right of the state to defend itself against its enemies, and all available weapons should be brought to bear against the 'criminal', the worst type of wrongdoer being the political criminal. It was not a matter of sentencing, he stated, but of eliminating these criminals and subversives.

Freisler's memorandum – produced in 15,000 copies for distribution among German jurists did not 'set out to provide an answer to decade-old academic and theoretical disputes within the science of criminal law', but 'to sound the depths of National Socialist ideology, to rise to the challenge of the duty of the state to administer justice to its people, and thus to establish the basis for the creation of a National Socialist criminal code', as he wrote in a pompously-phrased essay entitled 'National Socialist criminal law and constructive criticism' for the February edition of the journal *Deutsche Justiz*. The essay also responded to a critique of the Freisler memorandum, written by a professor of law from Jena on the invitation of the journal's editorial office. Freisler wrote:

Not only does the memorandum on criminal law accept criticism; it invites and encourages it. However, it will not reply to destructive criticism which surgically dissects the whole in an attempt to prove that here and there something is not logically consistent, that here and there some detail of the letter of the law needs refining. It will not deign to reply to such criticism, because such criticism falls short of the mark and is therefore of no consequence.

What it welcomes, on the other hand, is criticism that is prompted by the earnest desire to work toward improvement. It even invites criticism that is basically hostile, because National Socialist criminal law is strong enough to stand the test.

For some years now, Professor Gerland in Jena has been known as a teacher of criminal law who is not exactly an advocate of National Socialist virtues. The journal *Deutsche Justiz* asked him for a statement on the criminal law memorandum of the Prussian Minister of Justice . . .

To begin with seemingly peripheral details, Professor Gerland objects to the external form of the memorandum, where the specific section precedes the general section. The Professor's dialectical-logical argumentation is that it is not possible to work with terminology which has not been previously defined. He rejects the protection it offers to the citizens of our nation as too restrictive, since non-members of the national community living in Germany are also protected by the order of the peace. He considers the simplification of the definition of criminal acts as too extensive. In his view, terms such as 'gesundes Volksempfinden' (the sound instincts of the people) which are used by the memorandum are too relative. He sees a move towards a criminal code that punishes the threat of criminal activity as a tightening of the law that presents a major challenge in practice, in particular if the same penalty is imposed for committing, attempting to commit and planning a crime. He fears that to permit the analogous application of laws would lead to non-uniform court practice.

He believes that 'Willensstrafrecht' (a criminal code which prosecutes the subjective 'will' of the perpetrator rather than specific actions) is not in accordance with the sentiments of the

German people and accuses the memorandum of contradicting itself when it recognizes the sound instincts of the people as a source of law while at the same time stating the need for education of the people. He also feels that the discretionary powers of the judge are too broad, making the judge a legislator in particularly mild cases and shifting the boundaries between the law and the court.

A veritable plethora of critical suggestions!

In fact, Freisler was using the pages of commentary penned by the Jena professor, benevolently described here as 'constructive criticism', to stoke the fires of his own vanity. Freisler hoped that this public debate would bring him recognition as the designer and co-author of a new National Socialist criminal code, the acknowledgement of his achievement in legal circles. He had no intention whatsoever of changing his views. In the April edition of *Deutsche Justiz*, he published a comprehensive rejoinder. Point by point, he defended the content of the memorandum and refuted Professor Gerland's objections. And it was an easy matter to find a few words of praise for his critic at the end of his article. He could even invoke the words of the Führer:

> The Führer has repeatedly emphasized the importance of constructive, cooperative criticism. I am pleased to be able to state in conclusion that the criticism of the Prussian justice minister's memorandum expressed by Professor Gerhard was indeed constructive and cooperative, even where it rejected the memorandum. May all forces everywhere who feel the inner compulsion to work with us on a National Socialist renewal of the law express constructive criticism, thus enabling the emerging new German law to fulfil its role within the living organism of the German Volk.

And he assured readers:

> Our untiring efforts continue wherever the revolutionary inner transformation of the law requires external expression. The work of the criminal law committee of the Reich Ministry of Justice and the criminal law committee of the Akademie für Deutsches Recht has reached an advanced stage. The experts and those directly involved are engaged in putting the final touches to the future German criminal code.

Following these publications, in prolific essays, on lecture tours and above all in his function as undersecretary, he did everything in his power to ensure that his proposed reforms would be implemented. Initially, his efforts did not bring the sweeping success he had hoped for, but the Law on Dangerous Habitual Criminals, which came into effect on 4 November 1933, was at least a step in the direction he envisaged. And a law passed on 24 April 1934 imposing more severe sentences – frequently the death penalty – for crimes relating to treason and high treason corresponded to his idea of a new criminal code.

Freisler's goal was a judiciary which passed harsh sentences and passed them quickly, particularly in the case of 'political criminals', who, for Freisler, were the worst traitors and enemies of the state. He summarised his views in an essay for publication in the journal of the Academy for German Law: 'Within twenty-four hours . . . charges must be brought . . . within a further twenty-four hours, the sentence must be pronounced, and the sentence must be carried out immediately . . . It is time to dispense once and for all with a habitual consideration of extenuating circumstances.'

On the face of it, Freisler's totalitarian legal theory may seem particularly fanatical and radical; yet he was by no means alone in his views. But – and this is what distinguished the industrious undersecretary from the majority of his colleagues – he knew better than any how to combine National Socialist ideology and the role of the National Socialist judiciary.

Following the dissolution of the Prussian Ministry of Justice in the course of the centralization of the judiciary, Freisler was transferred to the Reich Ministry of Justice on 1 April 1934 as an undersecretary. Here, too, together with his colleague, the much older undersecretary Dr Schlegelberger, he was soon recognized as a jurist absolutely committed to the Nazi cause. Freisler was placed in charge of a field of particular importance to the Party, namely that of criminal law. He was also responsible for the organization of the judicial system – and then there was Freisler's greatest challenge: the Volksgerichtshof.

The role Freisler envisaged for the People's Court becomes clear in an essay published in the March edition of the journal of the Academy for German Law. Under the title 'Volksgerichtshof', it lays forth his central aim of making the new People's Court the new Reichsstrafgericht (Reich penal court). He saw a People's Court as the 'focal point of a general German criminal code', which according to Freisler, could only be correctly evaluated and assessed by examining the present and future criminal justice system.

Although probably already nursing ambitions to become President of the Volksgerichtshof himself at some point in the future, Freisler nevertheless tirelessly supported the establishment of a German people's tribunal which would be the equivalent of the Reich civil court. 'It would be the custodian of legal unity, a champion of legal development, the guardian of legal certainty, all at the same time, and thus first and foremost the primary protector of the safety of the nation', he wrote in his essay. Freisler hoped to make the People's Court an all-embracing legal institution. The 'establishment of a court which is as close to the people as the Volksgerichtshof, transforming it into the supreme German criminal court anchored in the national consciousness' was a challenge which fascinated him.

In the new Reich Ministry of Justice under Dr Frank Gürtner, Freisler was even busier than under the former Prussian Minister of Justice Kerrl, and became such a whirlwind of frenetic activity that contemporary jurists soon perceived him as the most prominent personality in the ministry. Freisler was everywhere, he wrote and commented on everything. With innumerable publications and lectures, he cemented his reputation as 'raving Roland', a nickname given to him by NSDAP jurists, who did not always look favourably on his activities.

During this period, his unbounded loyalty to the Führer and his fanatical glorification of National Socialism became increasingly evident. He had already demonstrated often enough what a hard line he took when it came to treason against the people, the Führer or the Party. Following the bloody and legally-unsanctioned execution of Ernst Röhm, other SA leaders and numerous other political opponents of the Nazi regime on 30 June 1934, which became known as the 'Röhm Putsch' or 'The Night of the Long Knives', an essay by Freisler appeared in *Deutsche Justiz*. In it, he supported the post-hoc legal justification of this blatant violation of the law and defended 'The Führer's deed' in grandiloquent words:

> A cleansing thunderstorm has swept over Germany. It bore away with it the sultry and oppressive climate. In its wake, it leaves air that is fresh, pure and cool, and everyone is now setting about their work again with renewed energy and the infinitely increased certainty of victory. This cleansing storm began abruptly, and it performed its task of purification with the precision of a well-oiled machine. How many long and sleepless nights the Führer must have spent before it, racked by worry and sorrow – weeks in which he was increasingly convinced that such betrayal must be impossible: yet weeks in which the frivolity and lack of character of the traitors themselves furnished grain upon grain of evidence, finally tipping the scales inexorably against them, until

the Führer realized with painful certainty that the impossible had become reality – betrayal! And then came the time for judgement, by a tribunal more equitable and essential than any the world has ever seen, a tribunal whose judgement drew on the clear, profound source of our German moral order; a court, then, that implemented law in its highest sense.

The ramblings of a pathological fanatic? Just a few years later, the undersecretary who here glorifies the murderous acts of the Nazis in the flowery, conservative language of old German would himself hold a key position and perform his task of 'cleansing' the state of 'traitors' with all the precision of a well-oiled machine. But all that still lay in the future.

Freisler was in fact only stating what thousands of jurists thought. When the *Reichsgesetzblatt* (Reich Law Gazette) announced on 13 December 1934 that the courts no longer held jurisdiction over legal claims in connection with the 'Röhm case', once again, there was hardly any protest.

In connection with the 'Röhm Putsch', Freisler was active not only as a publicist but also in his old profession as a lawyer. In December 1934, Hitler, as the leader of the NSDAP, had filed a suit against the newspaper *Kasseler Volksblatt*. The paper had published the so-called 'Röhm paper', in which it was claimed that Hitler was aware of the SA leader's homosexual leanings and tolerated them, which was demonstrably true. In the action for an injunction, a civil court ordered the *Kasseler Volksblatt* to black out all references to Hitler's knowledge of Röhm's homosexuality in any remaining copies of the paper, on the grounds that there was no concrete evidence to support the claim. The success of the action – which later resulted in the newspaper closing down due to repeated harassment by the Nazi district administration – was due in part to the lawyer who represented Hitler before the court in Kassel: Dr Roland Freisler. This legal victory was more than just a flattering but essentially insignificant triumph in one of his old haunts; it was to benefit the power-hungry undersecretary in his later career.

Not everyone felt comfortable with Freisler and his overweening ambition. Without question, he was considered a competent undersecretary, a jurist with an exceptionally sharp intellect, a man who could present complex legal issues clearly and objectively, but who, when it came to 'the great and sacred National Socialist achievements', assumed the implacability of a Grand Inquisitor.

He was also known as a man driven by his emotions and the mood of the moment. He often veered off into fanatical tirades on National Socialist ideology. This was a man who could captivate others, but could also strike fear into them, especially anyone who opposed his thoughts and ideas.

Freisler knew how to exploit any situation in his own interests – that was what made him so inscrutable – and so dangerous. But in no way was this an obstacle to his career in the Nazi legal system. Quite the contrary.

A man like Freisler was always on hand to deal with political questions in the field of jurisprudence. At times, his immense capacity for work and his flexibility perplexed his fellow jurists – but they seldom admired him. He was considered an authority, his skills and his loyalty were held in high esteem. Yet he was not particularly popular within the ministry, the Party or the judiciary.

Freisler was not someone who particularly needed to be liked. He saw himself as a lone warrior, fighting for the great common goal. In his eyes, he was rendering an important contribution to the establishment of the new National Socialist jurisdiction – and always driven by his own strong instinct for the source of power.

He did indeed play a major role in the systematic extension of the brutal Nazi laws, not only as the author of numerous essays in the influential professional journals – or of the memorandum mentioned above – but above all as the co-author of the two-volume report on the 'work of the official criminal law commission' published in 1935 by Reich Justice Minister Gürtner under the title *Das kommende deutsche Strafrecht* ('Future German Criminal Law'). It was Freisler's 'masterpiece' to date. After the publication of the report, he persistently continued his efforts to promote the implementation of his concept of law with unabated zeal and strategic calculation, in personal meetings, in lectures and presentations, but in particular, in his position as undersecretary, by issuing a flood of directives and regulations.

A diligent and very busy man indeed. His prolific publications did not stem from his craving for recognition within the field of jurisprudence alone. First and foremost, Freisler wrote because he was convinced that this would increase his legal and political influence. Three key factors determined Freisler's thinking, three factors without which it is impossible to understand his later career – and with it, the history and practice of the Volksgerichtshof.

Firstly: The role of treason. Like many, if not the majority, of his fellow Germans, Freisler believed that the German Reich had only lost the First World War because its army had been betrayed by the civilians on the home front. There was an unshakable belief in the 'Dolchstosslegende' (the stab-in-the-back legend). The Germans seized on this conspiracy theory, shocked by the defeat of the seemingly invincible German army and the subsequent 'humiliating provisions' of the Treaty of Versailles.

43

In a speech in the Reichstag on 18 November 1919, Hindenburg had already attempted to explain the reasons behind the German defeat:

> Despite the immense effort demanded of the army and its leaders, despite the being outnumbered by the enemy, we could have brought the unequal struggle to a favourable outcome if determined and unanimous co-operation had existed between those at war and those on the home front . . . But what happened?
>
> While on the side of our enemies, all parties and all social classes, though their troop strength and material resources were already superior, closed ranks to form a close-knit front in their will for victory . . . . here, where such a united front was far more important in view of our inferior position, diverging party interests began to manifest themselves, and under these circumstances, very soon led to fragmentation and a weakening of our will to win . . . the collapse was inevitable.

The National Socialists, and with them the majority of the German people, vowed that such a 'stab in the back' must never be allowed to happen again. The Nazis had already proclaimed before they came to power that the penalties for treason and high treason would be increased. Freisler was in full support of this. In his eyes, the main threat to the state and its government was treason and high treason. In other words, here we can already see evidence of the fanatical attitude Freisler would later adopt towards so many of the defendants brought before him as President of the People's Court.

Secondly: For the National Socialists, treason was no isolated crime of conscience, but an attack on the entire 'national community', and the National Socialist regime saw itself as the highest embodiment of the national community. It was determined not to allow a situation to arise in which any one part of the people could rise up against another. Society was no longer made up of different classes, but of one Volk. Anyone who violated the laws of the state was no longer part of the national community and became a 'Volksfeind' (enemy of the people).

For Freisler, with his National Socialist world-view, the law and the judiciary were exclusively instruments for the maintenance of internal and external order and the protection of the people. Both were bound to serve the people – where necessary, with the utmost rigour.

The third and last factor in Freisler's thinking was the National Socialist 'Führerprinzip' (leader or Führer principle). In *Mein Kampf*, Hitler had already defined the role of the Führer, whose power

44

extended from the smallest community to the leadership of the Reich. This power was not subject to any limitations. It was absolute. It followed that not only were the orders of the Führer to be carried out unquestioningly, but that the will of the Führer became the yardstick for all actions. The order, issued from above and implemented via a network of institutions and public authorities, became the decisive instrument of the NS state. In 1937, the official publication *Deutsche Verwaltungsblätter* stated:

> The authority of the Führer is not a competence. The Führer does not make the office. The Führer forms the office in accordance with his mission . . .
> The authority of the Führer knows no gaps in responsibility . . .
> The authority of the Führer stands above all competence . . .
> The authority of the Führer is absolute.

This Führer principle was also to be applied in the courtroom. The presiding judge was the sole authority in a trial. His directives were more important than the files documenting the case. In Freisler's view, assessors and lay judges should also accord the role of the judge as Führer priority over the law. Later, this Führer principle would be applied in practice, especially at the Volksgerichtshof. Nowhere was the role of the judge as Führer emphasized more strongly.

Unqualified loyalty was the logical consequence in a state where the Führer principle had exclusive validity. Anyone who opposed the Führer and the national community was guilty of a breach of loyalty – and that, too, was treason.

Freisler was not interested in motives here. For him, the mere intent to commit treason was tantamount to having committed it. The intention and the crime itself, he argued with particular fervour, should be punished with equal severity. Anyone who committed a crime claiming that it was in order to improve the Reich was – according to Freisler – just as much a traitor as any other person guilty of treason. The Führer Adolf Hitler alone determined the character of the state.

Again and again, he compiled lengthy lists of 'crimes', many of them no more than offences, which had not yet been entered in the German criminal code and which, in particular in the years following 1938, he elevated to the status of crimes by extending the definition of treason. Even the slightest criticism of the regime, claimed Freisler, should be classified as treason, because this alone would ensure that the law would once again become 'the ethical code of the Volk'.

45

The central themes of Freisler's prolific publications were always the same: the Führer, the Volk, the Party, the law, the judiciary. The titles of just a few of his essays will serve as examples: 'Judge, jurisprudence and the law' (*Deutsche Justiz*, 1934), 'The deed of the Führer is our duty' (*Deutsche Justiz* 1934), 'The task of the Reich legal system developed from a biological understanding of law' (*Deutsche Justiz*, 1935), 'The duty of the criminal code to protect the people against parasites on the body of the nation' (*Deutsche Richterzeitung*, 1938), 'The Reich and the law' (*Deutsche Justiz*, 1939), or 'The preserver of German criminal law thinks, speaks and writes in German' (*Deutsche Justiz*, 1941).

And indeed, Freisler thought, spoke and thought in the German of the people. His essays were free of cumbersome legal rhetoric, their argumentation was cogent and consistent, but as the same time liberally seasoned with the usual Nazi propaganda jargon.

Freisler stated his case from the perspective of a committed – and indeed, following the outbreak of the War, a fanatical – National Socialist. His starting point and context were always his unshakable National Socialist world-view.

Again and again, he defined the Nazi state, in which the individual had no free and subjective choices, as a 'Rechtsstaat'. In 1937, in an essay entitled 'Der Rechtsstaat'. he wrote: 'Only the concentrated power of the Volk, as concentrated fire power once tamed the tank that threatened our front line, will enable us [to do this]. The organized form in which we bring concentrated fire power to bear for the protection of our Volk is our vision of the "Rechtsstaat".' The state as the sum of its people – a statement that appears, at first glance, almost radically democratic. However, three clear Nazi perversions correct this false impression:

Firstly: There was a clear and explicitly racial definition of the Volk. In 1933, in his proposals for the reform of the criminal code, Freisler had stated that 'Blut und Boden' (blood and soil) were the 'most sacred German values'. And in his previously-mentioned essay 'The task of the Reich legal system developed from a biological understanding of law', he explained:

> National Socialism is characterized by its biological perspective. It looks at the Volk, its internal and external growth, biologically, sees its history as biologically determined, biologically determined through the people's selection of its life goal and the selection of the correct path to achieve this life goal. The National Socialist also sees the law as biological. Our view of the nature of the law differs from that held by others who wrestled with themselves and the world to achieve knowledge of and insight into the law.

The new German law, stated Freisler, needed to be based on the idea of the 'biological substance of the Volk', whose 'ethnic unity' had to be preserved. And he warned that the 'tide of racial mixing in Germany over the course of centuries must be stemmed', for example in his essay 'The protection of race and inheritance in the new German criminal code', published in 1936.

In other words, Freisler agreed with the radical 'Social Darwinist' propagandists who exerted considerable influence on Hitler, Himmler and other prominent Nazis. The National Socialist racial cult – the tenets of which Freisler wanted to see applied in the future legal reform – quickly found its application in law. On 15 September 1935, the Law for the Protection of German Blood and German Honour came into force. In effect, this law was a piece of blanket legislation covering every imaginable 'attack on the race' and thus all possible violations of the Nuremberg Laws, monstrous racial laws which marked the beginning of the systematic persecution and murder of the Jews.

In this context, it is interesting to note that Freisler never explicitly occupied himself with the so-called 'Jewish problem'. Nevertheless, he was one of the circle of leading jurists who gave the racial mania of the National Socialists a pseudo-legal veneer. It was his conviction from an early date that the protection of the race was also a primary task of the judiciary. For, as he wrote in 1936, 'It is the duty of the German nation and of every individual to practise racial hygiene; failure to fulfil this duty is tantamount to treason'.

To return to Freisler's ideas of the Rechtsstaat: for him, the question of whether an individual belonged to a national community or not was not a question of a subjective choice. The irrefutable Führer principle degraded the individual to a passive recipient of commands and excluded him from any form of active choice.

Freisler's definition of a National Socialist Rechtsstaat also rejected the idea of an absolutist state, but not in order to protect the rights of the individual; he saw therein a danger of the state becoming an end in itself, and the end purpose was neither the individual nor the state, but the Volk, the Germanic race itself. The institutions of the state, he demanded, must be infused with the spirit of National Socialism in order to create an organic bond between the national community, the Führer and the Party.

There was no place in this vision of the Rechtsstaat for a separation of powers, which Freisler in any case saw as the outdated legacy of a past characterized by mistrust between the people and its political leaders. In National Socialist Germany, the separation of powers had made way for an organic unity between the Führer and the people and 'the confidence in the healthy unity of the people and the belief in the strength of this people to maintain this unified stance throughout history', as he wrote in an essay published in the *Deutsche Juristenzeitung*.

In Freisler's view, one of the main prerequisites for the maintenance of the NS state was a strong and efficient judiciary whose task it was to preserve the Volk and the state. At the same time, the law needed to be capable of development and adaptable to changing circumstances, he explained in the essay quoted above, 'for the law which is good today can be bad tomorrow'. The law, wrote Freisler, was no longer a normative absolute, but an instrument of political expediency.

In other words, the National Socialists completely subordinated the administration of justice to the achievement of their political aims. Step by step, the German Civil Code valid at the time was substantially amended and stripped of its original content. Criminal law in particular, on the pretext of protecting the rights of the people and the state, became a weapon in the arsenal of National Socialism.

And Undersecretary Dr Freisler was always right there in the front line. Untiringly, he propagated the defence of the 'most sacred German values'. In the fight against the enemies of the people, he believed, the Volksgerichtshof should assume the central role within the overall German legal system. In it, the leadership principle should be realized in particular manner as an example for all subordinated German courts. The president of each senate, stated Freisler, would be the leader, and his directives were to be followed unquestioningly by the professional and lay judges. This was the only way to achieve the 'Germanic' form of trial, a vision which Freisler developed in an essay published in 1935 under the title 'Details of a future German court with power over life and death'.

He stated that sole responsibility lay with the presiding judge, whose task it was to see to it that cases were processed as quickly as possible. Freisler accorded the lay judges at most an advisory function. Nevertheless, all parties involved in a 'Germanic trial', from the most experienced judge right down to the youngest lawyer, had to be 'soldiers of the law'.

The punishments meted out by these 'Germanic courts' were to be consistent and harsh and of course, included the death penalty. Freisler referred to alleged 'Germanic' ritual executions. For example, in an essay that appeared in *Deutsche Justiz* under the cynical title 'The active administration of justice', he advocated self-execution by means of a 'poisoned chalice'.

He also turned his attention to the court proceedings themselves, which he regarded as inefficient. He suggested considerably reducing the number of cases reviewed, not only because they were unnecessarily time-consuming, but also because they undermined the confidence of the people in the judiciary. And reviews should be dispensed with entirely where they would mean only insignificant changes in the sentence. Freisler, in other words, was quite prepared to accept the risk of miscarriages of justice. His main priorities were efficiency and the confidence of the people in the supposed infallibility of the judiciary. And it was in accordance with exactly these principles that the Volksgerichtshof would later be run.

And devoting such attention to the role of the judge as Freisler did, it was logical that he also had something to say about the training of the judiciary. In the essays 'The training of German legal professionals' and 'Aptitude for the profession of a German legal professional', both published in 1941 in *Deutsche Justiz*, he proposed that in future, recruits should no longer be selected by the judiciary, but by institutions of the NSDAP itself. The criteria for selection: Firstly, the candidates had to be healthy – in view of the heavy burden that rested on the shoulders of a judge. Secondly, they should come from racially healthy stock. And thirdly, the candidate should prove his leadership qualities, for example through earlier membership in the Hitler Youth or NS student organizations.

Finally, candidates should provide proof that they would find full satisfaction in working for the national community, which according to Freisler, would in turn result in 'awareness of the needs of the Volk and of the factors essential for its existence'.

In his essay, 'Deutscher Osten' ('The German East'), after the Wehrmacht invasion of Poland, Freisler described his vision of 'Germanic law' and how the future judge should deal with 'inferior' races such as Jews and Poles. The 'Polenstrafrecht', a criminal code that applied solely to Poles, he said, should be applied without any sentimentality. The interest of the German Volk was all that mattered. 'All those who have proved themselves in the east', he stated in the essay, which was published in 1941, 'will place their stamp on the judiciary of the entire Reich.'

Especially after the outbreak of the Second World War, such Nazi propaganda was the tenor of almost all the essays Freisler wrote. The catalogue of his rigorous demands became increasingly extensive, inhumane and excessive. No new law or directive escaped his public commentary.

After the start of the War, the National Socialists imposed a total of eleven new laws and decrees. To give an example, Freisler commented on one of them, the 'Decree on Extraordinary Measures for Wireless Owners', which prohibited Germans from listening to enemy and neutral radio stations and from disseminating news derived from them. In Freisler's opinion, what was being punished here was not curiosity, but the 'deliberate self-mutilation of the German soul', which, 'in addition to the damage caused by the spreading of news from foreign radio stations', could even have 'a defeatist effect'.

Freisler's trauma, his fear that the events of November 1918, the 'stab in the back from the home front' could be repeated, is evident in many of his publications. And it was not without effect.

Hardly any other profession saw itself subjected to such a barrage of National Socialist demands and maxims and to such close surveillance by the organs of the state and the Party as the judiciary. In 1935, Freisler wrote triumphantly in his essay 'The unity of party and state in the staffing policy of the judiciary': 'The German judiciary has every reason to be proud of being the first state institution to have implemented the unity of the movement, the Volk and the state in its staffing policy, throughout the Reich and on all levels of the civil service.' Freisler himself supported this process – as undersecretary and publicist – from the very beginning and 'in the front line', as he had sworn to do when the Nazis seized power in 1933. He negated the independence of the judiciary. In his view, it had become as obsolete as other individualistic tendencies, because National Socialism drew its strength from the ever-flowing fountain of the people. It was the task of the judiciary, he wrote in his 1936 essay 'Law and the lawmaker', to 'keep this water clean'. In other words: the task of the judiciary was to subordinate itself completely to the totalitarian demands of the National Socialist regime.

Freisler's maxim 'Harshness towards the enemy of the Volk ensures the well-being of the Volk' had been implemented step by step since 1933, with increasing consistency, brutality and inhumanity, not only at the Volksgerichtshof, but by special courts throughout the Reich, later also in the occupied territories, and in the barbarous actions of the Einsatzgruppen.

This development coincided with Freisler's guiding principles, which had remained the same through the years. In 1935, he wrote:

> It is indeed possible that though the letters, words and paragraphs of the law have not changed, a judge's decision underpinned by the objectivity of a neutral age may differ from a judge's decision underpinned by the exercise of judicial freedom in the spirit of National Socialism. One cannot approach the question of the judge's position on right and law in his professional work only from the same standpoint as that from which a soldier who has been assigned a task sets about doing his duty: respect for the will of the Führer as the natural expression of law and pride in the trust invested in us . . . and the sense of obligation to take

into account all circumstances in accordance with the National Socialist directive.

Following the death of Reich Minister of Justice Gürtner in 1941, Undersecretary Schlegelberger took over as acting minister. As a consequence, due to the additional administrative workload, Freisler was forced to curtail his flood of publications.

Eighteen months after Gürtner's death, NSDAP member Otto Thierack, then President of the Volksgerichtshof, was appointed his successor as Reich Minister of Justice, and Thierack's chair in the People's Court was filled by a man who, more than any other, brought with him the prerequisites for the job: Roland Freisler.

At last he was in a position where he could carry out the orders of his masters and relentlessly put into practice all the maxims he had so fervently recommended as a publicist on matters of German law.

Chapter 5

# Against Traitors and Parasites

It is impossible to give an account of the Freisler era which began on 15 October 1942 without first providing a brief overview of the criminal code as it was to be applied and interpreted by the Volksgerichtshof. The following pages will therefore focus on the laws governing high treason and treason, individual procedural regulations, areas of responsibility and the influence of the Gestapo (Geheime Staatspolizei, secret state police).

Not only for Freisler was National Socialist thinking based on three main maxims; the role of treason, the concept of the Volksgemeinschaft (national community) and the Führer principle. Nowhere were these three pillars of National Socialist ideology more consistently applied than at the Volksgerichtshof, which had moved and was now based at Bellevuestrasse 15 in Berlin. Anyone brought before the senates of the Volksgerichtshof was considered a traitor, and the criminal code had been extensively supplemented and stiffened to deal with them.

For example high treason (Hochverrat) and treason (Landesverrat, literally 'treason against the country'): paragraph 81 defined high treason as an act committed with the aim of changing the constitution or the territory of the Reich, while paragraphs 83 and 84 covered conspiracies with the intent to commit high treason and finally, paragraph 86 defined preparation to commit high treason as a punishable offence.

Initially, Landesverrat was covered by the same paragraphs as high treason in the Strafgesetzbuch (German criminal code). Landesverrat was defined as conspiracy between a German and foreign agents to prepare for a war against Germany. Paragraph 90 listed all acts constituting Landesverrat: from incitement to desertion to betrayal of operational plans, espionage, the sabotaging of war material and incitement to mutiny within the German armed forces.

The 'Decree of the Reich President for the Protection of People and State' and the 'Decree against Treason on the German People and Activities of High Treason', both passed on 28 February 1933 in reaction to the Reichstag Fire, had increased the penalty for treason and high treason from imprisonment to death. And to demonstrate that the regime meant business, the National Socialists – this time on the basis of the Enabling Act – had introduced execution by hanging or decapitation for all acts of treason and high treason committed between 31 January and 28 February 1933. Marinus van der Lubbe, the young man brought before the Reichsgericht as the Reichstag arsonist, was condemned to death and executed on the basis of this law.

The message of the Nazi regime was clear: acts of high treason and treason, even the mere intention to commit treason, were to be punished promptly and harshly. It was the senior Reich prosecutor who decided whether alleged traitors would be tried in front of the Volksgerichtshof. He had the power to delegate the case – for example, if the charge was intent to commit treason – to the next lower court, the Oberlandesgericht (regional court of appeal). From an early date, however, Freisler exhibited a tendency to view these courts as mere 'subsidiaries' of the Volksgerichtshof.

The jurisdiction of the Volksgerichtshof had already been extended in 1935: 'Wehrmittelbeschädigung' (damage to military resources) and 'failure to report treason and high treason' were now also punishable crimes and treated as acts of treason in themselves. Despite tougher penalties, the Ministry of Justice had criticised the sentences imposed by the People's Court as too lenient to have the desired deterrent effect.

And indeed, the Volksgerichtshof cannot be accused of being excessively harsh in its judgements in the early days of its existence. In 1934, for example, the First Senate sentenced a man accused of having distributed illegal pamphlets and weapons in the police force to two years' imprisonment for preparation of high treason and violation of the firearms act, and the seven months' he had already spent in detention awaiting trial were taken into account. A defendant accused of distributing subversive literature within the Reichswehr was sentenced to one year and nine months in prison for preparation of high treason, also reduced by seven months for time already spent in detention. In view of the fact that under the decrees of 28 February 1933, such offences could be punished by imprisonment with hard labour for up to three years, these were indeed mild sentences. It also did not escape the attention of the lawyers in the Reich Ministry of Justice that in November 1934, senates of the Volksgerichtshof allowed two defendants awarded prison sentences for acts of treason to retain their 'honour and rights as citizens'.

It was not until 1936, when loyal Party man Otto Thierack was appointed President of the Volksgerichtshof, that its sentencing policy changed dramatically. Thierack advocated – quite in line with National Socialist ideology – that the judicial system should subordinate itself entirely to the requirements of the political leadership and that the Volksgerichtshof, which defined itself primarily as a political court, must play a dominant role. These words, from a letter written by Thierack to Freisler in 1942 – by that time, the former was Reich Minister of Justice, the latter President of the Volksgerichtshof – already applied at the beginning of his presidency, and they underscored the primacy of National Socialist views: 'At the Volksgerichtshof more than any other court, the administration of justice must be in accord with the leadership of the state. And it will primarily be your responsibility to guide the judges in this direction.'

For the time being, Thierack himself directed the Volksgerichtshof judges under his charge. For him, 'commitment to the German cause' was a key requirement for the judiciary. This extract from a staff report reveals what was considered to be the ideal career history for a German judge:

> Landgerichtsrat _____ is an upright, open-minded man with a goal-oriented attitude, paired with the due restraint and good conduct. He has fought in the organs of the Party since its early years and is now SA Führer and head of the regional NSDAP office. His professional and private conduct are without reproach, and his active involvement demonstrates his positive attitude towards the National Socialist state.

The perfect German judge. And to maintain and ensure the survival of the National Socialist system, the entire judiciary was to be carved from the same wood. Jurists who were loyal and obedient Party members guaranteed the smooth running of the NS legal system and in particular, that of the Volksgerichtshof, although it first required a statutory basis to legitimate its dictatorial concept of law.

In the course of time, a whole series of laws had been passed, considerably broadening the jurisdiction of the Volksgerichtshof. The following list of laws, offences against them and the punishments meted out documents the extended activities of the People's Court.

| Law | Paragraph | Offence | Sentence |
|-----|-----------|---------|----------|
| Criminal Code | §80 | Treason against the territory and constitution of the Reich | Death |
| | § 81 | Treasonable compulsion | Death or imprisonment with hard labour |

| Law | Paragraph | Offence | Sentence |
|---|---|---|---|
| | § 82 | Preparation for high treason | Death, imprisonment with hard labour or imprisonment |
| | § 83 | Minor cases of high treason | Imprisonment with hard labour or imprisonment |
| | § 89 | Treason against the country | Death or imprisonment with hard labour |
| | § 90 | Espionage | Death or imprisonment with hard labour |
| | § 90a | Treasonous forgery | Imprisonment with hard labour |
| | § 90b | Betrayal of former state secrets | Imprisonment |
| | § 90c | Treasonous relationships | Imprisonment |
| | § 90d | Disclosure of state secrets | Imprisonment |
| | § 90e | Negligent disclosure of state secrets | Imprisonment |
| | § 90f | Treason against the Volk through the spreading of malicious lies | Imprisonment with hard labour |
| | § 90g | Treasonable betrayal of confidence | Death or imprisonment with hard labour |
| | § 90h | Treasonable destruction of evidence | Imprisonment with hard labour |
| | § 90i | Treasonable bribery | Imprisonment with hard labour |
| | § 91 | Causation of danger of war | Death or imprisonment with hard labour |
| | § 91a | Supplying arms | Death or imprisonment with hard labour |
| | § 91b | Aiding and abetting the enemy | Death or imprisonment with hard labour |
| | § 92 | Wilful acts of treason | Imprisonment with hard labour |
| | § 94, par. 1 | Attack on the Führer | Imprisonment |
| | § 139, par. 2 | Serious cases of failure to report acts of treason and high treason and damage to military resources | Death or imprisonment |

| Law | Paragraph | Offence | Sentence |
|---|---|---|---|
| Wehrmacht protection decree of 25 Nov 1939 | | | |
| | § 1, par. 1 | Serious cases of damage to military equipment | Death or imprisonment with hard labour |
| | § 5 | Endangering allied armed forces | Imprisonment with hard labour or imprisonment |
| Decree for the Protection of the People and the State of 28 Feb 1933: | | | |
| | § 5, par. 2 | Endeavouring to kill the Reichspräsident or a member of the government | Death or imprisonment with hard labour |
| Law against Economic Sabotage of 1 Dec 1936: | | | |
| | § 1 | Transfer of property abroad | ? |
| KSSVO (Special Wartime Penal Code) of 17 Aug 1938: | | | |
| | § 1 | Espionage | Death |
| Decree for the Protection of the Armaments Industry of 23 Jan 42: | | | |
| | Par. 1 | False statement on economic requirements or stocks | Death, imprisonment with hard labour or imprisonment |
| KSSVO, supplement to the ordinance regulating allocation of responsibilities of 29 Jan 1942: | | | |
| | §1 No. 5 | Public undermining of the war effort | Death, imprisonment with hard labour or imprisonment |

The vast array of new laws made it increasingly difficult to separate the responsibilities of the Volksgerichtshof and those of the Reichskriegsgericht (Supreme Reich Military Court), which had been reinstated as the highest military court under a law passed on 26 June 1936. Cases of treason or high treason against active or former members of the Wehrmacht were tried before the Reichskriegsgericht. In order to achieve uniform administration of justice, it was agreed that the sentencing policy of the two courts must be brought into line. Officers assigned to the Reichskriegsgericht were also made honorary members of the Volksgerichtshof.

Nevertheless, there were problems with the demarcation of the crimes over which the Reichskriegsgericht and the Volksgerichtshof had jurisdiction – particularly following the outbreak of the Second World War in September 1939, as cases not only of treason but also subversion of the war effort or damage to military resources against civilians could be transferred to the Reichskriegsgericht. All that was necessary was for the President of the Reichskriegsgericht to declare that there were specific military reasons for their prosecution. The Reichskriegsgericht was then empowered to take cases away from the Volksgerichtshof as being of specifically military relevance.

It was not until May 1940 that responsibility for the prosecution of civilians for undermining the war effort was transferred back to the ordinary criminal courts. Later – from January 1943 onwards – such cases fell under the remit of the Volksgerichtshof, which could, however, still delegate them to subordinate courts where it saw fit. Finally, on 20 September 1944, Hitler – possibly due to an increasing lack of confidence in the military courts – decreed that all political crimes, including those committed by Wehrmacht personnel, were to be tried exclusively by the Volksgerichtshof and the special courts.

'Undermining the war effort' was the crime most frequently prosecuted by the Volksgerichtshof, followed by the so-called 'Nacht-und Nebel' (night and fog) trials, which were based on a decree passed by Hitler in December 1941 and will be discussed later. The majority of defendants brought before the Volksgerichtshof were 'defeatists' who had subverted the war effort by publicly questioning Nazi propaganda, especially in the last years of the War with the deprivations it brought within Germany. A careless comment on the 'coming defeat of the German Wehrmacht', a flippant joke about the Führer or the Party could mean the death sentence – there were informers everywhere.

This broadening of the range of offences over which the Volksgerichtshof held jurisdiction to include far more than treason against the people and the state, the crimes for which it had originally been created, was accompanied by a gradual increase in its geographical jurisdiction in step with the forced expansion of the Reich.

Following the 'Saar referendum' on 13 January 1935, the 'Decree on the Transfer of the Administration of Justice in the Saarland' made the Volksgerichtshof responsible for prosecuting cases of high treason and treason there. A further expansion of its jurisdiction followed the annexation of Austria on 13 March 1938. The provisions of the German criminal code with regard to high treason, treason and damage to military resources came into effect in Austria barely four months later, on 1 July 1938. An implementing regulation stipulated that Austrian cases were to be tried primarily by a specific senate of the Volksgerichtshof and that honorary judges from Austria were to be appointed to the Volksgerichtshof. Under a further directive, issued on 13 March 1940, cases could be delegated to the regional court of appeal in Vienna, which, however, was to administer justice in accordance with the 'procedural regulations of the German Reich'.

A similar course was followed after the Munich Agreement of 29 September 1938, which permitted Nazi Germany to annex the 'Sudetenland', areas along the borders of Czechoslovakia which were mainly inhabited by German-speaking people. In fact, the decrees were almost identical to those issued for Austria.

And when the remaining Czech territories became the German protectorate of Bohemia and Moravia, German criminal law was also introduced for German citizens there. For non-Germans among the population, a series of provisions from the German criminal code applied, notably those governing high treason and Landesverrat, attacks on the Führer and damage to military resources. The Memel Territory also fell under German jurisdiction, under the law of 23 March 1939.

Finally, after the invasion of Poland, Polish law was abrogated step by step in the regions of West Prussia and Posen, which were newly created by Hitler. And in June 1940, the German criminal code and German procedural regulations were introduced in the occupied eastern territories with the understanding that they also applied retroactively, that is, to offences committed prior to their introduction. A directive issued on 5 September 1939 by the Commander-in-Chief of the Army had already declared the German criminal code applicable in as far as it stipulated that criminal acts were to be tried by the Wehrmacht tribunals and the special courts. A further directive brought the Gerichtsverfassungsgesetz (Constitution of Courts Act) into force in the 'incorporated Eastern territories' from 15 June 1940.

In the West, too, Reich law was introduced in its totality during the invasion of Western Europe. The courts which were immediately set up in Belgium, Luxembourg and France also saw themselves as responsible for certain political crimes, which often meant a conflict of competence with the Volksgerichtshof. The situation in the occupied Netherlands was a unique one. Alongside the Dutch courts, the Nazis established German courts which were responsible for offences committed by Germans and citizens of the protectorate as well as for specific political crimes and could apply both Dutch and German law.

As acts of high treason and treason committed by foreigners abroad were also punishable under German law and fell under the jurisdiction of the Volksgerichtshof, the Reich commissioner for the occupied Netherlands territories ordered that all cases of high treason were to be initially forwarded to the senior Reich prosecutor; the Reich Ministry of Justice would then decide which criminal code would be applied. If a case was not allocated to the foreign courts, it was transferred to the German courts in the occupied Netherlands, where it was tried under German law, subject to the approval of the Reich commissioner for the occupied Netherlands territories. Similar principles applied to cases of Landesverrat.

The examples outlined here show that the geographical and legal remit of the Volksgerichtshof was vastly expanded from the beginning of the war in September 1939 onwards. Its original maxim, to protect the Reich against traitors from within, was now supplemented with additional tasks, all with the same goal: to maintain and safeguard the National Socialists' claim to power in its continually expanding territory.

As the powers of the Volksgerichtshof increased, the procedural rights of the defendants brought before it and their legal counsel shrank. From its creation on 24 April 1934, it had already been clear that this was a special court in which fundamental rights had been suspended.

For example, the Volksgerichtshof was the court of first and last instance (Art. III, § 3, par. 1) and no legal appeal was possible. There was a clear further erosion of legal guarantees for the defendants and the accused in that the requirements for the preliminary examination, which had formerly been obligatory, were relaxed; eventually not only in the case of simple offences, but also in complex and comprehensive criminal proceedings, the court president could decide whether an offender would be tried or whether a warrant of arrest should be issued or an existing warrant remained valid.

The process of the review of remand in custody was abolished. Instead, an inspection procedure was to ensure that suspects were held in detention for as short a time as possible. The power of the court to confiscate defendants' assets was also extended – which often meant financial ruin for defendants and the accused, even if in the end they only received minor sentences or – an increasingly rare event in the era of the Volksgerichtshof – were acquitted.

A further example is the fact that the procedural regulations of the juvenile criminal court law were no longer applied. In many cases, juveniles were brought before the Volksgerichtshof, tried as adults without consideration of their moral or mental maturity and received draconian sentences, including the death penalty.

This erosion of legal guarantees affected not only the defendants and the accused, but their defence counsel. The foundation charter had already contained massive intervention by the Nazi jurists in the rights of defence lawyers. A defence counsel was mandatory: no defendant could be tried without legal representation. However, the choice of defence counsel had to be approved by the presiding judge, who could subsequently withdraw his approval at any time. The introduction of mandatory approval by the court therefore restricted the defendant's choice from the outset, and the defence counsel was dependent on the goodwill of the presiding judge. Although an official explanation of the foundation charter stated that the accused's choice of defence counsel was not limited to a list of officially-approved defence lawyers, making the approval of the presiding judge mandatory rendered the principle of free advocacy an illusion. It weeded out even those few lawyers who had so far managed to escape the far-reaching purges of the Nazi regime.

Any defence lawyer who was considered by the system as politically unreliable or made an unfavourable impression on the court could expect the judge's approval to be withdrawn or could not count on being approved to appear as a defence counsel in future. Those who nevertheless acted as defence counsel – or more aptly, were allowed to act as defence counsel – faced the prospect of possible official reprimand which threatened their future careers. Professional tribunals closely monitored whether defence lawyers upheld the interests of the Volk at all times while representing such 'enemies of the people' or 'traitors'. For example, the official directives for Volksgerichtshof defence lawyers contained clear warnings against any expression of 'un-German sentiments contrary to the sound instincts of the Volk'.

In other words, lawyers faced censorship from three sources: the court, the Party and the professional tribunals. The consequence: no real defence was possible for the accused. It was merely the upholding of a farce, an empty convention. The regulations in an information sheet which was handed out to defence lawyers on the instructions of the President of the Volksgerichtshof on their appointment or approval as defence counsel and for which confirmation of receipt was required show the extent of the constraints placed upon them. Information sheets on cases of high treason and treason had been issued for the first time in October 1936. Both contained clear instructions for the defence.

A further obstacle for the defence was a directive issued by the Reich Minister of Justice on 24 June 1939, which stated that any content of the indictment classified as secret was not to be included in the lawyers' copies of the bill of indictment. This meant that before the main trial, defence counsel only learned of such content during access to the court files and was therefore not able to prepare his case. And after the trial, the defence lawyer had to return the bill of indictment. The accused himself received no copy of the indictment, even if it did not contain any confidential information. If he was still at liberty, the accused was merely notified that the bill of indictment had been forwarded to his defence lawyer. If the accused and his defence counsel lived far apart, the indictment was to be sent to a selected judge who was requested to inform the accused of its content. If, as in most such cases, the accused was already under arrest, he was to be allowed access to the bill of indictment in the presence of an officer of the prison where he was being held, after which the indictment was to be locked away safely; here, too, confidential information was not to be divulged. Court officers were to translate the key points of the indictment for foreign defendants.

During the War, the large number of trials in rapid succession placed another obstacle in the path of the defence: the indictment was delivered only shortly before the date set for the main hearing. Often, the accused did not learn what charges were being brought against them until the evening before the trial. A defence lawyer was frequently not allowed to speak to his client until a late stage and was only given access to the court files when the application was lodged, so that it was almost impossible to prepare a defence in the brief time span between the arraignment and the main hearing. As a rule, a defence counsel was not appointed until charges had been filed with the court, which left the defendant without a lawyer during the key phase of the preliminary proceedings.

A letter from the NSDAP Reich leadership to Thierack dated 15 October 1942 illustrates how important it was to the Party that defence lawyers should toe the line. The letter states that at the session of the Volksgerichtshof in Vienna from 21 September to 2 October 1942, two defence lawyers had delivered pleas which were exemplary in all respects. It went on to propose that, in order to make profitable use of this type of defence and to provide 'orientation' for others, a team comprising the two best and one of the least promising lawyers should be appointed as defence counsels at the next session of the Volksgerichtshof in Vienna. All available lawyers would be instructed to observe the trial, which would be followed by a 'critical discussion'. Goebbels felt that this 'practical method of alignment' was the 'most powerful and sustained'.

A practical demonstration of how a German lawyer should deliver a German speech, a demonstration given right where German justice was dispensed and German sentences passed – in the courtroom. But the Reich Ministry of Justice rejected such proposals, as it did Goebbels' suggestion that politically-relevant judgements from the Volksgerichtshof should be made accessible to German jurists for training purposes. Later, however, individual sentences were forwarded to the Party Chancellery of the NSDAP.

In the meantime, it was not long before blood-red placards on advertising columns were informing not German jurists but the German people at large of the death sentences meted out by the People's Court to 'traitors and national parasites', not only as public evidence that all conspiracies against the state and the German people were being rigorously pursued and mercilessly punished, but also as a clear warning to anyone tempted to betray 'the German cause'. In the course of the preceding years, the National Socialists had anchored the Volksgerichtshof both in the minds of the jurists and the consciousness of the German people as exactly the kind of tribunal they intended it to be.

At the end of 1941, the Volksgerichtshof consisted of six senates. Volksgerichtshof President Thierack chaired the First Senate. In the senates, seventy-eight professional judges and seventy-four public prosecutors administered German justice. All but five were NSDAP members. They had all joined the Party after 30 January 1933 in a 'landslide change of opinion', as Freisler called it. Of the eighty-one lay judges, seventy-one were members of NSDAP organizations, the others from the three sections of the Wehrmacht. In other words, this was a National Socialist court through and through and totally committed to serving the Führer, the Party and the 'German cause'.

The Nazi regime could therefore rely on the Volksgerichtshof to guarantee the rigid pursuit and liquidation of any form of opposition. Close cooperation with the Gestapo also helped to further this aim. Almost all cases of treason tried by the Volksgerichtshof were processed by the Gestapo. The influence of the latter – criticised by some Volksgerichtshof judges – was in some cases so strong that the Nazi lawyers and the Volksgerichtshof seemed little more than an extension of the secret state police. Following their arrest, suspects often spent many months in police custody, during which they were subjected to bullying and brutal beatings. Later, especially during the last years of the War, they were even tortured. The Volksgerichtshof judges were aware of this abuse, but they took no measures to stop it, even where defendants withdrew their confessions on the grounds that they had been extorted under the violent interrogation techniques of the Gestapo.

The all-encompassing power of the Gestapo is shown by the fact that suspects released from detention awaiting trial, those who were acquitted or prisoners released after serving their term or granted pardons were likely to be re-arrested by the Gestapo and shipped off to concentration camps, irrespective of the decisions of the courts, the organs of law enforcement or parole boards.

At a conference on 'Justice and the Gestapo' which took place in Berlin on 11 November 1936, Freisler, at the time an undersecretary, showed surprising sympathy for the methods employed by the Gestapo, but insisted that they needed to be placed on a legal basis. It was a fight over areas of responsibility and competence, a power struggle between the judiciary and the Gestapo. Berlin was trying to stake out the borders and come to an arrangement. The conference ended with agreement on both sides that closer cooperation was necessary in order to effectively counter 'treasonous activities'. A short time later, the chief of the SS, Heinrich Himmler, ordered that the Gestapo and the prosecutors and judges of the People's Court should regularly exchange files relating to cases of treason. This order was promptly complied with.

Even though there was some dissatisfaction – not only among Volksgerichtshof jurists – over the increasing influence of the Gestapo, everyday legal practice revealed a different picture: on the basis of a directive from Heydrich, the head of the security police, on 'Principles of inner state security during the War', the Gestapo established its own criminal justice system, which henceforth dealt independently with offences of all kinds, thus excluding the ordinary administration of justice. Despite its displeasure and occasional protest: the judiciary was forced to look on as the Gestapo usurped more and more of its areas of responsibility. And even where the judiciary retained its power, it could expect Hitler to intervene personally at any time and demand that sentences which had aroused his disapproval should be corrected.

On the other hand, the People's Court itself supported the intervention of the Gestapo in legal affairs by advocating that insignificant cases should be handed over to the secret state police. In a letter to the Reich Minister of Justice dated 14 August 1940, Volksgerichtshof President Thierack wrote 'It is wrong to give every hanger-on, even the smallest one, the honour of appearing before the Volksgerichtshof' and added that it would be better to show the culprits the error of their ways by detaining them in concentration camps, which was more expedient than taking the lengthy, cumbersome and expensive path of a trial.

There can be no doubt about it: despite considerable unease, the representatives of the German legal system, and in particular the judges, bowed to the dictates of the National Socialist regime – at the very least, it can be said that there was no significant criticism.

There were few prominent critics. One of them was Hans Frank. Former president of the Academy for German Law and a profound believer in the National Socialist cause, recently released from his duties as head of the Reich legal department of the NSDAP, the tyrannical and merciless Governor-General of Poland complained of a growing legal uncertainty within the borders of the German Reich, which in his opinion was due to the dominant role played by the Gestapo and the interference of the police. He repeatedly stated the need for and importance of an 'independent judiciary'. He attempted to explain what he meant by this in a speech laced with pithy slogans which he gave in July 1942:

> No Reich without law – not even ours! No law without judges – not even German law! No judge without real power – not even a German judge! As someone who has always defended the principle of law to every man within the movement, it is a disappointment to me to hear voices emerging here and there claiming that the authoritarian state in which we live has no need of judges or of an independent administration of justice. I will never cease to assert with all the force at my command that it would be a disaster if the police state were presented as the ideal of National Socialism while completely disregarding Germanic concepts of law.

In Frank's view, Germany needed to return to 'ancient Germanic law' and the associated principles. At around the same time, he wrote in his diary:

> I never encountered difficulties when pronouncing these principles, which I did solemnly and before a vast audience of 25,000 at the last 'Tag des Deutschen Rechts' in Leipzig in 1939. It was only with the rise of the Gestapo apparatus and the increasing influence of the authoritarian views of the police leadership that my standpoint began to stand more and more in contrast to that of a growing opposing faction. In recent years, in which I have repeatedly noted and on many occasions witnessed the Führer's personal dissatisfaction with the jurists, in which there has been increasing intervention by the state in the judicial system and in which the conflict between the organs of the police and the judiciary has resulted in the almost complete dominance of the former over the latter, it became clear that it would now be more and more difficult to proclaim the idea which is so sacred to me. I began to encounter obstacles of all kinds and became progressively aware of the displeasure with which those in power at this time view my observations.
>
> My position was further complicated by the increasingly obvious inability of the judiciary to counter anti-judicial arguments presented with bombastic and demonstrative force. Before long, no judge dared to pass sentence without first obtaining the

approval of a higher authority, which of course, in turn allowed a terrible despair over legal development in Germany to take hold. The 'Schwarze Korps', the official newspaper of the SS, apparently with approval on the highest level, referred to all legal institutions and preservers of the law in an increasingly aggressive and offensive tone . . .

Frank saw his vision of National Socialist law and thus the continued existence of the state as threatened. In his diary, he criticised these anti-judicial views, and even expressed criticism – albeit veiled – of Hitler:

Unfortunately, even on the level of the National Socialist leadership, the prevailing standpoint is that removing the legal certainty of the citizens under its rule fortifies the authority of the state. The powers of the executive organs of the police, which are open to the most arbitrary application, have been extended to such a degree that at present, one could say that the individual Volksgenosse has been completely stripped of his rights. Of course, the justification put forward is that this is a necessity in wartime or that it is important to focus all national energies on one goal and above all, that it is essential to rule out any possibility of sabotage of our national striving for liberty. I, however, am of the opinion that the German character has such a strong, innate sense of justice that if that sense of justice is satisfied, the joy of the national community and the enthusiasm of our people for the national cause would be much more effectively aroused and sustained than will ever be achieved by the application of rigid controls.

The difference in standpoint between Frank and the NS leadership was obvious. As a result, Hitler ordered Frank to resign from all his legal positions. He was also barred from delivering speeches in public, except to make statements as Governor-General of Poland. He wrote in his diary:

When at the beginning of last week, the Führer appointed the President of the Volksgerichtshof, Thierack, with whom I and the entire legal profession are at odds – it was he who, as President of the Volksgerichtshof, first admitted representatives of the police as public prosecutors in the criminal proceedings in Prague, excluding the Volksgerichtshof's own senior Reich prosecutor, thereby and in his further conduct providing practical evidence of his absolute commitment to the new course – Reich Minister of Justice, he also became the head of the National Socialist Association of German Legal Professionals and President of the Academy for German Law, which I myself founded . . . In doing so and in issuing a decree authorizing the new minister of justice Thierack to deviate from the existing law where necessary in order to establish a National Socialist administration of justice, the Führer was signalling his intention to break completely with the views I represented. Coming as no surprise, this development had no power to wound me. I see in it not a crisis of the law, but a crisis of the state, and I pray to God that when the time comes, the inevitable consequences may be as limited as possible.

In October 1942, SS Gruppenführer Otto Ohlendorf from the Reichssicherheitshauptamt (Reich Main Security Office) responded to the accusations of Frank and his sympathizers. In a public statement, he retaliated aggressively, pointing out that a National Socialist judge was primarily bound by the principles of National Socialism and only secondarily by the law. He stressed the threat faced by Germany and maintained that all associated measures made it necessary to 'focus not on the individual, but on the community'. Legal certainty, said Ohlendorf, meant certainty for the community rather than for the individual, and all political actions were to be evaluated from this standpoint alone.

Irrespective of the disputes between the judiciary, the Gestapo and the police, Germany was at war – and war has its own laws. In view of this, Ohlendorf emphatically called for a politically and ideologically uniform judiciary. His conclusion: in future, it should be possible to remove a judge who was found to have been negligent in the performance of his duties without much ado. The 'exclusive connection' between judge and law no longer existed, he argued. The first priority was the judge's commitment to National Socialist ideology. As long as judges saw this ideology as their ruling principle and conducted their trials accordingly, they were completely free and independent representatives of the law.

Ohlendorf's views were fully in line with those of the NS leadership and of Hitler, who was increasingly critical of the judiciary and pressed for changes which all followed but one goal: to eradicate the last vestiges of independence.

The totalitarian maxims of the NS state tolerated no other sources of power. And so the institution of the judiciary was now experienced exactly what Hitler had repeatedly demanded and the majority of the judges themselves had advocated: a total symbiosis of judiciary and state.

At the summit of the system: the Führer, this time in his role as supreme judge – and once again, the jurists followed him. All too willingly, they turned a blind eye to the fact that he held the legal profession in low regard and had made no secret of it. During dinner-table conversations in the past, he had repeatedly voiced his doubts about the legal system in general and was often enraged by the sentences meted out by the courts. In private conversation at the end of March 1942, he had vowed to whittle the legal administration down and to separate the 10 per cent wheat from the chaff, once again making it perfectly clear what he thought of the legal profession. Lawyers, he asserted, were either 'defective by nature' or were bound to become so in the course of time. This particular outburst was prompted by a ruling of the regional court in Oldenburg in a case against a construction worker whose wife died in an asylum after becoming depressed following years of physical abuse at the hands of her husband. On 19 March 1942, the court sentenced the husband to five years' imprisonment with hard labour. Hitler heard about the case and was beside himself with rage at what he perceived as the leniency of the sentence. Not for the first time, he telephoned Undersecretary Schlegelberger and demanded a tougher sentence. When Schlegelberger confessed that he was not familiar with the case, Hitler screamed at him that this was typical of the entire legal system. Hundreds of thousands were risking their lives at the Front while a murderer was sent off to prison for five years, where he lived at the expense of the state. He threatened to hand over all criminal cases to the SS.

This was no isolated occurrence. Hitler's sudden outbreaks of rage over what he saw as scandalous sentencing policy were commonplace, frequently throwing his entourage into a burst of hectic activity. In his speech to the Reichstag on 26 April 1942 – his last speech delivered at what was to be the last meeting of the Reichstag – Hitler revealed the full extent of his distaste for the judiciary. The time had come, he felt, to speak a few clear words on the subject of law and justice and to formulate demands:

> However, I do expect one thing: that the nation grants me the right to intervene immediately and to take action myself whenever a person has failed to render unqualified obedience in the service of great and vital tasks. The front and the homeland, transportation, administration and judiciary must obey only one thought, and that is victory. No-one can in this time insist on his vested rights, and all must know that today, there are only duties to be fulfilled. I therefore ask the German Reichstag to confirm expressly that I possess the legal authority to see to it that every

individual performs his duty and that I may imprison subject to legal review or remove from office or position any person who in my considered opinion has failed to fulfil their duties, irrespective of who they may be or what rights they may have acquired . . .

I also expect the German judiciary to understand that the nation is not there for their convenience but that they exist to serve the nation, and that the entire world, including Germany, must not be allowed to perish so that there is formal law, but that Germany must live on, notwithstanding what the formal interpretation of justice may be . . . From now on, I will intervene in these cases and remove from office any judge who evidently does not recognize the demands of the hour.

The members of the Reichstag rose to their feet in an expression of approval. With that, the Reichstag granted him the powers he had requested. Hitler's attack on the judiciary had been successful. The last vestiges of judicial independence had been eradicated. While the speech caused a considerable stir and major uncertainty among jurists, not one judge or public prosecutor anywhere in the German Reich resigned in response to Hitler's attacks.

A few days later. Goebbels – also no friend of the judiciary – wrote in his diary that it would be necessary to administer a 'little dose of encouragement' to the humiliated judges at the next available opportunity. An unnecessary precaution – the jurists were completely subservient to the Führer. Some may have been unsettled, humiliated and depressed, but even they followed their 'supreme judge' without protest.

On 22 July 1942, Goebbels addressed the Volksgerichtshof. The People's Court and its judges had been – almost conspicuously – spared in Hitler's scathing attack. Goebbels now proceeded to set the record straight. His comments, he assured them, bore special political significance because Hitler himself had approved the manuscript of his speech. He condemned the attitude of many judges, who, he said, were still clinging to 'outdated ways of thinking' and also criticised individual sentences handed out by the Volksgerichtshof. Judges who delivered such sentences, he went on, were to be removed from office: even generals could be removed. Judges, said Goebbels, were to proceed less from the law than from the principle that the criminal was to be eliminated from the national community. In wartime, it was not a matter of whether a sentence was fair or unfair, but only of whether the decision was expedient.

The state had to ward off its internal enemies in the most efficient way possible and annihilate them completely. Goebbels stated that in such times, one had to discard the idea that it was necessary for a judge to be convinced of the defendant's guilt. The prime task of the judiciary was not retribution or even improvement, but to uphold the state. The starting point for the judge's decisions was not the law, but the necessity for this offender to be removed. These drastic measures, he said, were the task of the judiciary, which had exposed itself to ridicule through certain actions and also needed to recognize its political duty when it came to the treatment of the Jews; any emotional consideration was inappropriate here. In conclusion, Goebbels pointed out once more that the state must employ all means at its disposal to ward off its enemies at home and abroad and that it was the idea of the expedient decision must therefore be the first priority in the administration of justice.

It hardly comes as a surprise to that Thierack, as President of the Volksgerichtshof, thanked Goebbels for his observations and requested that he might continue to furnish such inspirational and motivating instructions in future. Later, following his appointment as minister of justice, Thierack was to introduce the so-called 'Richterbriefe' (Judges' Letters), circulars in which he made every effort to 'guide' the judges in the administration of this new German justice.

The aim of the Richterbriefe was to ensure that the decisions made by the judges were in line with National Socialist principles. The first Richterbrief was issued on 1 October 1942 and began with the appeal:

German judges!
According to the ancient Germanic interpretation of the law, the leader of the nation was always its supreme judge. Therefore, when the leader of the nation invests another person with the authority of a judge, this means not only that the latter derives his judicial power from the leader and is responsible to him, but also that leadership and judgeship are related in character.

It follows that the judge is also the guardian of national self-preservation. He is the protector of the values of the nation and the annihilator of the unworthy. He regulates those functions of life which constitute diseases affecting the body of the nation. A strong judiciary is indispensable for maintaining a true national community.

This task makes the judge the direct assistant of the leadership of the state. This position renders him prominent, but also shows the limits of his tasks, which cannot, as a liberal doctrine assumed, lie in the supervision of the leadership of the state, because if a state is not such that it grants leadership to the best, the activities of the administration of justice can be no substitute for this selection . . .

A corps of judges like this will not cling slavishly to the letter of the law. It will not anxiously search for support in the law, but with satisfaction in its responsibility, will find within the bounds of the law the decision which is best for the life of the community.

In times of war, for example, the requirements placed on judges are quite different from those of peacetime, and judges need to adapt to these differing requirements. They can only do this if they are familiar with the intentions and goals of the leadership of the state. The judge must therefore be in harmony with the leadership of the state at all times. This is the only way to ensure that he can carry out his essential task in the interest of the national community and to prevent the administration of justice – divorced from its true responsibilities in the life of the community – being perceived as an end in itself. The importance and necessity of guidance in the administration of justice derive from this.

Goebbels and Hitler had every reason to be satisfied. Thierack, who had rendered such obedient service as President of the Volksgerichtshof, was now appointed not only Minister of Justice, but President of the Academy for German Law and head of the National Socialist Association of German Legal Professionals.

Thierack reported not only to the Führer, but also to the head of the NS Party Chancellery, Martin Bormann. Hitler had paved the way for this with a decree granting special full powers to the Reich Minister of Justice:

A strong administration of justice is necessary for the fulfilment of tasks of the Greater German Reich. I therefore commission and empower the Reich Minister of Justice to establish a National Socialist administration of justice and to take all necessary measures in accordance with my directives and instructions and in agreement with the Reich minister, the head of the Reich Chancellery and the leader of the Party Chancellery. Hereby, he may deviate from existing law.

The appointment of Thierack to the position of Reich Minister of Justice was accompanied by further personnel changes within the Ministry of Justice. Long-serving undersecretary Schlegelberger retired with an endowment of 100,000 Reichsmarks and was replaced by Dr Curt Rothenberger. Freisler had initially been considered for the position of

President of the Academy for German Law, but knowing of his support for Frank's ideas, Hitler decided to offer him Thierack's old position as President of the People's Court instead.

In the last years of its existence, then, the Volksgerichtshof was under the presidency of a man who had perhaps been more deeply involved in the establishment of a National Socialist administration of justice than any other: as a lawyer, a public speaker, Party member, publicist and undersecretary. And always in the limelight – or should one say in the front line on the 'home front'? And now Freisler was President of the Volksgerichtshof. This was the beginning of the last stage in his professional career and at the same time the start of the bloodiest era in the history of the Nazi People's Court.

# Chapter 6

# The Political Soldier

On 15 October 1942, the new President of the Volksgerichtshof wrote to Hitler:

> Mein Führer! I beg leave to report: I have taken up the office to which you appointed me and have settled in to my task. My gratitude for the responsibility you have conferred upon me will find its expression in loyal and devoted service to the cause of the security of the Reich and the inner unity of the German Volk, both by my own example as a judge and as the leader of the Volksgerichtshof, with pride in the responsibility you, mein Führer, as the supreme law lord and judge of the German people, have assigned to me for the administration of justice in your highest political court. The People's Court will take great care to judge each case in the manner in which it trusts that you, mein Führer, would yourself judge it. Heil, mein Führer! Your most obedient political soldier, Roland Freisler.

For almost a decade, Freisler had played a leading role within the legal system, had experienced the rise and triumph of National Socialism, enjoyed proximity to the seat of power and furthered his career. He had harboured ambitions to become Reich Minister of Justice, and he viewed his failure to achieve this office as a personal defeat. Nevertheless, he endeavoured to quickly come to terms with his new position as the chief judge of the Volksgerichtshof, and he did this in his accustomed manner: dutifully, energetically, almost fanatically.

Shortly after his appointment, Freisler had sought an audience with the Führer in order to report to him personally that he had taken up his duties. However, Thierack, while claiming to support Freisler's request, had taken no action to bring about such a meeting. He was aware of Freisler's ambitions, and if anyone was to have direct contact with Hitler, it would be Thierack himself, the Reich Minister of Justice.

Thierack and Freisler: two men who respected, but did not particularly like, each other. However, their high status demanded that they work together on a professional level. On 16 October 1942, one day after his letter to the Führer, Freisler wrote to Thierack:

> I have now settled down to work in my new position and have divided up the work of the Volksgerichtshof in such a manner that I personally, also in my role as a judge, am in a position to identify any form of treason and high treason committed by Germans or foreigners within the Reich, to assess the nature and scope of such crimes and the level of danger they represent and to combat them by means of judge's decisions which I hope will provide guidance for the court.

Freisler was fully aware that the 'judge's decisions' with which he hoped to set a shining example for the judiciary would be based on purely political and never on merely legal considerations. Even before his appointment to the Volksgerichtshof, in a private letter, he had quoted Reichswehr minister Gustav Noske, who said in 1919, 'Someone is going to have to be the bloodhound'. And Freisler was ready and willing to assume this role.

Some weeks previously – on 9 September 1942 – in a letter to his successor, Thierack had underscored the importance of the Volksgerichtshof using concrete examples and invited Freisler to refer to him in all confidence for support:

> In no other court does it emerge more clearly than in the case of the People's Court that the administration of justice must be in harmony with the leadership of the state. It will be primarily your task to guide the judges in this direction. You must therefore examine all charges brought before the court in order to identify those cases where it is necessary, in confidential and convincing discussion with the presiding judge, to emphasize what is necessary from the point of view of the state. I stress once again that this must be done in a manner which convinces rather than orders the judge, who alone bears the responsibility for his verdict. And it goes without saying that such direction of judges must be restricted to the essentials. Excessive exertion of influence will only lead to judges making irresponsible decisions and will be perceived as a severe burden by responsible judges: judges must seek you out in cases where such direction is necessary, and you must make it clear to them when they seek you out unnecessarily.

As a general rule, the judge of the People's Court must accustom himself to regarding the ideas and intentions of the state leadership as the overriding consideration and the individual human fate which depends on him only as a secondary factor. The defendants brought before the People's Court are merely minor representatives of a much larger circle of enemies of the Reich, and this is particularly true in wartime.

And the Reich Minister of Justice gave examples:

1) If a Jew, and a leading Jew at that, is charged with treason – even if he is only an accomplice therein – he has behind him the hatred and the will of Jewry to exterminate the German people. As a rule, this will therefore be high treason and must be punished with the death penalty.

2) If, after 22 June 1941, a German within the Reich disseminates Communist propaganda or even attempts to influence the Volk with Communist ideas, this must be seen not only as preparation for high treason, but as aiding and abetting the enemy – namely the Soviet Union.

3) When the Czechs in the Protectorate of Bohemia and Moravia, influenced by propaganda broadcasts from London, repeatedly commit acts against the Volk, even in the form of agitation, this is not only preparation for high treason but is also aiding and abetting the enemy.

At the end of his letter, Thierack assures his esteemed Party comrade Freisler of his support: 'If you should ever be in doubt as to which line to follow or which political necessities have to be taken into consideration, please address yourself to me in all confidence. I will always be in a position to clarify matters for you.'

Thierack's concern that his newly-appointed successor might lack orientation turned out to be completely unfounded. Freisler threw himself into his new office with his customary energy. His motto, 'Right is whatever serves the interests of the Volk' now became the guiding principle of his administration of justice. All that mattered was the Volk, the Reich, the Führer – and the success of the German cause. Anyone who stood in the way of these goals was punished with the full rigour of the law. No sentence was too harsh in the fight for the Führer and German victory. This was Freisler's conviction.

A plethora of new offences such as 'Verdunkelungsverbrechen' (crimes of collusion), 'Heimtücke' (malice) or 'Wehrkraftzersetzung' (subversion of the war effort) made it possible to declare almost any opponent of the regime an enemy of the state on the basis of careless and usually harmless remarks and to liquidate him – in the name of the people.

Soon, it was considered a waste of time to send those convicted of 'subverting the war effort' or 'making defeatist statements' to prison. Instead, they were put to work, for example in the armaments industry. To simplify procedure, the formality of due process was increasingly dispensed with, especially when the accused were so-called 'Untermenschen' (sub-humans), for example Poles or Jews, who were classified as 'lawless' and thus had no right to a fair trial.

Meanwhile, judges could regularly read the latest directives on sentencing in Thierack's Richterbriefe. And the over-zealous NS jurists always endeavoured to follow the instructions of their Minister of Justice to the letter.

On 29 January 1943, all cases of 'subversion of the war effort' were transferred to the Volksgerichtshof. And although they had the power to delegate cases to subordinate courts – for example the regional courts of appeal – at their own discretion, the Volksgerichtshof judges were unwilling to provide anyone with grounds for doubting their competence. In 1943, the Volksgerichtshof tried 241 cases in Berlin alone. And the sentence meted out by the judges – especially after Stalingrad – was usually death. Between January 1943 and January 1944, a total of 124 defendants were sentenced to death and immediately executed for 'Wehrkraftzersetzung'.

The majority of those executed were condemned as 'defeatists'. In other words, they had been imprudent and careless enough to make comments in public expressing scepticism and doubt: of the Führer, the armed forces of the Reich or the course of the war.

In the eyes of Freisler and his colleagues in the Volksgerichtshof, these people were Marxists and Communists, agents of world Jewry, un-German and lacking in any sense of military virtues. A distinction was made between 'private' and 'public' utterances, but this was a merely theoretical discussion which had no impact on the verdict reached by the Volksgerichtshof.

On 8 September 1943, for example, the Volksgerichtshof sentenced the defendant Fritz Gröbe to death for 'public subversion of the war effort'. The court's written statement on the ruling, comprising no more than one type-written page, states as the reason for the sentence that on 27 July 1943, the accused had commented to a close acquaintance: '. . .that this was the end, that the government should stand down, that things were going the same way as in Italy, it was time to put a stop to the murdering . . . Göring and Goebbels had already transferred their money abroad.'

The court had the following to say on the use of the term 'public':

> He admits everything but refuses to see that he has done anything particularly wrong, insisting that he was only talking to a good friend, as he would talk in his own home!!!
>
> All the worse if that is the kind of comments that are made in his home! However, if the defendant's intention was to state that his was not a public statement, he is wrong, because National Socialism wants the whole German nation to participate in political life, and any political utterance must therefore also be seen as a public statement. It must be expected that any Volksgenosse hearing such statements will report them to the competent authority in the Party and the state, in other words, that such comments will be passed on. A criminal cannot therefore make any claim based on confidentiality.

The 'criminal' Fritz Gröbe paid for his comments with his life. His acquaintance, who had denounced him, may have been shocked by the death sentence. But had he not merely done his duty as a German citizen?

The verdict against Gröbe even drew Thierack's disapproval. Two days after the sentence, on 11 September 1943, he wrote to Freisler criticising the First Senate's interpretation of 'public' as too broad: 'If every political utterance were deemed to have been a public utterance, this would invalidate the carefully formulated definition of the "public sphere" in the § 5 of the Special Wartime Penal Code. I would prefer the senate to refrain from expressing such views in future.'

Freisler, however, remained unconvinced. On 28 September 1943, he replied to the minister:

> You expressed the view that my senate's definition of a political utterance was too general. This prompted me to subject the cases adjudicated by the Volksgerichtshof to a close review.
>
> However, this review did not persuade me that the interpretation detailed in the judgement against Gröbe is irreconcilable with the National Socialist concept of the structure of our Reich. On the contrary, I believe that it arises naturally from this concept. It is . . . also in keeping with the goal of ensuring the security of the Reich.

> It is my conviction that a charge of aiding and abetting the
> enemy can be brought in all such cases, and I shall therefore first
> examine every case to ascertain whether a just verdict on a charge
> of aiding and abetting the enemy will also serve to uphold the
> security of our Reich.

What was being handed out here was anything but a 'just verdict'. The harsh line pursued by the jurists of the Volksgerichtshof was frequently contrary to the majority opinion of the legal commentators and commentaries drafted by the undersecretaries of the Reich Ministry of Justice. The Volksgerichtshof had chosen to take a particularly tough stance and had set its own independent course. With increasing frequency, this bloody tribunal took its own view of the administration of justice, and its main spokesperson was Freisler himself.

A further example of issues on which the Volksgerichtshof followed its own independent course: In reaching a verdict, judges were supposed to differentiate between 'agitation' and 'idle grumbling'. In a commentary on the Kriegssonderstrafrechtsverordnung (KSSVO – Special Wartime Penal Code), the Reich Ministry of Justice had emphasized that not 'every by-the-way political comment' constituted Wehrkraftzersetzung. But as the Volksgerichtshof had long lost any sense of reality, here, too, its sentences remained inexorable, and almost without exception, comments expressing dissatisfaction with the current situation were interpreted as agitation. Neither did the Volksgerichtshof judges have any problem establishing the 'subjective motivation'. All legal commentaries considered 'conditional intent' a prerequisite and stated that is was necessary for an offender to be aware of the subversive nature of his comments, to understand that they were liable to 'paralyse or undermine the defence efforts of the people', yet in practice, the sentencing policy of the Volksgerichtshof negated these findings. People could be sentenced to death for saying that German fighter planes could not fly as high as Allied bomber planes, that the war was lost after Stalingrad or that the Führer should resign to pave the way for the signing of a peace treaty with the Allies.

Many of the sentences bear Freisler's signature. As president of the First Senate, he was particularly keen to set a 'shining example' for his fellow judges. And this was noticeably the case in trials which attracted a lot of publicity. This was the stage he craved as Hitler's 'political soldier', the courtroom as the impregnable bastion on the home front.

One of his most spectacular cases was the trial of the members of the 'White Rose' movement, a resistance group made up of students of Munich

University, among them sister and brother Hans and Sophie Scholl, and Professor Kurt Huber.

On 18 February 1943 – the day on which, 600km away in Berlin, Goebbels gave his famous Sportpalast speech, calling on the German people to mobilize their last reserves for the German cause and asking his audience if they wanted total war, to which the crowd responded with a resounding 'JA!' – Hans and Sophie Scholl were on their way to the university, carrying a suitcase full of leaflets denouncing the crimes of the Hitler regime, stating that the Germans had incurred a lasting burden of guilt through the murder of Jews, questioning the apathy of a nation that stood by and allowed such things to happen and calling on the German people to offer passive resistance wherever it could and to commit acts of sabotage in order to bring down the National Socialist government.

They left piles of leaflets in the hallways of the university, so that hundreds of students could read them as they left the lecture halls. Sophie threw the rest of the them into the central courtyard from the second floor. But the caretaker, who had witnessed this, locked the doors and notified the Gestapo. Hans and Sophie Scholl were arrested and taken to prison, where the interrogation began. Later, further members of the White Rose were arrested, including their friends and fellow campaigners Christoph Probst, Willi Graf, Alexander Schmorell and Professor Huber.

The accused received the official indictment on the afternoon of 21 February. The trial began just one day later, in Munich's Palace of Justice. The defendants and their lawyer had been allowed no time to prepare a defence. The presiding judge was Roland Freisler. The young students were charged with incitement to high treason and aiding and abetting the enemy with intent to commit treason and undermine the German war effort.

In their last pamphlet they had written:

> The name of Germany is dishonoured for all time if German youth does not finally rise up, take revenge and at the same time make atonement, smash its tormentors and establish a new Europe of the spirit. Students! The German people look to us! As in 1813 the people expected us to shake off the Napoleonic yoke, so in 1943 they look to us to break the stranglehold of National Socialist terror through the power of the spirit. Beresina and Stalingrad are burning in the East . . . Our people stands ready to rebel against the National Socialist enslavement of Europe in a fervent new breakthrough of freedom and honour.

And now they themselves stood before Freisler, who seemed to have his temper under control during the proceedings and was unusually restrained and focussed. Once during the trial, Sophie Scholl said with emphasis 'What we said and thought are what many people are thinking. They just don't dare to say it out loud!' Freisler made no comment. In conformity with the trial procedure, each of the three prisoners was allowed to make a final statement in their defence. Sophie chose to remain silent. Christoph Probst asked for clemency, for the sake of his children. Hans Scholl attempted to speak up for his friend Probst, but was interrupted by Freisler, who barked: 'If you have nothing to say for yourself, keep your mouth shut!' Then the verdict was pronounced: the death penalty. The prisoners were executed that same day in Munich's Stadelheim prison. Sophie was beheaded first. The executioner was later to say that he had 'never seen anyone go to their death so bravely'. Before laying his head on the block, Hans Scholl called out in a voice so loud that the walls rang 'Long live freedom!'

Germany in February 1943: The North Group of the German Sixth Army capitulated at Stalingrad. Hundreds of thousands of 'Untermenschen' were sent to their deaths in Auschwitz and other Nazi concentration camps. In the Reich, all schoolchildren who had reached the age of 15 were drafted as 'Luftwaffenhelfer' (air force helpers). In Berlin, the film *Sophienlund*, directed by the popular actor Heinz Rühmann, had its première.

Joseph Goebbels, who just days before had concluded his Sportpalast speech to thunderous applause with the resounding appeal 'Now, nation, rise up, and let the storm break loose!' – was a guest at the première, this time in his capacity as President of the Reich Chamber of Culture. He called on the German film industry 'to make more family films'.

Germany in February 1943: a deluded people. A nation of perpetrators, hangers-on and opportunists – and victims.

On 19 April 1943, Freisler was back in Munich. It was a Monday, and an eyewitness reports that courtroom 216 of the Munich Palace of Justice was packed with members of the Wehrmacht, the Party and the Gestapo. The president of the regional court of appeal was there, as were the chief public prosecutor and Munich Gauleiter Wagner. On the stroke of nine, Freisler and the assessors entered the chamber. Justizrat (judicial counsel) Roder was to defend Professor Huber, at the defendant's own request, but his first and only official act was to rise to his feet and declare that he had only just heard of the grave insults to the Führer contained in the White Rose leaflet written by his client. Under these circumstances, he stated, he felt it impossible to continue to defend Huber and asked to be released from the case. Freisler now designated one of the remaining five lawyers, the defence counsel of one of the other thirteen defendants, as Huber's lawyer for the remainder of the proceedings. When the man protested that he had not seen the case file, Freisler announced scornfully 'That does not matter. I will read aloud everything that is important, and you may be certain that I will read it truthfully'.

According to witnesses, Freisler behaved like 'a buffoon' during the questioning of the accused, gesticulating wildly with his arms, drumming his fingers on the bench, screaming and ranting. When a young female student, one of the other defendants, referred to 'Professor Huber', Freisler shouted: 'I don't know a Professor Huber or a Doctor Huber, only the defendant Huber. This man does not deserve to be called a German. He is a scoundrel!'

By this time, the other Volksgerichtshof judges were familiar with the way their President conducted trials. In particular, the other members of the First Senate, which Freisler chaired, were aware of the deep repugnance and seething contempt he felt for the prisoners brought before him. They knew that there could only be one star in the courtroom: Freisler. And that Monday was no different. The other judges and assessors were reduced to the role of onlookers. Their President did all the talking and determined the course of the trial.

The Reich prosecutor demanded the death penalty for the three main defendants Huber, Graf and Schmorell for 'intent to stab the Fatherland in the back in its hour of grave danger'.

The court-appointed defence counsels attempted to portray the Professor as an ivory-tower idealist, a scholar of high repute, and to emphasize the altruistic convictions of his young co-defendants. All to no avail.

Together with the young students Graf and Schmorell, Professor Huber was sentenced to death. The other defendants got off with – in some cases long – prison sentences.

No-one was beyond the reach of the Volksgerichtshof – which increasingly collaborated with the officers of the Reichssicherheitshauptamt – no matter how well connected or prominent they were. Two examples:

During a concert tour in Berlin in March 1943, the talented pianist Karlrobert Kreiten had made negative comments about Hitler's Germany, prophesying a revolution in which the Nazi leaders' 'heads would roll'. He was denounced, brought before the First Senate of the Volksgerichtshof and sentenced to death for public subversion of the war effort on 3 September 1943. In its findings, the court stated: 'In our present struggle – despite his professional achievements – he endangers our victory. He must be condemned to death, for our Volk is determined to march strong and united towards victory'. Werner Höfer, at the time a columnist for the Berlin newspaper *12-Uhr-Blatt* and in the post-war years the popular host of the TV discussion show *Internationaler Frühschoppen*, published a commentary on the verdict which was quite in tune with the propaganda of the Nazis: 'It would be incomprehensible today if an artist who stumbled was shown more leniency than the lowest of our Volksgenossen.' Certainly, Höfer – who had also worked for Goebbels' elite newspaper *Das Reich* – met with no understanding for his comments in later years. When his past caught up with him, his employers, broadcasting company Westdeutsche Rundfunk, sent their star journalist into early retirement – albeit with a generous pension. Höfer himself was brought down by his early enthusiasm for the National Socialist cause: a rare enough event in post-war Germany.

The second example:

Elfriede Scholz, sister of the author Erich Maria Remarque, was accused of criticising the NS regime and sentenced to death by the People's Court in a trial presided over by Roland Freisler. Her brother had fled to Switzerland following the public burning of his books by the Nazis, and after being deprived of his German citizenship, he had emigrated to America. His novel *All Quiet on the Western Front*, which described the devastating effects of war, was translated into almost every language in the world. The Nazis hated him, and because the writer himself had escaped their clutches, they took their revenge on his sister.

Germany in 1943: On 4 December – Freisler had been President of the Volksgerichtshof for sixteen months – internal reports from the Reichssicherheitshauptamt had indicated the necessity for 'intensified efforts' to combat 'dissolutionist tendencies', mentioning the concentration of cases on the Volksgerichtshof as an example of such efforts. In Freisler's era, the court was already working closer together with the Gestapo than it had under Thierack. This resulted in many people who were denounced and under suspicion being sent off to concentration camps without a trial. Under Freisler, the judges of the Volksgerichtshof had already streamlined business to an unprecedented level. The following statistics serve as an example of just how efficient they were:

By April 1943, the total number of prisoners held on remand by the Volksgerichtshof had increased to 4,128 compared with 1,230 in December 1938. And whereas 'only' 57 court sessions were held in its founding year of 1934, the Volksgerichtshof judges tried 1,258 cases against 'enemies of the Volk' in 1943.

The six senates of the Volksgerichtshof dealt with more cases than other courts, including the special courts and courts martial, whose sentencing policy Freisler often criticised as too lenient. No other court pronounced more 'blood judgements' than them. And the zealous Freisler sent semi-annual reports to the Reich Minister of Justice as evidence of its efficiency. A report dated 11 January 1943 and covering the period from 1 January 1942 to 31 December 1942 reveals that of the 2,573 defendants brought before the People's Court – in just this one year – 1,192 received the death penalty, 107 were acquitted and the rest sentenced to life imprisonment or detention in prison camps. In the first six months of 1943 – the period in which Freisler had sole responsibility for the Volksgerichtshof – the court tried 1,730 cases and passed 804 death sentences. The number of acquittals was a mere 95. Item 15 of Freisler's report lists 'Cases (persons) dealt with by other means', in other words, people sent to concentration camps or handed over to the Gestapo. In 1942, the Volksgerichtshof reported 495 such cases; in the first half of 1943 – under Freisler – 561.

Freisler's First Senate was the most zealous. It was here, where the most important cases, the cases that received most publicity, were tried that the most death sentences were handed out. Shortly after assuming his position as its President in 1942, Freisler had begun to exert a dominant influence on the administration of justice by the Volksgerichtshof. He personally assigned all cases which met the conditions described above to the First Senate, over which he himself presided, 'in order to participate actively in the administration of justice by the Volksgerichtshof'. The thought that his fate might rest in Freisler's hands was enough to fill every defendant with dread. This abuse continued until the Reich Minister of Justice called for an end to the practice on 22 November. In compensation, Freisler transferred to his own senate cases of offences committed by intelligence personnel and economic crime, which in turn considerably boosted his influence.

The crime most often tried by the Volksgerichtshof was subversion of the war effort, followed by the so-called Nacht-und-Nebel-Prozesse (Night and Fog trials) – based on Hitler's 'Nacht-und-Nebel decree' of December 1941. The background of this decree was as follows: after the occupation of large areas of Northern and Western Europe by the German Wehrmacht, there were repeated attacks and acts of sabotage against the personnel and facilities of the German occupiers. Hitler ordered the death penalty for anyone who participated in acts of terror or sabotage. Keitel, Chief of the German Armed Forces High Command, stated in a directive at the end of 1941:

> It is the considered will of the Führer that, in the occupied zone, criminal acts directed against the Reich or the occupying force should henceforth be countered with other measures.

The Führer is of the opinion that punishing such crimes with prison sentences, even life sentences, will be interpreted as a sign of weakness. An effective and lasting deterrent can only be achieved by death sentences or measures that leave the relatives and the public uncertain as to the fate of the perpetrator.

Deportation to Germany serves this purpose.

And so the alleged perpetrators vanished without a trace 'into the night and fog' and were murdered. But what court was to pronounce the death sentence?

Amid the wrangling over responsibility for this task, Freisler pointed out that the Volksgerichtshof could handle the 'Night and Fog' cases if they were placed under its jurisdiction. The 'political soldier' once again stepped up to do his duty, just as he had promised the Führer when he was appointed.

The first 'Night and Fog' trials began in August 1942. By the end of the year, more than 1,000 cases had been assigned to the Volksgerichtshof. Due to the excessively high workload, Freisler transferred over 800 cases to special courts and regional courts of appeal, while the other cases were retained by the Volksgerichtshof and tried by Freisler's own First Senate. In some of the trials, there were more than 100 defendants, and the death penalty was the rule rather than the exception. So many death sentences were handed out that some prisons could not keep pace with the executions. Despite transport problems caused by the Allied air raids, some prisoners were therefore transferred, for example from Berlin, to prisons in other areas, where execution commandos carried out their bloody task. The relatives of the condemned were never notified, and farewell letters were destroyed. The 'Night and Fog' trials, in which the Wehrmacht judges were also involved, and which ensured that all death sentences handed out in occupied areas were carried out within twenty-four hours, were classified as 'Geheime Reichssache' (top secret Reich affair).

Any defendant acquitted in one of these trials – and there were very few verdicts of 'not guilty' – was handed over to the Gestapo. And that meant certain death. Most were hauled off to concentration camps and murdered there.

Despite occasional wrangling over areas of responsibility, despite contrasting opinions on definitions and interpretations in the jungle of laws and ordinances against enemies of the Volk, the 'home front' comprising the police, Gestapo, the Party and the legal system stood united – at least on the surface.

Nevertheless, some parts of the judiciary repeatedly laid claim to a special position. To boost the status of the judiciary, Thierack had already published a circular, on 12 October 1942, according judges a special status among civil servants. In Nazi Germany, a judge was no longer to be classified as a civil servant, but as a judge. Thierack's motive, however, was to bind the entire judiciary even more tightly to the NSDAP.

Not long after his appointment to the office of Reich Minister of Justice, he had begun to gather 'top secret' information on trials and sentences, particularly those at the Volksgerichtshof, which he passed on to Hitler himself as 'Führerinformationen'. In Thierack's view, it was especially important now, in wartime, to streamline the entire judicial procedure and bring it in line with Nazi ideals. And he seems to have achieved this without difficulty. Nowhere in the Reich was there appreciable resistance from the jurists. It was as if a variation of the combat slogan 'Command, Führer, and we will follow' had become their motto: 'Command, Thierack, and we will follow.'

Freisler, on the other hand, often pursued his own goals. This had not escaped Thierack's attention, and he saw his old reservations with regard to Freisler confirmed. He also noted that Freisler grabbed for himself the cases that attracted most publicity and often presided over the courtroom as if he were playing the leading role in a drama. Thierack found Freisler's courtroom manner too crude and blustering. Nevertheless, Thierack could not deny that the Volksgerichtshof President was running his court efficiently. The sentences it meted out were harsh – in Thierack's estimation – but they were in keeping with the grave situation and therefore quite exemplary. After all, were there not saboteurs, subverters of the war effort, defeatists, aiders and abetters of the enemy everywhere in the Reich? Like Freisler, Thierack was convinced that harsh sentences were necessary, because Germany was at war. Anyone who was not with them was against them, an enemy of the state and therefore was to be dealt with by the courts.

Freisler shared this view. In a letter in October 1943, he wrote: 'I am fully conscious of the fact that my administration of justice is one-sided, but only in pursuit of one political aim: to use every means within my power to prevent a repetition of 1918.'

There we have it again: Freisler's trauma, his fear that the home front could collapse as a result of sabotage and treason. In a letter dated 4 February 1944, he expressed concerns about the national identity of the Germans, questioning whether they possessed that 'healthy' nationalistic spirit that was so vital in times of war. Speaking of the rigorous legislation which he had helped to initiate, he wrote:

I believe that the corresponding laws would never have been passed if we Germans were a truly united nation with a national consciousness and pride such as that of the French and British . . .

Sometimes, when I have the time to deliberate and follow a train of thought to its end, I am surprised that we made such progress between 1933 and 1939 and that we have achieved such great military successes since 1939 despite our inner weakness.

All the more reason to be cautious, even if this means fighting to the end in a battle whose debris will bury us.

Again and again, during his numerous journeys through the Reich, Freisler witnessed at first hand the ruins of war. Evidence of the Allied air raids was everywhere. And they also affected the working of the Volksgerichtshof. The beginning of trials was often delayed because the lay judges and defence counsels could not reach the court on time. This was of particular consequence for the defence lawyers, who then had very little time to confer with their clients. In a letter dated 9 February 1943, senior Reich prosecutor Lautz had suggested that the responsibility for deciding whether a defence counsel was appointed at all should lie solely with the judge. After this letter, with increasing frequency, defendants were tried without legal representation, though this never became the rule. At the end of 1942, those condemned to death had already been denied spiritual assistance. The defendants had been reduced to defenceless objects.

While the Reich sank into the rubble under the onslaught of the Allied attacks, the judges of the People's Court, now, under a new directive, exclusively Party members, relentlessly continued their work.

This was in complete accordance with the instructions of its President, who on 1 December 1944, described the sentences handed down by the Volksgerichtshof as a 'continuous self-purification of our nation' and described the task of the blood tribunal as follows:

The Volksgerichtshof is the highest court in the Greater German Reich and ensures its political strength. In our present struggle for life and liberty, it is therefore our task to protect the Reich against treason and the German people against the subversion of its will to fight. And our focus lies steadfastly on this task.

As National Socialists, as followers of the Führer, we do this by always looking forwards to where our Führer stands. As the Führer of the Volk and the Reich, he is also its judge. And so we strive to act as his deputies.

We therefore draw the justification for our actions, the collective political axioms on the basis of which we administer justice, directly from the collective spirit of National Socialism.

Freisler increasingly expressed doubts concerning this 'collective spirit', but never publicly. On the contrary: in public, he used the vocabulary of Nazi propaganda when speaking of the national unity:

Our nation can consider itself fortunate to have [this sense of unity] . . .! This alone gives it its sound foundation. And whoever, as a judge, takes his position and direction from this sense of unity can never lose his way in the maze of theories and hypotheses, will not sink into weakness and lack of orientation through doubt; he will remain capable of action, will continue to march within the closed formation of our nation. And if this is the principle of our administration of justice, the German people also knows that when called upon to give account, that is, when it is a question of honour, freedom, life, the Volksgenosse will not be judged by the yardstick of some 'secret science', but according to the inner law of the soul of our nation, our innate sense of decency. What the Führer asks of us, has so often told us and demonstrates by his example, is the law of our own life, the law under which we took up arms.

It is our conviction that if we make our decisions based on these convictions, any decent man will not only understand our judgements – that would be too little – but will perceive them as his own. In this way, our work effects a continuous self-cleansing of our nation . . .

Our most dangerous enemy is defeatism. Its essential nature is: pestilence! And we are burnt children who have learned to dread the fire: 1918! . . .

To avert danger from our nation in the hour of war, to ward off the dagger that would strike it in the back, can never be denunciation. It is a duty!

This must be made clear to all those who turn to us in doubt.

The harsh punishment we mete out to those who are defeatists through weakness, cowardice, inadequacy, protects the healthy and the strong against infection with this same weakness. On the front, the coward cannot excuse himself on the grounds of weakness when he is dragged out from the hole in which he cravenly concealed himself while his brave comrades heroically advanced; that hole will become his dishonourable grave.

And weakness spreads like pestilence!

Our task as the representatives of the People's Court of the Greater German Reich, sustained by our belief in the National Socialist cause, fired by the energy of our political world-view, is to remind the nation of its duty, to call for unity and rigour and to preserve the strength of our nation at home and abroad.

The 'law of the soul of our nation', as Freisler called it, was to find its expression in the draconian sentences handed out by the court. And these sentences were to be such that 'any decent German citizen' could identify with them. To this end, Freisler drafted his judgements in a way that was completely new to the German legal system. In pronouncing his verdict, he focused not on the crime itself – for example, treason or high treason, subversion of the war effort or aiding and abetting the enemy – and announcing the punishment, but on a description of the perpetrator himself, using coarse and emotive language. The defendant was portrayed as a particularly evil, ruthless and unique criminal, which, of course, meant elevating even minor offences to the status of outrageous violations of the law. In contravention of the rules of procedure, the legal basis for the sentence was frequently not mentioned at all. Instead, the judge spoke of the 'monstrosity' of the crime and the 'wantonness' of the criminal – and then announced the 'just punishment'. 'In the name of the people . . .'.

The findings of the court glorified National Socialism, and any criticism of National Socialism was a crime against the German nation. Freisler never tired of portraying National Socialism as the only way of life in accordance with the character of the German people, a code which embodied all the virtues which he considered quintessentially German: loyalty, courage, manliness. These were the sole yardsticks against which the defendant was to be measured. In outlining the reasons for the sentence, Freisler frequently used Germanic figures of speech – for example that 'the deed judged the man' or that the traitor was 'wolfsfrei' (outlawed).

In addition to the glorification of National Socialism, the tenets of which, in Freisler's view, all Germans willingly embraced, the Führer was praised in the highest terms. In Freisler's findings, Hitler is described as a wise father figure, an outstanding statesman solicitously guiding the fate of his people, as an ingenious military commander who had been forced unwillingly into war and under whose leadership victory was certain. To doubt the Führer, the Party or the Wehrmacht was nothing less than treason and was branded as a crime so heinous that it called for the harshest punishment.

Yet for all his grandiose rhetoric, despite his invocations of the Greater German Empire and the 'Endsieg' (final victory), Freisler knew that the Wehrmacht was foundering, and he saw the ravages caused by the air raids; he perceived the first signs of impending doom. But his court findings gave no indication of the disastrous events that were unfolding around him. On the contrary: Anyone who doubted that Germany was marching to victory and questioned the leadership of the Führer was to be annihilated – 'in the name of the Volk'.

In handing down such barbarous sentences, was he also exorcising his own deep-seated doubts? A form of self-punishment? On the outside, not even Freisler's immediate environment – and least of all the defendants brought before him – noticed his latent ambivalence.

Freisler's sentencing style, the distinctive and macabre hallmark of a judiciary that sat in judgement on those whose only crime was that their political views did not coincide with those of the Nazi regime, remained blatantly contemptuous of human life. And it was emulated, at least at the Volksgerichtshof. Many judges did their very best to copy Freisler's style when pronouncing their verdicts. But few, of course, could match his efficiency and perfection. Instead of relying on the services of the court reporter for his written grounds for the verdict, he dictated them himself immediately after the end of each session. He frequently recorded a death sentence on just a few pages. And no-one dictated more death sentences than Freisler.

In addition to the trials, he performed his administrative tasks as President of the Volksgerichtshof, chaired meetings and gave lectures. He had very little private life and hardly any time for his two sons Roland and Harald, who were now five and seven years old. They and their mother, Freisler's wife Marion, saw him increasingly rarely. In these days, when the threat to Volk and Vaterland, Führer and Party was so obvious, duty came first. Germany was fighting for the 'final victory', and the fate of the nation hung in the balance. Freisler was the 'political soldier', and the front on which he fought was the courtroom.

For Freisler, the courtroom was a political stage. To ensure that the machinery of the court ran smoothly and efficiently, he would set out his view of each case to the lay judges who formed the other members of the panel in advance, which meant that the verdict was usually a foregone conclusion. His handling of the defendants during the trial depended on how they conducted themselves. Any attempt to play down the facts of the case was countered with sarcasm, hatred and contempt. He conducted the trials in an authoritarian manner and with disregard for the law. He screamed at the defendants, often shouting them down. He interrupted them constantly, subjected them to a barrage of insults, tried to intimidate them and humiliated them by mocking and ridiculing them in front of the audience. The defence lawyers were reduced to the role of mere bystanders. Motions to take evidence were rejected summarily, often on the grounds that the production of further evidence could have no effect on the verdict of the court. Instead, Freisler's gestures and comments left the public prosecutor in no doubt as to what verdict he should call for. And the lay judges, too, were little more than window-dressing.

The First Senate did not need to retire to consider its verdict. On the rare occasions when another member of the court voiced a different opinion, Freisler reacted with such vehemence and such cutting remarks that the majority preferred to keep their mouths shut and vote as he wanted. Freisler was only prepared to listen to other opinions and answer questions when the other members of the panel were generals of the Wehrmacht. But here, too, when the judges had concluded their 'deliberations', the outcome was almost always the verdict which Freisler had decided upon long in advance. The court was Freisler. Any defendant brought before his bench was doomed. In line with his conviction that the sentences of the Volksgerichtshof effected a 'continuous self-cleansing of our nation', he handed out death penalty after death penalty,

Of the almost 1,200 death sentences passed by the Volksgerichtshof in the year 1942, almost 650, more than half, were handed down by Freisler's First Senate. It was the same in 1943, when 779, almost 50 per cent, of the 1,662 death sentences were pronounced by the First Senate. And finally, the First Senate dispensed 866 of the total of around 2,100 death sentences in 1944.

Freisler was contemptuous of any divergent and more lenient views expressed by other judges of the Volksgerichtshof. He called these judges 'jurists of the old school' and sent communiques to the President of the Fourth Senate, criticising his sentencing policy and instructing the senate to take a tougher line. When his warnings had no effect, Freisler took all cases in which the defendant was charged with subversion of the war effort, the crime in question, away from the Fourth Senate. In any case, as President of the Volksgerichtshof, he had the authority to overturn any verdict of a senate which he disagreed with by means of an 'extraordinary objection' and replace it with his own. In the year 1944 alone, the 'special senate' over which Freisler presided handed out the death sentence in seventy-five cases. In such cases, Freisler was often seeking to change a previously-pronounced prison sentence to a death sentence.

Freisler, the indomitable 'political soldier'. He sent thousands to their deaths. A murderer in a blood-red judge's robe.

The evidence of his reign of terror can be seen today in the Federal Archive in Koblenz. Thousands of death sentences, each file a silent witness to a barbaric administration of justice and a merciless judiciary. In the name of the Volk.

Chapter 7

# In the Name of the Volk

The function of the Volksgerichtshof was not to dispense justice, but to crush any opposition to the regime. And the judges in blood-red robes, led by Freisler, performed their task with consistent fanaticism. But by no means did the court carry out its grisly work under a cloak of secrecy.

The Germans were aware of it. Blood-red placards publicising the death sentences handed down by the Volksgerichtshof were everywhere. Visible for anyone with eyes to see. The problem was that hardly anyone wanted to see them. Neither the Party members who – despite the advance of the Allies – still remained convinced of the 'final victory', nor the Hitler supporters, who in their nationalist delirium steadfastly refused to hear the evidence that the tide of the War had turned against the Germans, who continued to applaud, to march – and to denounce. The opportunists and hangers-on kept their vague doubts about the Führer, the Wehrmacht and the Reich to themselves, blotted them out – and carried on as before. Hitler's Germans – a nation of collaborators, lookers-on and people who looked the other way.

The others, the opponents and critics of the regime, had long been arrested and murdered, had fled into exile – or were awaiting death in concentration camps. So who was there left to stop the blood judges of the Volksgerichtshof, who was there left to protest or feel pity for the victims?

The 'self-cleansing of the nation' which Freisler had repeatedly expounded in such glowing terms was working.

The death sentences issued by the Volksgerichtshof were pronounced and indeed carried out 'in the name of the Volk'. The German people had become accomplices of the Nazis' blood justice. A nation of perpetrators and accomplices. And the victims?

Files are the silent witnesses. From thousands of death sentences, ten were selected for this account. All ten were passed by Freisler's First Senate. The sentencing policy of the other five Volksgerichtshof senates was the same. The ten death sentences and their 'Grounds' on the following pages stand as examples of the 5,243 issued by the Volksgerichtshof, documenting its fanatical intolerance of any criticism of the regime, however insignificant and harmless. One careless remark, one subtle joke was enough to merit the death penalty.

The inflammatory and annihilating language in which the sentences were written was not a product of Freisler's 'demonic nature'. These were not the hate-filled tirades of one individual: this was the language of an inhumane judiciary, a tyrannical regime – and a blinded people.

---

## Sentence 1

### 'His honour and rights as a citizen are forfeited for all time'

In the name of the German people

In the action against
the miner Dietrich Tembergen from Kamp-Lintfort, born on 21 November 1887 in Baerl near Utford, at present imprisoned on remand by the court for crimes including preparation for high treason, the Volksgerichtshof, First Senate, pursuant to the trial held on 7 January 1943, in which the officers were:

Judges:
President of the Volksgerichtshof Dr Freisler, chairman
Landgerichtsdirektor (regional court director) Dr Klein,
Generalarbeitsführer (general labour leader) Müller,
SS-Brigadeführer Polizeiführer (chief of police) Bolek,
Stadtrat (town councillor) Kaiser,

Representatives of the senior Reich prosecutor:
Landgerichtsrat (regional court judge) von Zeschau,
as Clerk of the Court:
Justizobersekretär (senior court clerk) Peltz,

finds:
that the accused did in wartime aid and abet the enemy by stating in a public tram, with reference to English propaganda leaflets, that the German people should revolt. On this account, he is to be punished by death.

His honour and rights as a citizen are forfeited for all time.

The costs are to be borne by the accused.

The correctness of this transcript is certified and the enforceability of the sentence confirmed.

Grounds:

The accused travelled by tram from Lintfort to his place of work every morning, taking tram 6, which departs at 6 a.m.

In the second half of July 1942, on the morning after a heavy British air raid on the neighbouring city of Moers, he boarded the said tram, entering the car where Volksgenossin V. was the conductor. The car was otherwise only moderately full.

The accused took out some English propaganda leaflets, showing them to the occupants of the car and stating that the leaflets spoke the truth. When the conductor told him to put the leaflets away, that it was not appropriate to be displaying them in public transportation, the accused asked her if she always had enough to eat. Volkgenossin V. replied that she only had what her ration card entitled her to, but that it had always sufficed. The accused replied that he went to bed hungry and that the war only benefited the 'fat cats'. In his opinion, he said, the people should join hands and start a revolution. The 'fat cats' could then bash in each other's heads. When the conductor asked if the accused meant there would be more food if the Russians marched in, he replied in the affirmative. The conductor answered: then we might as well all take a rope and hang ourselves.

Volksgenossin V. repeated these statements to the police and in her testimony before the Volksgerichtshof. In the eyes of the court, she is a good and credible witness.

The incident is therefore already verified by her statements.

Moreover, her description of the incident is corroborated by the credible testimony of Volksgenossin O., who witnessed the first part of this scene. She confirmed that the accused produced leaflets – or at least papers which she cautiously described as having the appearance of leaflets – that she heard him say that 'if you eat your fill before you go to bed, you have nothing to eat the next morning' and stated that he was still complaining when she got off the tram.

The testimony of Volksgenossin V. is even confirmed by the statements of the accused himself. When first questioned by the police, he denied everything and claiming that he had merely spoken to another passenger about his pay slip, but during a second interrogation, when confronted with the testimony of Volksgenossin V., he declared that while he was not disputing her words, he had no recollection of having made such statements. During examination by the judges, he claimed that he could not remember whether he said that the war only benefited the 'fat cats', that the Volk should unite and start a revolution and that people would have more to eat if the Russians came. Before the Volksgerichtshof, he attempted to deny the charges by means of clearly foolish and brazen statements, but admitted three things:

1. that he had spoken of 'leaflets'. He maintains, however, that he meant pay slips (!);
2. that he referred to 'the fat cats'. He claims that he did not mean the government, but the factory owners;
3. that he said the people should join hands and start a revolution.

These statements can therefore rightly be said to corroborate Volksgenossin V'.s account of the scene.

The defence counsel maintained that the accused was merely a habitual grumbler. The Volksgerichtshof cannot concur with this. Anyone with enemy leaflets in his hands who states in public that the people should revolt is dangerously eroding our home front at a time when the German solider is risking his life in heavy fighting. He is stabbing our army in the back. This is highly dangerous – as shown in 1917–18 – even if the first, the second and many other stabs miss their target. And everybody is well aware of this, even the somewhat mentally deficient defendant! He is therefore no mere grumbler, but a dangerous enemy of our fighting Volk. He is doing exactly what the English speculate on when they drop their mixed cargo of bombs and leaflets upon us: wearing down the spirit of the Volk, weakening its defensive power in a total war and aiding and abetting the enemy. (§ 91 b StGB)

To claim that the actions of the accused could cause no more than minor damage to the Reich is patently incorrect. They are a weight tossed onto the scales of destiny, tipping them towards the side of 'failure of our nation'. The accused has therefore removed himself from the community of our fighting nation and deserves the death penalty.

As a traitor to our soldiers, he has forfeited his honour for all time.

Signed: Dr Freisler                                                      Dr Klein

On 25 February 1943, a clerk working for the 'Senior Reich Prosecutor at the Volkgerichtshof', Senior Public Prosecutor Dr Drullmann, sent a parcel of files by registered mail from the Volsgerichtshof in Bellevuestrasse across Berlin to the Reich Ministry of Justice in the Wilhelmstrasse. It was addressed to the Reich Minister of Justice, for the attention of Oberregierungsrat Ulrich. The parcel contained the Senior Reich Prosecutor's indictment, a folder containing a plea for clemency with statements, two copies of the sentence and an accompanying letter signed by Dr Drullmann:

> Enclosed, I am forwarding the files containing the verdict pronounced on 7 January 1943 by the First Senate of the Volksgerichtshof, in which the above-mentioned defendant was sentenced to death and permanent loss of honour and rights as a citizen as requested by the prosecution. The condemned is currently housed in Plötzensee Prison in Berlin. None of the bodies I interviewed has appealed for clemency.
>
> Following an enemy air raid in the area of his town of residence, the condemned spread defeatist propaganda by producing enemy leaflets in a public place and in particular by advocating that the people should rise up against the state in order to bring about the end of the war. In view of the dangerous nature of the crime and in the interest of deterrence, I consider the death penalty to be justified.
>
> I therefore recommend that no pardon should be granted.

On 30 March 1943, Reich Minister Thierack approved the recommendation. He also found that 'justice' should be allowed to 'take its course':

> In the case of Dietrich Tembergen, who was sentenced to death by the Volksgerichtshof on 7 January 1943, I have decided, with the approval of the Führer, not to exercise the right of clemency, but to allow justice to take its course . . .

Nine days later, the miner Dietrich Tembergen was led from his cell in Plötzensee prison and executed. In a brief letter to the Reich Ministry of Justice dated 10 April 1943, in the name of Dr Drullmann, his colleague Parrisius confirmed that the death sentence had been duly carried out:

> The death sentence pronounced by the First Senate of the Volksgerichtshof on 7 January 1943 against the miner Dietrich Tembergen from Kamp Lintfort was enforced in the prescribed

manner on 8 April 1943. The execution was carried out without incident and took 14 seconds from presentation of the condemned to announcement by the executioner that the prisoner was dead.

A day later, a brief announcement appeared in a few German newspapers:

> 55-year old Dietrich Tembergen, sentenced to death by the Volksgerichtshof for aiding and abetting the enemy, was executed on 8 April. Tembergen had publicly attempted to undermine the resistance of the German Volk.

---

## Sentence 2

### 'Spreader of subversive enemy propaganda . . .'

In the name of the German people

In the action against
the businessman Wilhelm Alich from Wiesenthal near Rogätz (Madgeburg district), born on 28 August November 1886 in Nordhausen, at present imprisoned on remand by the court for subversion of the war effort, the Volksgerichtshof, First Senate, pursuant to the trial held on 29 September 1943, in which the officers were:

Judges:
President of the Volksgerichtshof Dr Freisler, chairman,
Kammergerichtsrat Rehse,
SA-Brigadeführer Hauer,
Undersecretary in the Wehrmacht high command
Dr Herzlieb,
Local group leader Friedrich,

Representative of the senior Reich prosecutor:
Senior Public Prosecutor Dr Heugel,

finds as follows:
Shortly after the betrayal of Mussolini, Wilhelm Alich declared that it was now time for the Führer to step down, too, as he had brought

such misfortune upon our nation that the rest of his life could not suffice to atone for it; he also stated that if no-one else was willing to shoot the Führer, they should bring him out, and he himself would do it!

As a spreader of subversive propaganda for our enemies, he has thus forfeited his honour.

He is sentenced to death.

Grounds:

Wilhelm Alich is a businessman who apparently takes little interest in our life as a national community: he is not even a member of the NSV (Nationalsozialistische Volkswohlfahrt – National Socialist Public Welfare Organization) – as he has always been too busy pursuing his own business interests. And that despite the fact that with his salary and sales commission, he can expect to earn at least 700 Reichmarks a month.

Shortly after the betrayal of Mussolini, the accused entered the Rogätz branch of the Kreissparkasse bank and told the branch manager, Volksgenosse Ollendorf, that Mussolini had resigned. He then pointed to the portrait of the Führer on the wall, saying that he should also resign, as he had brought down such misfortune on the German people that the rest of his life would not suffice to atone for it. He stated that the Führer should be shot and said that if no-one else was willing, he, the accused would do it. Initially calm, he became increasingly agitated as he spoke.

Alich denies the accusations. In each of three interrogations, he has told a different story. Before the court today, for example, he maintained that he said that Mussolini's resignation had brought misfortune on the German people for which he could never be brought to account, and that the Führer would never resign; he would shoot himself first. Firstly, this statement about Mussolini is so far-fetched as to be highly improbable. Secondly: Alich expressly denied to the police that he had spoken of the Führer at all! And finally: a man who changes his story so often cannot possibly be believed. Volksgenosse Ollendorf, on the other hand, described the incident in exactly the same way three times – to his regional head, to the police and before the court today. The court's impression of the witness was that of an upright, conscientious and reliable man who was clearly at pains not to exaggerate. The Volksgerichtshof has no doubt that the events took place exactly as he described them.

The defence requested a psychological examination of the defendant. It suggested that due to his contracting syphilis in 1923 and a car accident in 1924, the defendant could not be held legally responsible for his actions today. However,

1. neither the syphilis nor the accident prevented Alich from pursuing his business activities very successfully over the course of two decades;
2. neither can protect him from subsequent punishment; the court therefore holds him liable for his actions;
3. during the trial, the accused defended himself in such a manner – first through vehement denial and then with tearful pleas – that the Volksgerichtshof has no doubt whatsoever that he is so far in possession of his senses that he can be held criminally responsible. The court requires no expert to verify this in this case. Even if it is true that the accused is somewhat excitable as an after-effect of syphilis – where would the German Reich be if it accepted this as a mitigating circumstance or as grounds for the lenient treatment of the perpetrator of such a horrendous crime?

The nature of the crime is such that the testimony of character witnesses whom the defence wished to call could not alter the opinion of the court. This is a case where, indeed, the deeds must judge the man.

Anyone who, like Alich, declares himself ready and willing to shoot the Führer if given the chance – has in our eyes forfeited his honour for all time. In the most heinous manner, he has knowingly rendered himself the tool of defeatist enemy propaganda (§ 91b StGB).

Anyone who declares intent to lay hand on the Führer thus condemns himself.

Such an individual must be cut out from our midst.

For this reason, the Volksgerichtshof has sentenced him to death.

Having been found guilty, the accused must bear the costs.

Signed: Dr Freisler                                           Rehse

## Sentence 3:

### 'By means of the most execrable seditious speeches ...'

In the name of the German people

In the action against
the master hairdresser Bernhard Firsching from Nuremberg, born on
10 October 1894 in Obertheras, at present imprisoned on remand by
the court for subversion of the war effort, the Volksgerichtshof, First
Senate, pursuant to the trial held on 30 September 1943, in which the
officers were:

Judges:
President of the Volksgerichtshof Dr Freisler, chairman
Kammergerichtsrat Rehse,
SA-Brigadeführer Hauer,
SS-Brigadeführer Heider,
SA-Oberführer Hell,

Representative of the senior Reich prosecutor:
Public Prosecutor Dr Bruchhaus

finds as follows:
For months, Bernhard Firsching systematically attempted to incite his
customers, soldiers and other Volksgenossen in his barber's shop by
means of the most execrable seditious speeches.

In doing so, he has made himself the propaganda agent of our
enemies in war, seeking to undermine the spirit of the nation.

He has forfeited his honour for all time.

He is sentenced to death.

Grounds:
Bernhard Firsching is a man who has undergone a complete change
of convictions. In the First World War, he was awarded the Iron Cross
Second Class. In 1925, he became a Party member and in 1930, after
leaving the Party in 1926, he joined the NSDAP again. He was active
in the movement during the period of combat. In the current war, he

99

once again served in the medical corps, with the rank of Feldwebel, from 1939 to the spring of 1943, in Poland, France and Russia.

However, he has now become a different man. During his time as a soldier, he was sentenced to eight months' imprisonment for making defamatory statements and was expelled from the NSDAP.

From spring until autumn of this year, in the period immediately preceding his arrest, he systematically used his barber's shop as a base from which to spread defeatist and seditious propaganda among soldiers and other members of the Party who were his customers.

Three soldiers have borne testimony to this today.

The first witness was Obergefreiter Schiller, who related the following: Firsching spoke of the terror attacks on Schweinfurt and Regensburg and added that another terror attack, lasting three hours and the heaviest so far, had been mounted on the city. The accused stated that the papers would probably claim that there had only been some minor damage to property. He claimed that the Mayor of Nuremberg had left the city two weeks before the attack and that all the medal-bearers were now also running. When it came to Russia, he said, all our talk had been just so much hot air and sabre-rattling. Firsching said that he himself had of course gone looking for the murdered Ukrainians in Kiev. Russian culture was far superior to that of the Germans, but the soldiers never saw it because they were kept out of the cities. The defendant stated that Stalin was a great politician who had hired 6 million Chinese and 2 million Iranians as workers for the armaments industry, freeing a further 8 million Russians to mount the offensive against us. In his opinion, the serious disputes in . . . and within the NSDAP would soon lead to a major breakdown, and the Communists were ready and waiting. Germany could not win the war.

The second witness was Unteroffizier Mederer, who testified that on 23 July, he visited Firsching's barber's shop in the company of a Gefreiter Gäbelin. The accused had stated, also in the presence of civilians, that Russian culture was at least equal to ours and that the Russians had better tanks and engineers, too. He claimed that the German 'Tiger' was a copy of a Russian tank. Unteroffizier Mederer contradicted him, whereupon Firsching said that as an infantryman, Mederer had been too busy jumping from one hole in the ground to another and had therefore seen nothing of Russia.

The last witness to take the stand was Obergefreiter Neener. He testified that in his presence, Firsching told civilians in the barber's

shop that he did not know any Volksgemeinschaft and that it was no matter to him if others perished. He stated that they would all see where Germany was six weeks' from then, a revolution had already begun in Italy, the German 'Tigers' were only a copy of Russian tanks and as our opponents had not yet cranked up their arms industry to full capacity, things were going to get much worse. Goebbels, he said, had been booed in the Rhineland, and had promised retribution a few months ago, but that was not going to happen now.

There can be no doubt: what these three soldiers calmly and authoritatively reported is a true account of events. This is confirmed by the fact that Firsching's only defence has been to claim again and again that his statements were misinterpreted . . . His words, however, were quite clear. The statements of these three witnesses, presented to the Volksgerichtshof in evidence, are decisive proof that Firsching was in the habit of speaking to his customers in this manner. He has therefore shown himself to be a propagator of defeatist and inflammatory enemy propaganda (§ 5 KSSVO, 91 b StGB). Moreover, he himself stated that he considers himself as standing outside the national community and has thus permanently forfeited his honour. To thwart Churchill's plans and prevent a repetition of 1918 and in order to make it clear to all others who strive to undermine our fighting spirit in like manner what punishment awaits them, the Volksgerichtshof had no other choice but to impose the death sentence.

Having been found guilty, the accused must bear the costs.

Signed Dr Freisler              Rehse

## Sentence 4

### 'In order to safeguard our domestic security. . .

In the name of the German people

In the action against
postman Georg Jurkowski from Berlin-Weissensee, born on 31 July 1891 in Berlin, at present imprisoned on remand by the court for subversion of the war effort, the Volksgerichtshof, First Senate,

pursuant to the trial held on 14 October 1943, in which the officers were:

Judges:
President of the Volksgerichtshof Dr Freisler, chairman,
Kammergerichtsrat Rehse,
Mayor and Gauhauptstellenleiter (head of the regional Party office) Ahmels,
Ortsgruppenleiter Kelch,
Kreisleiter Reinecke,

Representative of the senior Reich prosecutor:
Senior Public Prosecutor Domann,

finds as follows:
At the beginning of August, Georg Jurkowski was heard to make subversive and defeatist statements on a public street in Danzig, in particular that the Führer would soon suffer the same fate as Mussolini and would be dead by January.

He has therewith forfeited his honour for all time. As an enemy propaganda agent, he is sentenced to death.

Grounds:
Georg Jurkowski is employed as a post office guard on the Reich railways and as such, was on duty on 3 August in Danzig together with postman Schönherr from Berlin, who was also working on the Reich railway. He planned to return to Berlin at roughly 10.30. At 10 o'clock, Jurkowski and Schönherr were on the Stockturm, on their way to the station. Volksgenossin Rosemarie Grande happened to be walking along the same street behind the two men and quite clearly heard Jurkowski tell Schönherr that Hermann Göring had obtained his sixth property in Italy, thus enriching himself by acquiring the property of others. Hearing this, she approached the two men and addressed Jurkowski, while Schönherr, believing the Volksgenossin to be an acquaintance of Jurkowski's, walked on ahead, which meant that he did not witness the rest of the conversation. Volksgenossin Grande warned Jurkoswki that he should choose his words more carefully and keep such opinions to himself, not trumpet them in a public place. Jurkoswki answered: 'Fräulein, two months from now, you will be

singing a different tune. All I can say is, Il Duce has been arrested, and the same fate awaits Hitler. He will be dead by January'. Inwardly shaken by the impertinence of such statements and in order to lend her words more weight, Volksgenossin Grande informed Jurkowski that she worked for the Gestapo. Jurkowski's reply: 'Well then, you know what is going on even better than I do, and you will soon be in hotter water than we are'.

Volksgenossin Grande now went in search of a policeman and, having found one, spied Jurkowski and Schönherr standing at a tram stop. When he saw her with the police officer, Jurkowski immediately attempted to flee. However, he was apprehended by passers-by and taken to the police station. Sitting there with Volksgenossin Grande, he said to her: 'I will give you whatever you want. Here, take my watch, but let me go'. Volksgenossin Grande testified with great certainty to all this, both to the police and in court on this day. The court finds Volksgenossin Grande to be a credible witness who neither abbreviated nor embellished her statements. She is absolutely certain that she was not mistaken, despite the noise of the street which Jurkowski refers to.

Jurkoswki denies having made the above-mentioned statements. He admits that he did indeed say that Volksgenossin Grande would be singing a different tune in two months' time, but insists that he was referring to our retaliatory attacks, though he did not state this at the time. According to the defendant, before this, he had merely been telling Schönherr how he had once planned to visit a castle – he said today it was Burg Neuhaus in Franconia – but had been unable to do so because Reichsmarschall Göring was there. The defendant denies having threatened Volksgenossin Grande when she claimed to be working for the Gestapo (in reality, she works in the office of the Reich governor). The fact that Jurkowski attempted to flee, however, is evidence of his guilty conscience, although he offers the highly improbable excuse that he was afraid of missing his train, a statement which Schönherr, testifying before the court today, also found extremely surprising. Jurkowski also says – another highly improbable claim – that he only offered Volkgenossin Grande his watch at the police station, when he had already missed his train, because he wanted to avoid getting into trouble. That the accused had a guilty conscience is thus proven. Moreover: the testimony of Volksgenossin Grande is such that the Volksgerichtshof has no doubt that the events in question happened exactly as she described them; it requires no corroboration by the witness Schönherr, who was not able to hear the conversation well because in the crowded street, he was repeatedly separated from Jurkowski, was not really paying attention as he had no great interest in what the defendant was saying and who walked on ahead a short distance when Volkgenossin Grande approached Jurkowski.

Volksgenossin Rosemarie Grande's resolute and appropriate intervention is to be commended. Such are the actions required of a German citizen today. She unmasked a dangerous defeatist and subversive, and one who has so ignominiously broken his oath to the Führer (§ 5 KSSVO, § 91 b StGB). Anyone acting in such a way at the end of this fourth year during which Germany has been at war must be considered to have forfeited all honour. In order to safeguard our inner security, and deprived of honour for all time, he must therefore be condemned to death.

Having been found guilty, Jurkowski must also bear the costs.

Signed Dr Freisler                                                                 Rehse

On the same day on which postman Georg Jurkowski was sentenced to death, Dr Max Josef Metzger, a priest from Baden, was brought before Freisler's senate.

Metzger played a key role in founding numerous religious organizations – in particular, the 'Una Sancta' movement. He was arrested by the Gestapo because of a manifesto addressed to the Swedish archbishop of Uppsala and in which he drafted a model, in disguised form, for a democratic form of government in Germany after the war. During his trial, the priest tried to explain the 'Una Sancta' movement, which aimed to bring together the Catholic and Protestant churches, but was interrupted by an angry Freisler with the words: 'Una Sancta, Una Sancta, Una Santissima, Una – We are Una Sancta, and there is nothing else!'

Metzger was sentenced to death – Freisler's second death sentence on 14 October 1943.

In Freisler's eyes, as a traitor to the Volk, Metzger had forfeited his right to live. An excerpt from his death sentence:

Roland Freisler, the President of the Volksgerichtshof, or the People's Court, photographed on 1 September 1942. (Bundesarchiv, Bild 183-J03238/ CC-BY-SA 3.0)

Roland Freisler, the laywer, with one of his clients, Otto Strasser, in 1930. (Author)

The inaugural gathering of Prussian law clerks at a camp in Jüterbog, north-eastern Germany, in 1933. Freisler, having been appointed the Director of the Prussian Ministry of Justice that year, is seen here, fifth from the right, on the first day of the gathering. (Bundesarchiv, Bild 183-H26606/CC-BY-SA 3.0)

The inauguration of the newly-appointed Attorney General, Heinrich Lautz, at the District Court in Berlin, on 31 August 1936. Lautz is seen here being congratulated by Freisler. (Bundesarchiv, Bild 183-H25930/ CC-BY-SA 3.0)

A meeting of the four men who imposed Nazi ideology on the German legal system before and during the Second World War. From left to right are Roland Freisler, Franz Schlegelberger, Otto Georg Thierack and Curt Rothenberger. (Bundesarchiv, Bild 183-J03166/CC-BY-SA 3.0)

The Reich Minister of Justice, Otto Georg Thierack (on the right), greets the new President of the Volksgerichtshof, Roland Freisler, in his office at the end of August 1942. (Bundesarchiv, Bild 183-J03230/CC-BY-SA 3.0)

The opening of a session of the Volksgerichtshof for the trials of those involved in the 20 July 1944 assassination attempt on Adolf Hitler. From left to right are Hermann Reinecke, Roland Freisler and Ernst Lautz, the Chief Public Prosecutor. (Bundesarchiv, Bild 151-39-23/CC-BY-SA 3.0)

Two pictures of Roland Freisler taken during the 20 July 1944 trials. (Bundesarchiv, Bild 151-17-15 and Bild 151-29-35/CC-BY-SA 3.0)

Dr Carl Friedrich Goerdeler, the former Mayor of Leipzig, speaking during his trial for his involvement in the 20 July plot. Had the plan succeeded, Goerdeler would have served as Chancellor in the new government. After the plot's failure, Goerdeler managed to escape from Berlin, but he was arrested on 12 August 1944 in Marienwerder. Found guilty in the trials, he was executed by hanging on 2 February 1945. Freisler can be seen presiding on the left. (Bundesarchiv, Bild 151-58-16/CC-BY-SA 3.0)

Roland Freisler faces a witness as the latter gives the Nazi salute on entering the Volksgerichtshof during the trial of the 20 July plotters. (Bundesarchiv, Bild 151-10-11/CC-BY-SA 3.0)

Another of the accused in the 20 July trials, Carl Wentzel, appears in front of Roland Freisler, whose back is to the camera on the right. A German farmer and agricultural contractor, Wentzel was found guilty and executed on 20 December 1944. (Bundesarchiv, Bild 151-53-30A/CC-BY-SA 3.0)

Ferdinand Freiherr von Lüninck appearing before the Volksgerichtshof for his part in the 20 July plot. Found guilty and sentenced to death on 13 November 1944, he was executed at Plötzensee Prison in Berlin the next day. (Bundesarchiv, Bild 151-52-31A/CC-BY-SA 3.0)

Roland Freisler discussing plans of the Wolfsschanze complex during the trials after the 20 July plot. (Author)

The ruins of the People's Court, or Volksgerichtshof, in Bellevuestraße, part of Berlin's Tiergarten district, photographed in 1951. (Bundesarchiv, B145 Bild-P054489/CC-BY-SA 3.0)

A memorial plaque on the site of the Volksgerichtshof. Translated, it states: 'The entrance to the Volksgerichtshof stood at this spot 1935-1945. The court, in violation of fundamental principles of justice, condemned more than five thousand people to death and an even higher number to loss of freedom. Its goal was the destruction of opposition to the National Socialist regime.'

## Sentence 5

### 'A traitor to the people who has forfeited his honour for all time . . .'

In the name of the German people

In the action against
the Catholic priest Dr Max Josef Metzger from Berlin, born on 3 February 1887 in Schöpfenheim (Baden), at present in police custody on suspicion of preparation for high treason,the Volksgerichtshof, First Senate, pursuant to the trial held on 14 October 1943, in which the officers were:

Judges:
President of the Volksgerichtshof Dr Freisler, chairman,
Kammergerichtsrat Rehse,
Mayor and Gauhauptstellenleiter Ahmels,
Ortsgruppenleiter Kelch,
Kreisleiter Reinecke,

Representative of the senior Reich prosecutor:
Senior Public Prosecutor Dr Drullmann,

finds as follows:
Max Josef Metzger, a Catholic diocesan priest, convinced of our defeat in the fourth year of the war, attempted to send a 'memorandum' to Sweden to prepare the ground for an inimical, pacifist-democratic, federalist 'government' with the personal defamation of the National Socialists. As a traitor to the people, forever without honour, he is sentenced to death.

Grounds:
Max Josef Metzger is a Catholic diocesan priest who in 1917 – in the midst of war! – was active in the foundation of a world peace organization in Austria, that is, he was already involved in undermining the war effort, like Erzberger in Germany.

And he has continued with these subversive activities to this day. He says himself that he is certain that Germany will collapse. For this reason, he says, he considered writing a letter to the Führer requesting him to step down in order to pave the way for peace negotiations! However, he did not in fact send any such letter,

1. because he was certain his letter would not reach the Führer;
2. because he did not believe that his request would be successful;
3. because he feared that he would then be arrested.

Instead, the accused drew up a 'memorandum', planning to send it to Swedish Protestant archbishop Eidem, whom he knew through his involvement in Una Sancta (a movement which aims to reunite the Catholic and Protestant churches). This document was to be delivered by Irmgart von Giessen, a former Swedish national who now holds German citizenship.

> Nordland' ('The United Nordic States') is a confederation of democratically governed free states (Norway, Sweden, Finland, Denmark, Iceland). Under the Nordland constitution, the free states remain independent in matters of internal policy, cultural and social affairs and administration, while pursuing a common foreign policy under the leadership of the confederation. According to its constitution, internally and externally, Nordland strives sincerely to achieve a peace based on moral integrity and loyalty and social justice.
>
> Its internal peace policy is based on acknowledgement of the eternal moral law, the recognition and assurance of equal fundamental rights for all citizens, a progressive social policy (job security, wages and the possibility to earn a living for all; the nationalization of all mines, power stations, railways and ownership of major real estate holdings such as fields, forests and lakes, a social fiscal policy which protects the weak) and a fair nationality and racial policy (self-determination for the national assemblies, e.g. with regard to public spending on schools).
>
> In foreign affairs, Nordland's peace policy fully recognizes and respects the rights of foreign peoples. It advocates and indeed voluntarily practises disarmament (retaining only a police force to maintain internal order) in favour of a supranational armed force under the command of a non-partisan organization of 'The United States of Europe' and tasked with the protection of a just peace among the states.
>
> The constitution guarantees every citizen of Nordland the inviolable right to personal dignity and legal certainty, freedom of conscience, of language and culture as well as freedom of religion, freedom of speech and finally, the right

to hold personal property and to make use thereof within the clearly defined legal limits dictated by the common good.

All citizens of Nordland who are demonstrably guilty of complicity in the national misfortune and rape of its people and anyone convicted of base criminal acts forfeits all civil privileges (the right to vote or to hold public office) for a period of twenty years. Until such time as their moral and constitutional trustworthiness has been established, all functionaries of the anti-national and anti-social parties and their military self-defence organizations will be assumed guilty of such complicity. A register of such persons will be published.

Until the establishment of a definitive constitution, legislative power in Nordland will rest with a parliament to be elected by general and free plebiscite. The parliament will comprise leading representatives of all professions and classes as well as outstanding personalities from intellectual, cultural, and religious bodies who will initially be selected by the Nordland Friedensorden (Peace Order), an association of such persons from all states and former parties who have proven to the people and the world in general that they stand by the moral, social and political convictions of the new politics of peace, in particular through the fact that under the former regime, they suffered personal disadvantages because of their views and convictions. This political programme is drafted to deal with the eventuality that the end of the war could be followed by the outbreak of a revolution which would render it impossible to maintain the continuity of justice.

By his own admission, the defendant is the author of this manifesto and in it, Nordland stands for Germany, citizens of Nordland for German citizens, Sweden, Norway, Denmark, Finland and Iceland for German states such as Bavaria, Saxony, Württemberg, Baden etc. and anti-national and anti-social parties for the NSDAP and its organizations. The document is therefore the draft of a system of government for a Germany that is democratic and pacifist, defenceless, at the mercy of the terrorist armies of our enemies, not a unified state, not even a federal state, but merely a confederation of states, or in other words, the realisation of our enemies' most fervent dreams! Metzger says that it was his intention that in the event of the collapse of Germany,

Archbishop Eidem, whom he considers pro-German, should lay out these ideas before our enemies in order to establish such a government and 'save' Germany from enemy rule.

This is an absolutely outrageous idea, and one which could only arise from a deeply defeatist attitude. A shameful and traitorous notion of which only a person with a profound hatred of our National Socialist Germany could conceive. A highly treasonous idea which has as its foundation and goal the replacement of the National Socialist order, the way of life which corresponds to our national identity, by a form of government based on outdated 'ideas' which are foreign to the nature of our Volk. Anyone who sets forth such ideas in a time of war, for whatever reason, weakens our power of resistance and strengthens our enemies, should such a document fall into their hands. Our enemies would undoubtedly use such a document as propaganda against us by creating the impression that there are forces within Germany who entertain thoughts of a German defeat and who would then ingratiate themselves with the enemy in order to establish a powerless and un-German government and thus aid and abet our enemies in subjugating our nation to an oppressive regime.

Metzger claims that he did not believe his 'manifesto' would fall into enemy hands before the collapse of Germany, that he trusted that Archbishop Eidem, whom he considers to be pro-German and a man of discretion, would only present these ideas following the collapse of Germany and to men of influence, for example, high-ranking English clergymen. He also claims that such men would then be able to help. English clergymen? For example, the English clergyman who recently travelled to Moscow? However, the Volksgerichtshof is convinced that a man in Metzger's position must have considered the fact that it would be beyond his power to control such a document once it was disseminated, and certainly once it reached a foreign country. It is absolutely impossible to believe that any thinking man would not have considered this. Nevertheless, he attempted to smuggle the document across the border! His actions therefore aided and abetted our enemies (§ 91 b StGB).

Even if Metzger was indeed convinced that this document would not fall into the hands of those who would use it against us before the collapse of Germany, this would have no influence on the verdict of the Volksgerichtshof. Metzger's actions overall are so monstrous that it is irrelevant whether they fall under the legal definition of high treason (Metzger states that he never envisaged the use of violence) or that of aiding and abetting the enemy (Metzger claims that he only intended the manifesto to be used after the collapse of Germany), whether his actions were the result of defeatism (Metzger insists it was never his intention to demoralize) – all this is of no consequence: every German citizen knows that for any German to step out of our lines and leave our battle front is an outrage, a betrayal of our Volk in its struggle for life, and that such a betrayal must be punished by death; it is a betrayal which points towards high treason, a betrayal which points towards defeatism, a betrayal which points towards aiding and abetting the enemy, a betrayal which the sound instinct of the Volk considers deserving of death (§ 2, StGB). For this reason, it would have been necessary to condemn Metzger to death even if he had not considered the possibility that this document, while we are still at war, might fall into the hands of those who would use it against us.

During the trial today, Metzger attempted to show that his actions were only intended to make provision for the worst-case scenario that he foresaw. In a letter sent to his defence counsel by his archbishop and which was read aloud at the trial, the archbishop stated that Metzger is not a criminal, but an idealist. But that is a completely different world, a world that we do not comprehend. Here in the Greater German Reich, a man can only be convicted on the principles that are valid here, by National Socialist principles which are worlds apart from those on which Metzger's actions were based – so far apart that any discussion of them on a National Socialist basis is impossible – and which no German court can, may and will consider. Every man must accept judgement according to the German, National Socialist norm, and that norm clearly dictates that any man who acts in this way is a traitor to his own people.

Metzger, who through his actions has forever lost his honour, must therefore be condemned to death.

Having been found guilty, Metzger must also bear the costs.

Signed: Dr Freisler                                                      Rehse

When, following the rejection of an appeal for clemency, Father Max Josef Metzger was beheaded on 16 April 1944, he left behind him an unpaid bill: for 293 days in prison and his execution. On 8 August 1944, Metzger's family paid the 'outstanding costs'.

On 9 June 1944, unbroken and full of hope for a better future, Frankfurt citizen Johanna Kirchner, a Socialist, went to her execution in the Berlin-Plötzensee prison. It had taken the Volksgerichtshof, chaired by Freisler, just half an hour to sentence her to death.

What was Johanna Kirchner's crime? She had helped opponents and innocent victims of the Nazi terror regime. Her character and her standpoint were shaped by her origins as a member of a long-established Social-Democratic family and a member of the socialist workers' movement since her fourteenth year. She was married to Karl Kirchner, a municipal politician and chairman of the SPD (German Socialist Party) and worked at his side as a reporter at party and trade union congresses.

When the National Socialists came to power in 1933, she did not cut down on her welfare work in any way; indeed, there were now even more people who needed her help. She worked untiringly, always in search of a way to help the persecuted and anti-fascists to flee, to snatch them from the clutches of the Gestapo.

Until the outbreak of the Second World War, Johanna Kirchner lived in Forbach in France, where she worked closely together with the German resistance movement and found friends in the International Brigade. She was interned when war broke out, but freed from the concentration camp at Gurs with the help of the French Resistance. Later, however, she was arrested by the Vichy Regime and handed over to the Gestapo under an extradition order.

She had already appeared before the People's Court once, in May 1943. Her sentence: ten years' hard labour. The reason for this 'mild' verdict was that one of the judges assisting at her trial, like Kirchner from Frankfurt, spoke up in her defence, excusing her 'misconduct' with her desire to help others. Johanna Kirchner served almost one year of her sentence in the prison at Cottbus.

But her sentence was overturned and the case against the resistance fighter reopened. And on 21 April 1944, her fate was sealed. This time, the Volksgerichtshof condemned Johanna Kirchner to death.

---

### Sentence 6

#### 'Expunged from our midst in disgrace . . .'

In the name of the German people

In the action against
the former SPD employee Johanna Schmidt, formerly Kirchner (divorced), née Stunz, from Frankfurt/Main, without fixed abode,

---

last resident in Aix les Bains, Département Savoi, France, born on 24 April 1889 in Frankfurt/Main, currently serving a prison sentence for preparation for high treason, the Volksgerichtshof, special senate, pursuant to the trial held on 21 April 1944, in which the officers were:

Judges:
President of the Volksgerichtshof Dr Freisler, chairman, Volksgerichtsrat . . .

. . .

. . . [files illegible, author's note]

Representative of the senior Reich prosecutor:
Reichsanwalt Dr Franzke,

finds as follows:
In emigration, the long-standing Social Democrat Frau Johanna Schmidt, together with the traitors to the Volk Matz Braun and Emil Kirschmann, engaged in acts of high treason among émigrés and against our Reich, disseminated the most evil and traitorous Marxist propaganda on a wide scale, gathering cultural, economic, political and military intelligence and communicating the same to our enemies, even using her own daughter as a source of information.

Expunged from our midst many years ago in disgrace, with perpetual loss of honour, she is sentenced to death.

Grounds:
Frau Johanna Schmidt, a member of the SPD since 1907 and employed as a secretary in the Frankfurt office of the SPD in the years preceding our National Socialist renewal, moved to the Saar region in 1933. She claims that this was not from a desire to emigrate, but because she feared that she would be unable to find work for some time if she remained in Frankfurt. In Saarbrücken, she was employed as a restaurant buffet supervisor by Frau Juchacz, who shared her political leanings. When the Saar region declared its allegiance to Volk and blood and returned to the Reich, she remained unaffected by the general elation and moved to Forbach, which was at that time in France, where she took up a position on the Saarflüchtlingskomitee (Saar refugees' committee), which was run by the notorious traitors to the Volk Matz Braun and Emil Hirschmann. These two, however,

soon fled further, the former to Paris, the latter to Mulhouse in Alsace. Frau Schmidt, the secretary, now ran the refugees' committee, very loosely monitored by Braun, who rarely made the journey from Paris to Forbach, and under somewhat closer supervision by Kirschmann, who travelled over from Mulhouse two or three times a week.

The true spirit behind this committee can be seen in the fact that it was financed by the international trades union office and the Rote Hilfe (Red Aid, an aid organization affiliated with the Communist Party of Germany)! And the fact that a full 20–25 per cent of the committee's funds went on paying the salaries of Kirschmann and Frau Schmidt reveals just how seriously the committee took its 'humanitarian' task!

As part of its aid services, the committee prepared 'profiles' and 'recommendations' for émigrés, arranged residence permits and support payments. However, this Rote Hilfe for emigrants was not the only activity the committee engaged in.

The committee, and with it Frau Schmidt as its secretary, began to disseminate highly treasonous propaganda against our National Socialist German Reich. It published a magazine – 'Saarnachrichten' – about 500 copies per edition, and the templates were created by Frau Schmidt! The refugee committee also distributed 100 to 200 copies each of the 'Sozialistische Aktion' by the Social Democratic exile pack in Prague, the Sopade, and other propaganda magazines, enclosing them as supplements with its own magazine.

Frau Schmidt herself has stated that the main content of this magazine was reports of atrocities within Germany. And Frau Schmidt was involved in preparing all this heinous poison for distribution! Moreover, her treasonous activities did not remain outside the Reich. No, she was even working on a plan to reinstate the SPD (German Social Democratic Party) in her home town, Frankfurt am Main, from Switzerland! A woman who, by emigrating, had forfeited the right to any say or involvement in German affairs!

In addition to such systematic agitation, there is also evidence of further despicable treasonous acts. For example, a certain von Puttkamer, traitor to the German Volk, had been arrested in Spain and was to be extradited to Germany via Italy. In Italy, he managed to escape and fled to Switzerland. And on the Swiss border, who was there to welcome him but Frau Schmidt, who had travelled there expressly in order to meet him and arrange for him to be accommodated in a Swiss sanatorium!

All this pales, however, in comparison with the acts of treason committed by this woman against the German nation. Kirschmann needed cultural, economic, political and military intelligence for his propaganda publications. To this end, he had instructed Frau Schmidt and others in the refugee aid organization in Forbach to gather such intelligence. Frau Schmidt was to collate such material and pass it on to him, which she did. She engaged in a broad range of activities, speaking to informants who were her regular sources, for example a certain Harig, von Hünekens, Niebergall, Kim and others. She then forwarded the information she had gleaned to Kirschmann.

This included the name of a well-known former Communist who was now a Gestapo spy, information which, in the interest of our national security, should have remained secret. Her communication with Kirschmann also contained details of forced labour camps in the Hunsrück and 'what was happening on the Eberkopf'. From time to time, she also received military intelligence – on special orders from Kirschmann, who, for example, instructed her to report whether fresh troops had arrived in Saarlautern or which forces were located in Saarbrücken. And she did her best to obtain such information, information which in our opinion should have remained confidential, even more so in the initial years between the National Socialists' rise to power and the beginning of the War, when we had not yet built up our defences and were therefore more vulnerable.

The depths to which Frau Schmidt was prepared to sink can be seen in the fact that she enticed her two daughters to come to Hohwals in Alsace, at the time French territory, under the pretext of spending a holiday together, and then proceeded to inquire about political, social, cultural, economic and military matters, or, as Kirschmann referred to it in his letters to her and she herself stated in her replies to him, to pump them for information. Neither did she have any objection to Kirschmann exploiting this intelligence; she merely requested him, as a matter of caution, not to make it public immediately.

Kirschmann doctored the information he received through this channel, giving it his typical political and journalistic slant, and published it in his information journal. Such information therefore became accessible to the French authorities, a fact Frau Schmidt was well aware of. In other words, with these acts, she became guilty of treason against the German nation. And thus ended her descent into a state of complete dishonour; an inexorable descent which began with her emigration, as individuals who cut themselves off from their racial national community and country cannot hope to find a foothold on the slippery downhill path to treason.

In the face of these acts of high treason and treason against the nation (§§ 83, 89 StGB), it can be of no significance that Frau Schmidt claims to have voluntarily ceased passing on intelligence and to have stopped working for the traitor Kirschmann a good year before the War began, or that she then took up household employment. And as regards the judgement of this court, it is of no consequence whatsoever that she was interred in a concentration camp by the French when war broke out. She states that in 1940, she attempted to return to Germany, regretting her acts and hoping to be accepted back into the fold of the German Volk during the War. If this was indeed her intention, she made no particular effort to put her plan into action. She spent one whole year living in complete liberty in Aix les Bains, before she was arrested and brought to the demarcation line. If she had genuinely repented of her crimes and felt such a longing for Germany, she could easily have crossed the border into occupied France and returned to Germany during that year. One more thing must be said here: even if she had sincerely repented, the Volksgerichtshof would not have taken this into account. There can be no allowance made for repentance in the case of genuine treason against the Volk. In the case of genuine treason, any repentance must come too late, because treason is a crime where the deed itself judges the perpetrator.

The Reich cast Frau Schmidt from its midst in disgrace in early 1937. With her expatriation, she already forfeited all honour. Therefore, all that remains for the Volksgerichtshof is to sentence her to death for the crimes described above, to which she has confessed under the weight of the evidence produced against her by the police and before the court on this day. The self-respect of the Reich, the desire of the people for cleansing and the protection of Reich and Volk can admit of no other punishment.

Having been found guilty, Frau Schmidt must also bear the costs.

Signed: Dr Freisler

## Sentence 7

### 'Guilty of defeatism, he has forfeited his honour for all time . . .'

In the name of the German people

In the action against
curator and Professor Dr Walter Arndt from Berlin, born on 8 January 1891 in Landeshut (Silesia), at present imprisoned on remand by the court for subversion of the war effort, the Volksgerichtshof, First Senate, pursuant to the bill of indictment signed by the senior Reich prosecutor on 4 April 1944 and received on 27 April 1944, and in the trial held on 11 May 1944, in which the officers were:

Judges:
President of the Volksgerichtshof Dr Freisler, chairman,
Kammergerichtsrat Rehse,
SS-Obersturmbahnführer Wittmer,
SA-Obergruppenführer Hell,
Ortgruppenleiter Kelch,

Representative of the senior Reich prosecutor:
Public Prosecutor Kurth,

finds as follows:
Walter Arndt is a dangerous defeatist. At the turn of the fourth and fifth year of the War, he stated to compatriots:
This is the end of the German Reich. We are to blame for the War, and all that remains is to in how far the guilty are brought to account and punished.
As a result of this defeatism, he has forfeited his honour for all time and is herewith sentenced to death.

Grounds:
Walter Arndt is a curator and Professor of the Zoological Museum in Berlin, which is affiliated with the university of that city.
In his defence, he emphasizes that he has performed several deeds of outstanding bravery in his life, for example as a medical orderly during the First World War, where he remained with his charges in

order to tend to them and as a result, was taken prisoner, that he risked his life to extinguish a fire in the Museum after an air raid, thereby saving the Museum, and that he has carried out important scientific work in his field of expertise.

However, all this can carry no significant weight in the face of such defeatism as he has been guilty of.

Volksgenosse Dr Stichel, a zoologist acquainted with Arndt, has given evidence that as they walked along for a short distance together on 28 July 1943, Arndt said to him that this was the end of the Third Reich, that all that remained was to punish the guilty and to establish how far down the line of command those responsible would be brought to account. He also stated that he had known ever since the Reichstag Fire swindle (!) that it would come to this, because it would not be possible to uphold such an edifice of lies in the long term. Stichel also reported that when he (Stichel) expressed his amazement, Arndt replied: 'Yes, I dare say no-one has ever said anything like that to you before'.

Arndt does not deny this; he merely says that he has no recollection of the conversation. To be able to forget having made such statements, however, must mean that one was in the habit of expressing such opinions on a daily basis and could therefore not remember an isolated statement. Furthermore, you would expect a person wrongly accused of making such statements to deny it and not simply to claim loss of memory. Moreover, Dr Stichel delivered his testimony with such calmness and certainty that there can be no doubt that he is telling the truth.

The court also heard further evidence of defeatism on the part of the accused.

Frau Hanneliese Mahlhausen, a friend of the defendant since his youth, stated that on 4 September in the fifth year of the War, she and her mother met Arndt on a railway platform in Landeshut, and that after greeting them, he said that the air raid on Berlin the previous night had been the heaviest yet (he had just come from Berlin to deposit some suitcases in Landeshut). The accused also stated that it was a pity we all had to suffer for the mistakes others had made. Frau Mehlhausen protested that we were not to blame for the War. Arndt replied that of course we were to blame and that those responsible would now be brought to justice.

According to the witness, talk now turned to the course of the War, and Arndt stated that Germany was retreating on all fronts. Frau Mehlhausen's mother protested that on the contrary, we had advanced deep into enemy territory, to which the accused replied that such initial success was no more than a flash in the pan. The witness reported that Arndt also said Italy had got rid of Mussolini in just three days, and the same thing would happen here; in four weeks' time, she would see, the Party would be gone. Frau Mehlhausen argued that Fascism and National Socialism were quite different things. But Arndt merely asked her if she remembered their meeting in November 1938, saying that after what happened back then, it had been immediately clear to him that there would be another world war. Again, Arndt does not deny having made such obviously defeatist statements; once more, he claims that he cannot remember the details. Greatly alarmed by these comments, Frau Mehlhausen wrestled with her conscience and finally did her duty as a German: she reported the conversation to her Kreisleiter (NSDAP district leader), although it pained her to bring such accusations against her childhood friend.

At the trial, it was obvious to all how heavily this weighed on her heart, and it is certain that Frau Mehlhausen spoke nothing but the truth.

In sum, Arndt expressed defeatist opinions on two different occasions to two German citizens, in the fourth and at the beginning of the fifth year of the War. He offers the excuse that he was extremely agitated at the time. He states that there had been two terrorist attacks on German natural history museums shortly before his conversation with Dr Stichel and that the fall of Mussolini had immediately preceded it. However, if he had been particularly concerned by the destruction of the museums, this should, if anything, only have served to strengthen his resolve. And the hour of the betrayal of Mussolini was a moment of truth in which the firm stance of every German Volksgenosse, but in particular of our leaders, who bear particularly heavy responsibility, was put to the test. Failure in the moment of truth cannot be excused by saying that the test was too challenging. And the state of agitation in which the accused claims to have been during his conversation with Frau Mehlhausen and her mother can be ascribed to the fact that many houses near his own had been totally destroyed in the air raids of the previous night, that the stucco had fallen from the ceiling and the window panes had shattered in his apartment. But that is no excuse for making such statements. What about all those brave Germans who have lost not only their possessions, but also a loved one, during such a night?

And how could a man in a leading position, with a responsibility to set a good example to his fellow citizens, be excused on such grounds? No, the Volksgerichtshof had a duty to deal with Arndt as it deals with all defeatists (§ 5 KSS-VO) who stab our fighting nation in the back with their disheartening defeatist utterances and therefore forfeit honour for all time. It had no choice but to sentence him to death in order to preserve Germany's confidence in victory and so that its fighting spirit remains undaunted.

Having been found guilty, Arndt must also bear the costs.

Dr Freisler                                                                                           Rehse

## Sentence 8

### 'Attempted to undermine our will to fight for victory . . '

In the name of the German people

In the action against
Father Josef Müller from Grossdüngen in the district of Marienburg/ Hanover, born on 19 August 1893 in Saalmünster, in the district of Schlüchtern, at present imprisoned on remand by the court for subversion of the war effort, the Volksgerichtshof, First Senate, pursuant to the bill of indictment issued by the senior Reich prosecutor on 11 July 1944, and in the trial held on 28 July 1944, in which the officers were:

Judges:
President of the Volksgerichtshof Dr Freisler, chairman,
Kammergerichtsrat Rehse,
Section leader Ahmels,
City councillor Kaiser,
Section leader Bartens,

Representative of the senior Reich prosecutor:
Amtsgerichtsrat Krebs,

finds as follows:

Josef Müller, a Catholic priest, told two fellow citizens the following story: On his deathbed, a wounded soldier asked to see the people for whom he was laying down his life. A picture of our Führer was placed on his right side, that of Reichsmarschall Göring on his left. The soldier then said: now I can die like Christ.

Through these and other subversive statements, he has attempted to undermine our will to fight for victory.

He has therefore forfeited honour for all time, and is sentenced to death.

Grounds:

Witness Hermann Niehoff, a master electrician from Grossdüngen near Hildesheim, reported the following:

At the beginning of August 1943, he was called to the house of Josef Müller, the new Catholic priest in Grossdüngen.

As he worked, he fell into conversation with the priest on the subject of the war. Müller described the situation as serious, saying that there was a risk that Germany would lose the war and that as a former soldier, he felt it would be a shame if the current war generation returned home as he and his comrades had. Niehoff asked what the consequences of a German defeat might be, and Müller replied: no matter what the outcome of the war is – the customs barriers would be raised! Niehoff was dissatisfied with this and pointed out that the Bolsheviks would march in if we lost. Müller answered that the Bolsheviks were not a threat, they were bleeding dry. This prompted Niehoff to say: Then God help the German men, who will then be deported to Russia to help with reconstruction. Müller retorted: Yes, and we have given them a shining example of how that works!!!

In the further course of the conversation, the two men also spoke of recent events in Italy. Müller described fascism as an economic phenomenon and stated that if Germany lost the war, National Socialism would suffer the same fate. It owed its rise to the fact that in the face of high unemployment and inflation, many people had set great hopes on it.

A short time later, the witness stated, Josef Müller visited Niehoff's sick father. Niehoff joined them, wanting to hear more about Müller's views. However, Müller evaded any talk of the war. Niehoff started to tell Müller a joke: a farmer died and met Saint Peter, who gave him the choice between going to heaven or hell. The farmer asked to see hell first, and when they got there, there was a party going on, with wine, women and song. Müller interrupted him, saying that he had already heard that joke, but he could tell Niehoff a new one: on his deathbed, a wounded soldier asked to see the people for whom he was laying down his life. Photographs of the Führer and Reichsmarschall Göring were placed to his right and left. The soldier exclaimed: Now I can die like Christ. At that point, Niehoff was called to the telephone. When he returned, Müller had already left.

Müller's own description of the second occasion matches Niehoff's, except that he claims he did not say he wanted to tell a joke, but a parable.

Müller largely denies the first account. He admits saying that the situation was serious and that in his opinion, it would be bitter if the young soldiers returned under the same circumstances as the troops at the end of the First World War. He may have spoken of the possibility of a throwing open of the borders at the end of the war, and he may also have said that the Bolsheviks did not constitute a threat, as its supporters were rapidly deserting the cause. However, he denies saying that we had set an example for the Russians and that they would deport our men to help with reconstruction in Russia; on the contrary, he claims to have pointed out that we have the Ostarbeiter (workers gathered from Central and Eastern Europe to do forced labour in Germany) here, meaning that there was no question of our men being set to work for the Bolsheviks.

Müller also alleges that, although he may have spoken of fascism in terms similar to those described, what he said about National Socialism was quite different: namely that ideologically, he could not give an opinion on National Socialism. It seemed to him that the current government had in part attained its current position of power due to inflation, high unemployment and the incompetence of other parties!!!

Müller's description of this incident reveals what manner of man he is. His belittling view of National Socialism shows that in his eyes, it, too, is little more than an economic phenomenon, and speaks volumes, as do his comments that the Bolsheviks would not take over if Germany were defeated and that the borders would be thrown open as a result of the war.

Notwithstanding Müller's account, we are certain that the events in question took place just as Niehoff described them. No-one who saw or heard this witness could entertain any doubt that his account is reliable.

Far from any desire to see Müller punished and apparently guided by a particular conscientiousness, he speaks circumspectly, even when his testimony incriminates Müller. However, he delivered the statement above with absolute conviction. He also did not in any way urge the authorities to initiate proceedings against Müller. On the contrary, due to the inner conflict he found himself in as a result of Müller's statements, he agreed to reveal the details to his political supervisor only after the latter promised not to report the matter straight away.

We therefore believe Niehoff's testimony to be true.

This first incident is far outweighed by the second, the key details of which match in Müller's and Niehoff's accounts.

Niehoff understood Müller's 'joke' or 'parable' as follows: the soldier was dying between two criminals. This is the logical interpretation.

According to Müller, however, he described the scene with the sole intention of underscoring the idea of sacrifice; no other meaning was intended. He also states that he was not, in fact, speaking to the witness, Volksgenosse Niehoff, but to Niehoff's sick father.

But this is not true:

1. He would then surely have explained the 'parable' to Niehoff's father, which, by his own account, he did not do.
2. In the story Müller told, the soldier asked to see the people for whose sake he was dying. The pictures, however, were placed not in front of the dying man, but to his right and left, where he could not have seen them. The contradiction between the positioning of the pictures and the wish of the dying man can only be explained by a desire to invoke an association with the scene of the crucifixion at Golgotha.
3. The dying soldier then exclaims: Now I can die like Christ! This moment and the meticulous way in which it is set up in the 'joke' or 'parable' would be absolutely superfluous if the intention had been to establish a link between the idea of sacrifice and the death of Christ. The logical interpretation is therefore the only possible one, and Müller's professed intention is patently invalid.
4. Müller's behaviour during the first incident also indicates that he is a man capable of uttering statements against the Volk and the Reich. This assumption is not necessarily undermined by the proven fact that he was a good soldier and did his duty in the World War, nor by his sadness at the thought of the fighting troops

suffering defeat. Neither is it necessarily refuted by the argument that as a priest, he would not be likely to use what is most sacred to him for political purposes, as the defending counsel suggested. For all we know, the undermining of the war effort may have seemed to him as binding as one of the commandments. Ideologically (see the report of the first incident above), he evidently does not concur with the ideas of National Socialism.

It follows that if the logical interpretation was indeed the one intended by Müller with his 'joke' or 'parable', he carried out one of vilest and most dangerous attacks directed against our confidence in our Führer, and with the authority of a priest, an attack aimed at undermining our will to carry on our noble and legitimate fight to defend the way of life of our Volk. And this was not a unique occurrence, because his words in the first incident described above point in the same direction (§ 5 KSSVO). And he did this in the hour of our gravest battle!

Such conduct is more than just an irresponsible abuse of the position of authority held by a priest; it is a betrayal of the people, the Führer and the Reich. Anyone guilty of such treason forfeits honour for all time.

In order to deter others with similar treasonous intentions, such an attack on our morale in a time of war can be punished with nothing other than death.

Having been found guilty, Müller must also bear the costs.

Signed: Dr Freisler                                                    Rehse

## Sentence 9

### 'A handmaid of our enemies . . . who has forfeited honour for all time'

In the name of the German people

In the action against
Emma Hölterhoff, née Maass, a crane driver's wife, from Erkheim near Memmingen, born on 28 May 1904 in Homberg (Niederrhein), at present imprisoned on remand by the court for subversion of the war effort, the Volksgerichtshof, special senate, pursuant to the trial on 8 November 1944, in which the officers were:

Judges:
President of the Volksgerichtshof Dr Freisler, chairman,
Volksgerichtsrat Dr Greulich,
Major General of the state police, retired, Meissner,
SA-Gruppenführer Aumüller,
Reichshauptamtsleiter Giese,

Representative of the senior Reich prosecutor:
Senior public prosecutor Dr Weisbrod,

finds as follows:
In the fourth year of the war, Frau Emma Hölterhoff told soldiers that they should throw away their rifles and play dead.

In doing so, she dared to undermine the war effort, thus becoming a handmaid of our foes, devoid of honour for all time, and is sentenced to death.

Grounds:
Frau Emma Hölterhoff is approximately 40 years of age, a mother of four whose husband, as she says herself, has been in military service for four years.

Although she managed to rescue all her belongings, namely furnishings, clothing, linen and other possessions after an air raid on Homberg am Niederrhein, she was evacuated to the Memmingen area, as the house in which she lived had suffered extensive damage and was no longer habitable. In the January of the fourth year of the war, she was sitting in the combined kitchen-living room of the Goll family, with whom she had been quartered, playing Ludo with Frau Goll. Also present were Frau Goll's son, who had just been released from the Reich Volunteer Labour Service, two other young men and grenadier Arnold Häring, who was on his first leave from the front. The conversation turned to the war, whereupon, as testified by both Arnold Häring and Hans Goll, Frau Emma Hölterhoff uttered words to the effect of: You fools. If they sent me to the front, I'd throw my rifle away and pretend to be dead.

During the preliminary proceedings, both witnesses also reported that she went on to grievously insult our Führer and added the following to her previous comment: 'My husband would do exactly the same if he was sent to the front'. Despite the fact that Frau Hölterhoff denies having made the last statement or insulting the Führer, the two young men would hardly both have delivered the same report if it was not true. It was, however, not deemed necessary to have them travel here by rail in order to obtain their testimony during this main hearing, as Frau Hölterhoff herself confirmed the core of her statements. And this core already contains an incitement to the soldier and to the other young man who is soon to be a soldier to lay down their arms. At the end of the main hearing, Frau Hölterhoff still insists that she made no reference to her husband, but no longer denies phrasing her comments to the soldier in such a way that they must be construed as an incitement.

The defending counsel felt obliged to emphasize that the accused is a woman of little education. When considering the culpability of persons who have uttered such remarks, however, no allowance can be made for their level of education or intelligence. It is a simple question of a healthy attitude and of loyalty, which have nothing to do with intellect or learning.

Even if the defendant made such comments on one occasion alone, she must be considered as without self-respect and devoid of honour for all time, having stooped so far as to become the handmaiden of our enemies, who, by disseminating such talk, strive to undermine our morale at home and at the fighting front and would bring about a repetition of the year 1917, of the year 1918! But it is our duty to cast out from our midst those who become agents of our enemies (§ 91 b StGB) through such subversion (§ 5 KSSVO).

Their behaviour poses a tremendous danger to our fighting people and thus jeopardises our victory, our very life and our liberty. In such cases, where culpability has been established without doubt, our only consideration in pronouncing sentence must be the need to protect Germany, a consideration which, in order to prevent a repetition of such developments as in the First World War, calls for the death penalty.

Having been found guilty, Frau Emma Hölterhoff must also bear the costs.

Signed: Dr Freisler                                        Dr Greulich

And as the need to protect Germany brooked no delay, Reich Minister of Justice Thierack ordered the death sentence to be carried out just sixteen days after pronouncement of the verdict. He gave express instructions that there should be no announcement of the execution in the press or by means of placards in this case. An ordinary woman of the people, mother of four children – there should be no publicity here. Thierack supported Freisler's verdict: hard times required harsh penalties. But this case was not likely to serve as an effective deterrent to potential subversives. On the contrary, it might even arouse feelings of sympathy and pity for this woman.

The execution was therefore to take place in secret, as the senior Reich prosecutor at the Volksgerichtshof informed Frau Hölterhoff's lawyer, Dr Ilse Schmelzeisen-Servaes, the same female lawyer who, just nine days later, would again appear as a willing accomplice of the NS tribunal in the trial of the young Margot von Schade which is described at the beginning of this book. On 5 December, Dr Schmelzeisen-Servaes briefly confirmed receipt of notification from the senior Reich prosecutor regarding the 'execution of the sentence, Frau Hölterhoff'. There was no particular urgency here. All in a day's work for a German lawyer.

Finally, on 8 December 1944, the senior Reich prosecutor confirmed that the death sentence had been duly carried out:

> At 11.34, the condemned was led in by two prison warders and handed over to executioner Röttger from Berlin and his three assistants, her hands bound behind her back.
>
> Also present were:
> Prison official Reg.-Med.-Rat Dr Schmidt.
>
> Following verification that the prisoner was indeed the condemned person, the supervisor ordered the executioner to proceed with the execution. The condemned, who was calm and composed, offered no resistance as she was placed on the guillotine. The executioner performed his task and pronounced the sentence enforced. From delivery of the prisoner to the pronouncement of death, the execution took 8 seconds.

---

## Sentence 10

### 'In collusion with the traitors of 20 July . . .'

In the name of the German people

In the action against
Frau Ehrengard Frank-Schultz, née Besser, from Berlin-Wilmersdorf, born on 23 March 1885 in Magdeburg, at present imprisoned on remand by the court for subversion of the war effort, the Volksgerichtshof, First Senate, pursuant to the bill of indictment from the senior Reich

---

prosecutor received on 2 November 1944, and in the trial held on 6 November 1944, in which the officers were:

Judges:
President of the Volksgerichtshof Dr Freisler, chairman,
Landesgerichtsdirektor Stier,
SS-Brigadeführer Generalmajor of the Waffen-SS Tscharmann,
SA-Brigadeführer Hauer,
City councillor Kaiser,

Representative of the senior Reich prosecutor:
First public prosecutor Jaager,

finds as follows:
Frau Frank-Schultz had the audacity to state that a few years of Anglo-Saxon rule would be better than 'the current violent regime'.

She is therefore guilty of collusion with the traitors of 20 July, thus forfeiting honour for all time, and is sentenced to death.

Grounds:
Before this court and previously before the police, nursing auxiliary Frau Erika Roeder gave the following testimony: a certain Oberleutnant Wendelstein was a patient in the military hospital in which she worked. Through him, she became acquainted with his landlady, Frau Ehrengard Frank-Schultz, with whom she also met after Oberleutnant Wendelstein was discharged from the hospital.

Frau Roeder states that on 21 July, she telephoned Frau Frank-Schultz to inquire after the well-being of Oberleutnant Wendelstein. Frau Frank-Schultz invited her to her home, where she told her that Oberstleutnant Wendelstein, who had been employed in the High Command of the Wehrmacht, had been arrested with the conspirators in the plot of 20 July.

It was agreed that Frau Roeder would visit Frau Frank-Schultz at regular intervals of about a week to learn any news of Oberleutnant Wendelstein's fate.

Frau Roeder states that during her next visit, she commented that it would have been terrible if the assassination attempt had succeeded.

Frau Frank replied:
'What do you mean, terrible! It's a pity they failed! If only Stauffenberg had positioned the briefcase correctly, the full force of the explosion

would have been unleashed! I don't understand how they could have been so careless. They shouldn't have got involved if they couldn't do the job properly!'

One week later, Frau Frank-Schultz once again expressed regret that the plot had not succeeded, saying that the officers would now be degraded and sent to a labour camp; 'But that won't matter to them; they can be proud of themselves'. On a further occasion, Nurse Erika Roeder asked her what the conspirators had hoped to achieve. Frau Frank-Schultz answered:

'We would have had a few days' peace without any further air raids. A few years under Anglo-Saxon rule would be better than the current violent regime.'

Frau Frank-Schultz also stated that a new assassination attempt was planned in September and was certain to succeed. Volksgenossin Roder gave this testimony before us with such reticence and clear sense of duty that we could entertain no doubt as to the veracity of her account, even if Frau Frank-Schultz herself had not largely confirmed it.

The latter claimed that her reference to the conspirators being 'proud' had been misinterpreted; she merely meant that Wendelstein could be proud of the fact that he was sent to a labour camp although he was innocent. This claim is however, illogical, and contradicts the standpoint Frau Frank-Schultz expressed in the other statements which she has admitted making. We therefore have no doubt whatsoever that the witness account is also truthful in this respect.

In her defence, Frau Frank-Schultz states that she has a liver disease. However, there is no evidence that liver disease triggers such base sentiments and comments.

Frau Frank-Schultz also says that she had grown extremely fond of Oberleutnant Wendelstein, whom she met when he was eighteen years old, had taken on the role of a mother to him and was therefore extremely disquieted by his arrest. But even if this woman, whose own son is interned in South Africa, had really developed such feelings for Oberleutnant Wendelstein, that could hardly excuse such treasonous behaviour. Hundreds of thousands of German mothers live in uncertainty for months over the fate of their only, or perhaps only surviving, biological sons. Yet despite their anguish, none of them has stooped to such base treachery.

And finally, Frau Frank-Schultz states in her defence that as the great-granddaughter of theologian and biblical scholar Friedrich Schleiermacher, she is very religious. Such a religious outlook, however, does not lead to such acts of treason, and it certainly does not excuse them. And secondly, Schleiermacher, one of the main protagonists in the fight of our nation for liberation from Napoleon, would turn over in his grave if he knew that his great-granddaughter has such treason in her soul and does not hesitate to invoke his name in her defence.

In reality, Frau Frank-Schultz's treason can be attributed to two causes:

1. Weakness, as a result of which she succumbed to defeatism. But weakness can be no excuse in a time when we all need to be strong, and

2. The totally reactionary views revealed by her statements. According to the credible testimony of Nurse Roeder, the accused also expressed the opinion that it was terrible that a man like the Reichsführer-SS, from such humble origins and not even of the officer class, should be appointed commander-in-chief of the Ersatzheer (reserve army)!

All this shows Frau Frank-Schulz to have been in collusion with the perpetrators of the 20 July conspiracy, thus attacking the psychological strength of our Volk in time of war, even going so far as to look forward to a fresh assassination attempt and to maintain that 'a few years under Anglo-Saxon rule would be better than the current violent regime'.

Anyone acting in this way is the personification of infamy. Anyone acting in this way is a traitor to our nation, the aider and abettor of our enemies and devoid of honour for all time (§ 5 KSSVO, § 91 b StGB). We must cast out such persons from our midst. Anything other than the death sentence would give our soldiers fighting at the front just reason to doubt whether we have indeed succeeded in fully excising the poison of the 20 July from the body of our people so that we can march forward, healthy and strong, to victory.

Having been found guilty, Frau Frank-Schultz must also bear the costs.

Signed: Dr Freisler                                                          Stier

The execution took place on 8 December 1944. On 23 November, the sister of the condemned woman wrote the following plea to the senior Reich prosecutor at the Volksgerichtshof:

> If the death sentence imposed on my sister, Frau Ehrengard Frank-Schultz, is indeed enforced without pardon, I would ask that the urn containing the mortal remains of my sister be sent to me for burial in the cemetery where her husband and her daughter lie.
>
> For my sister's only son, a farmer in German South West Africa for many years and interned since the outbreak of the war, it would be unbearably painful not even to be able to visit his mother's grave on his return to Germany.
>
> For this reason, I humbly ask you to grant my request.

The request was denied. A representative of the senior Reich prosecutor, public prosecutor Jaager, replied with the terse words:

> Surrender of the mortal remains is denied' . . .!
> Charge for the death penalty
> Bill for the costs, criminal proceedings against Schulz

Chapter 8

# The 20 July Plot

The bomb exploded at 12.42 p.m. Hitler had just leaned over the heavy oak table to study a map showing troop deployments for Heeresgruppe Nord (Army Group North) on the Eastern Front. There was a deafening explosion, and the twenty-four officers and generals present, among them Wilhelm Keitel, head of the Wehrmacht High Command, were hurled to the ground. Part of the ceiling caved in. Four people were killed, and almost everyone suffered injuries. But the target of the attack – Adolf Hitler – survived, yet again, with only minor injuries. The right leg of his trousers was in shreds, his right arm hung motionless at his side. A piece of debris had struck him in the back, it was later discovered that the tremendous force of the detonation had perforated his eardrums, and there was a sharp pain in his right leg, but he had survived.

On the afternoon of that same day, he personally greeted Mussolini at Rastenburg station, not far from Führer headquarters, the 'Wolfsschanze' (Wolf's Lair). Colonel Claus Graf Stauffenberg, chief of staff of the Ersatzheer (Reserve Army), had also been summoned to the Wolf's Lair on that hot July day, in order to report personally to Hitler on the measures planned by the Ersatzheer to halt the advance of the Red Army.

But Count Stauffenberg was carrying more than just maps and official documents on that day. In his briefcase, between reports and slips of paper, nestled a bomb. It consisted of a 1kg block of high-grade plastic explosive and a detonator. A shirt had been placed over the contents of the briefcase, concealing the bomb. In the folds of the shirt, Stauffenberg had hidden a small pair of pliers which he needed to prime the charge. They has been specially adapted because of his war wounds – he had lost his right eye, his right hand and two fingers of his left hand. Again and again, Stauffenberg had practised the movements with which he would arm the bomb. The bomb that would kill Hitler.

The assassination attempt, planned for some time, had been repeatedly called off. The conspirators were almost exclusively generals and officers who had supported Hitler for many years and who had only decided to take action when it became apparent that Germany could not win the War, that the German Reich would crumble and fall. Stauffenberg was one of the leaders of the group and had played the major role in the planning and preparation of the mission.

His original idea, to blow himself up together with Hitler in order to be sure of success, had been rejected by his fellow conspirators, who felt that Stauffenberg was essential for the organization of the planned overthrow of the Nazi regime. Following the assassination, under the 'Valkyrie' plan, all centres of National Socialist power, that is, the offices of the NSDAP, the administration, police, the secret state police and the SS would be seized. However, this was not to be. The following is a timeline showing the events of 20 July shows how and why the plot failed:

| | |
|---|---|
| Previous evening: | Around thirty officers belonging to the group of conspirators – including Stauffenberg, Field Marshal Erwin von Witzleben, General Erich Hoepner and the Wehrmacht commander of Berlin, Paul von Hase, meet to discuss the final details. They learn that the bomb is to be set off the next day. After the meeting, Stauffenberg goes to his apartment in the city. |
| Soon after 6 a.m.: | Stauffenberg and his brother Berthold leave the apartment and are driven into the city by Stauffenberg's chauffeur. There, the two men are joined by Lieutenant Colonel Werner Karl von Haeften. Together, they travel to Rangsdorf airfield. |
| 7 a.m.: | A Heinkel He 111 with Stauffenberg and Haeften on board takes off for the flight to Rastenburg. With them, a briefcase containing a bomb with silent chemical-action fuses. From the airfield, Stauffenberg's brother Berthold travels to Berndlerstrasse, where the Reichswehr ministry and the general staff have their headquarters. |
| 10.14 a.m.: | Stauffenberg and Haeften land in Rastenburg. A staff car is waiting and takes them to the Führer command post, the Wolf's Lair. Arriving in the inner compound, Stauffenberg has breakfast in the mess and then meets with General Erich Fellgiebel, head of the |

131

Wehrmacht signals services, who is part of the conspiracy. His job will be to notify the others in Bendlerstrasse in Berlin of the success of the assassination attempt and cut all communications with the Führer command post.

**Around 11.30 a.m.:** Stauffenberg meets with Field Marshal Wilhelm Keitel, chief of the Wehrmacht high command. Keitel informs Stauffenberg that the briefing has been brought forward by half an hour to 12.30 a.m. and that due to the extreme heat, it will be held in a barracks hut instead of in the bunker.

**Just before 12.30 p.m.:** Keitel leaves to take part in the briefing. Stauffenberg inquires where he can change his shirt. Adjutant Ernst John von Freyend shows him to a bedroom. Here, Stauffenberg breaks a capsule containing acid, thus priming the bomb. He has brought a second bomb with him but has no time to arm it. While he is still stowing the first bomb in his briefcase, Freyend knocks and pushes open the door, warning him that it is time for the briefing. Stauffenberg hurries off to the barracks.

**Shortly after 12.30 p.m:** Keitel and Stauffenberg enter the conference room, where the briefing has already commenced. In addition to Hitler, there are twenty-three other persons present in the wooden hut. They have gathered around a heavy oak table with a thick tabletop and solid legs and are studying the maps spread out on it. Stauffenberg is shown to a place on Hitler's right. During the report on the situation on the Eastern Front, he places his briefcase under the table and pushes it as close as possible to Hitler with his foot.

**About 12.37 p.m.:** Five minutes before the bomb is scheduled to detonate, Stauffenberg makes an excuse to leave the room. In the meantime, one of the other persons present, trying to get a better look at the maps, moves the briefcase to a position behind the heavy oak leg of the table.

**12.42 p.m.:** The bomb explodes, but Hitler survives.

On that same evening, the putsch comes to a bloody end. Shortly before 11 p.m., officers loyal to Hitler storm the office in the Bendlerstrasse army headquarters in Berlin to which Stauffenberg and von Haeften fled shortly after the assassination attempt and where they and the other conspirators, Stauffenberg's brother Berthold, Beck, Peter Graf Yorck von Wartenburg, Eugen Gerstenmaier and Albrecht Mertz von Quirnheim have gathered.

The men are disarmed and placed under arrest. The retired General Beck asks to be allowed to shoot himself. He places the pistol against his temple and fires twice, but the shots are not fatal. A sergeant administers the *coup de grâce*.

General Fromm hastily convenes an impromptu court martial with himself as its commander and instructs the conspirators to write a few quick words to their families. He withdraws to his office and returns five minutes later with the words: 'Chief of Dtaff Colonel von Mertz, General Olbricht and . . .', he points at Stauffenberg 'the colonel whose name I no longer care to mention, and Lieutenant von Haeften are sentenced to death.'

Shortly before midnight, the four men are taken into the courtyard of the building in Bendlerstrasse, where the execution takes place. There, in the light of the headlamps of Wehrmacht lorries, Olbricht, Haeften, Stauffenberg and Mertz are placed in turn in front of a heap of sand and shot. The officers' rebellion is over.

Not so Hitler's revenge. Although at first surprisingly composed, even greeting Mussolini at the station as planned and giving him a tour of the ruined block where the attempt on his life had taken place, he later fell into a fit of raging fury, threatening all conspirators and their families with the most terrible retribution.

That same night, his voice rang out in a broadcast on all German radio stations:

Fellow Germans!

If I speak to you today, it is first in order that you may hear my voice and know that I am unhurt and well: second, in order to inform you of a crime unparalleled in German history.

A very small clique of ambitious, unscrupulous and at the same time senseless and criminally stupid officers have formed a plot to eliminate me and with me, the German Wehrmacht high command.

The circle which these usurpers represent is a very small one. It has nothing to do with the German armed forces, and above all, nothing to do with the German people. It is a very small clique composed of criminal elements which will now be exterminated without mercy . . .

This time we will settle accounts as we National Socialists are accustomed.

His retribution began with a broad wave of arrests, followed by brutal interrogation and torture. The German people should be left in no doubt as to how the regime would deal with conspirators, resistance fighters and traitors – in short, with all dishonourable criminals.

The great majority of the German people was still enthralled by the blustering Nazi rhetoric and the successful rise of the 'Greater German Reich'. Reporting by the compliant mass media ensured that although the consequences of the war were visible and indeed being felt by the population, their faith in the Reich, the Party and the Führer remained unbroken. Very few Volksgenossen experienced pangs of conscience, and the few acts of opposition came from a very small minority. No-one recognized or wanted to admit the extent to which the NS leadership had betrayed and abused their ideals, had callously sacrificed their lives for the sake of total war. Millions rallied behind the swastika flag, the majority of Germans still applauded the Führer, continued to believe that the final victory, the 'Endsieg', was within reach. And they breathed a collective sigh of relief that the Führer had been spared.

Just one day after the failed assassination attempt, on 21 July 1944, the chief of the Reich Main Security Office, SS-Gruppenführer Kaltenbrunner, wrote in a secret report by the party office of the NSDAP in Munich on 'initial effects of the attempt on the Führer's life on the mood of the nation'. He addressed the following report to his 'esteemed Party colleague Bormann':

Based on the information received so far from various parts of the Reich, the first radio broadcast via the Grossdeutsche Rundfunk [Germany-wide radio service] was heard by only a small proportion of the population. However, the news spread like wildfire, as even complete strangers told others on the streets or in shops . . .

All accounts agree that throughout the nation, the news of the assassination attempt triggered shock, the deepest consternation, horror, profound disgust and anger. From several cities (e.g. Königsberg and Berlin), there are reports of women breaking into tears in the shops and on the streets, often stunned and unable to comprehend what had happened. There was great joy over the relatively harmless outcome. Everywhere, people breathed a sigh of relief: 'Thank God, the Führer is alive!

The general rejoicing over the fact that the Führer had survived was in part overshadowed by a certain despondency as the Volksgenossen suddenly realized the dangerousness and gravity of the situation. After the initial shock and relief that the Führer had escaped relatively unscathed, a reflective mood descended.

Everywhere, the consequences of a successful assassination attempt are considered unthinkable. There were dark prognostications of the unimaginable harm it would have brought upon our entire nation. The current opinion of many Volksgenossen is that in the present situation, the Führer's death would have meant the loss of the Reich. 'That's all we needed. That would have been the end', is a view repeatedly expressed.

Many Volksgenossen, however, were convinced from the outset that the attack must have come from the Führer's immediate circle, that – similar to the case of Mussolini – it was an attempt by the opposition forces always suspected within the Wehrmacht and a clique of reactionary generals to seize power, possibly the very group of generals recently fired by Hitler and who, in the opinion of the population, were to be held responsible for the 'betrayal of Minsk', the collapse of the central section of the Eastern Front and other military setbacks . . .

That the Führer has been saved from the gravest peril has deeply moved all levels of German society. A large proportion of the population sees it as visible evidence of the hand of providence that the Führer's life was spared. There is a deep-rooted conviction that despite the difficulties of recent months, with the Führer, all will be brought to a successful end. Reports have been received from many places stating that the Führer must be under the protection of a higher power . . .

Accounts indicate that there is great willingness within the population to make every sacrifice for the war effort, 'now more than ever' to do everything in its power to achieve victory. Countless Volksgenossen have expressed a desire to be given an active role in the war and the fight for victory. In particular within the working class (e.g. in Berlin), there is now a demand for total war, an all-out effort, also on the part of those circles which have so far avoided large-scale involvement (for example in the women's voluntary labour service). There is a frequently expressed view that it is now high time for the 'merciless eradication' of the 'enemy within'.

Hitler himself specified how anyone in any way implicated in the plot was to be dealt with:

> This time, I will make short work of it. These criminals will not be tried by court-martial, but by the Volksgerichtshof. They must be allowed no opportunity to make grand speeches. And the sentence is to be carried out at once, within two hours of pronouncement of the verdict. They must be hung immediately and without mercy.

Initially, Hitler had envisaged a public show trial of the conspirators with press and broadcasting coverage. But Himmler, now commander-in-chief of the Ersatzheer, advised against this, saying that the situation had changed, it was no longer that of 1939 or 1940. Hitler finally admitted: 'You are right, Himmler. If I give these men a public trial, I must allow them to speak publicly. One of them might be talented enough as a speaker to represent himself as a bringer of peace to the German people. That could be dangerous.'

However, Hitler did not for a second waver in his intention to take exemplary action against the perpetrators of the attempted putsch. Not out of a desire for revenge alone, but also because he realized that making short work of 'these criminals' by bringing them before the Volksgerichtshof offered a welcome opportunity to boost his prestige at a time when the fate of the nation hung in the balance. And the trials were to be conducted by his most fanatical blood judge. 'Freisler will see to it. He's our Vyshinsky', Hitler is said to have once commented during a briefing. He trusted Freisler.

Andrei Vyshinsky had gained fame as the prosecutor at the Russian show trials. A loyal Stalinist and chief public prosecutor from 1935 to 1939, he was the legal mastermind behind the Moscow Trials during the Great Purge and had sent thousands into exile for decades or to their deaths, including Lenin's former comrades-in-arms Zinoviev. Kamenev and Bukharin. The fact that Hitler compared the President of the Volksgerichtshof with Stalin's prosecutor is revealing. He had already once described Freisler as 'by his very nature a Bolshevik'. For Hitler, at least, Freisler seemed the most appropriate judge to conduct the upcoming trials against the conspirators of 20 July.

The 20 July trials were the pinnacle of Roland Freisler's career. In the main chamber of the Kammergericht in Berlin, he found the stage he had always craved. And the Führer himself had paved the way for Freisler to appear in court over a period of many months. And Freisler would now no longer be deciding the fate of insignificant members of the public who had made defeatist remarks or been caught listening to enemy radio broadcasts, but that of generals and officers, of prominent civilians. Goebbels, who on 25 July, had been appointed 'Reich Plenipotentiary for Total War', a title he had coveted, demanded that 'the tribunal which must now be established must have historic dimensions'. This was Freisler's opportunity to demonstrate convincingly to his Führer that the National Socialist legal system made no distinctions of class. Whether complete unknowns or celebrities, all traitors and conspirators were equal before the law. And they all deserved the same punishment: death.

The proceedings against the first eight defendants accused of involvement in the bomb plot began on 7 August. They marked the beginning of a veritable avalanche of trials. Over the ensuing weeks and months, several hundred conspirators or suspected conspirators were charged with high treason and treason against the nation, brought before the Volksgerichtshof and in most cases sentenced to death.

Under valid law, the conspirators, at least those among them who were officers, should have been tried by the Reichskriegsgericht. But Hitler had serious misgivings about this institution; he mistrusted the Wehrmacht judiciary. It had incurred his displeasure, particularly in the recent war years, by returning verdicts which were to Hitler's mind too independent and which patently served the interests of the Wehrmacht.

So he circumvented the responsibility of the Reichskriegsgericht by establishing an 'Ehrenhof', a military 'court of honour', ordering it to expel from the Wehrmacht all officers who, based on a preliminary examination, were expected to be found guilty. By doing so, Hitler was killing two birds with one stone. While creating the impression that he was acting in accordance with military law, in reality he wanted to bring the conspirators before a court which he felt could be relied upon to pronounce the sentences he required: the Volksgerichtshof. The 'Ehrenhof' fulfilled its purpose excellently. The defendants – Field Marshal von Witzleben, General Hoepner, Major General Stieff and Lieutenant General von Hase – were discharged from the Wehrmacht. Now they sat in the packed main chamber of the Berlin Kammergericht in Elseholzstrasse, where the trials in front of the People's Court were now held, the Volksgerichtshof building in Bellevuestrasse having been destroyed in an air raid. Freisler opened the proceedings in a strident voice:

> The Volksgerichtshof of Greater Germany meets in the form
> of the First Senate, with the President of the Volksgerichtshof
> as the presiding judge, senate president Günther Nebelung

as Deputy President, Infantry General Reinicke, Hans Kaiser, landscape gardener, and Georg Seuberth, merchant, as honorary assessors, and with Emil Winter, baker, and Kurt Wernicke, engineer, as deputy honorary assessors. Volksgerichtshof counsellor Lemmle will take the minutes as reporting judge, and Oberlandesgerichtsrat Dr Köhle will act as reporting deputy judge. The prosecutor is Oberreichsanwalt Lautz himself, who will be assisted by Oberstaatsanwalt Dr Görisch. The defending counsels, appointed by me, are Dr Weissmann, Dr L. Schwarz, Justizrat Dr Neubert, Dr Gustav Schwarz, Dr Kunz, Dr Dr Falk and lawyers Hugo Bergmann and Boden.

The first éclat came just a few minutes later. After Oberreichsanwalt Lautz had introduced the indictment, Erwin von Witzleben stood and approached the bench with his arm extended in the 'Nazi salute', a fact which has not been revealed in the often overly-romanticized accounts of the conspiracy of 20 July.

Freisler bellowed:

> You are Erwin von Witzleben. In your place, I would no longer use the German salute. The German salute is reserved for Volksgenossen who are men of honour. This does not mean that any decision has been reached in advance. However, in your place, I would feel ashamed to still use the German salute.

Witzleben was then asked to state his place and date of birth, as were the defendants Hoepner, Stieff, von Hagen, von Hase, Bernardis, Klausing and von Wartenburg. Oberreichsanwalt Lautz proceeded to read out the indictment:

> Defendants von Witzleben, Hoepner, Stieff, von Hagen, von Hase, Bernardis, Klausing and von Wartenburg, I indict you on the charge that in the summer of 1944, within Germany, as part of a small clique of discouraged officers, you attempted to cravenly kill the Führer in order to overthrow the National Socialist government and seize power over the army and the Reich and end the war by negotiating an ignominious pact with the enemy. As traitors against the state and the nation, you have violated the following laws . . .

There followed a list of the relevant laws and decrees, after which Freisler summarized:

This is the most terrible charge ever raised in the history of the German people. Oberreichsanwalt Lautz states that he has evidence proving that you have committed the most monstrous act of treason which is known in our history. Our task today is to ascertain what you have done and then to reach a judgement in accordance with our German perception of law. I will discuss the accusations against each one of you with you individually, and will take as my starting point a brief outline of your career. Whether a more detailed description of your history may be of interest to the court will become clear once we have determined what you have done, because there are acts of treason so base as to invalidate any past achievements. If it is ascertained that you have committed such acts, it may therefore be that the details of your career are no longer of interest to us.

Defendant Helmuth Stieff, step forward! First, I shall tell you something that applies equally to all other defendants. The indictment, a copy of which you have all received, is one of the most important foundations of our present search for the truth. But it also serves another purpose, namely that of allowing us all to prepare for the main trial today. It can therefore be of no disadvantage to you when I now ask you to discuss the matter face to face in as far as you are able. However, before I open the proceedings, I will ask Oberreichsanwalt Lautz if he wishes to lodge any appeal with regard to the publicity of the trial.

Lautz promptly requested that the public should be excluded. After brief deliberation, Freisler ruled that all those present, by virtue of their office, had an 'official interest' in the trial and excluded only the 'general' public on the grounds that it might become necessary to discuss state secrets. Those present – all functionaries of the NS regime or officers of the Wehrmacht – were allowed to stay. Freisler instructed them as follows: 'This is a non-public session of the Volksgerichtshof. Anyone passing on details of a non-public session renders themselves guilty of a serious crime under prevailing law.'

Freisler then began his examination of the accused. Now the time had come to 'make short work of it'. This was Freisler's hour. Although the tone and tactics of the proceedings over which Freisler presided did not vary, and although they almost invariably ended with the predetermined result, a death sentence, these first '20 July' trials were akin to a new challenge for Freisler. After all, was this not a particularly illustrious group of conspirators? Surely the dramatic developments in the war – which

Freisler was aware of – demanded an even more resolute demonstration of militant resolve? And did the Führer not place great faith in Freisler's capabilities as a judge?

Freisler did not disappoint Hitler. The transcript of the proceedings, taken down on the orders of the Volksgerichtshof by shorthand experts from the Reichstag, shows that, although the death sentence was a foregone conclusion, Freisler never passed up an opportunity to humiliate, berate and scorn the accused. A tribunal without mercy, with himself as its grand inquisitor, master over life and death. And he almost always chose death, just as Hitler expected of him.

In his brief closing statements, Oberreichsanwalt Lautz, predictably, demanded the death sentence for all defendants. He did so in an almost indifferent tone. The defending counsels were conspicuously passive. In his closing words, Witzleben's lawyer stated: 'The defendant's action stands, and the guilty man falls with it.'

Klausing, Bernardis and Stieff spoke briefly, requesting execution by firing squad. On the next day, the remaining conspirators – with the exception of Yorck von Wartenburg – followed suit. But Freisler denied their request even before pronouncing sentence. The accused were to hang.

The verdict was announced in the afternoon. The courtroom was full to bursting, the atmosphere one of calm expectancy. Then Freisler's piercing voice rang out through the high-ceilinged room:

> In the name of the German Volk! The honourless, ambitious oath-breakers Erwin von Witzleben, Erich Hoepner, Hellmuth Stieff, Paul von Hase, Robert Bernardis, Peter Graf Yorck von Wartenburg, Albrecht von Hagen, Friedrich Karl Klausing have betrayed the fallen soldiers, the Volk, the Führer and the Reich. Their betrayal is without precedent in German history.
>
> Instead of fighting manfully and following the Führer to victory like the rest of the German people, they hatched a cowardly conspiracy to murder the Führer in an abominable, traitorous act, with intent to put our nation at the mercy of its enemies and enslave it to the dark forces of reaction. They have betrayed everything we live and fight for and are herewith sentenced to death. Their property is confiscated by the Reich. The Volksgerichtshof of the Greater German Reich justifies its verdict as follows: A villainous act beyond the bounds of comprehension and exceeding all rational measure has been committed. At the end of the fifth year of war, our people is engaged in a bitter

struggle for liberty and survival. And at this very moment, a detonation of British explosives and triggered by British chargers tears open a yawning abyss of horror in the soul of our nation and in every one of us.

The conspirators' cowardly plan was to assassinate our beloved Führer. It was thwarted by the strength of the Volk, whose ever-vigilant guardians eradicated the traitors, and a tide of outrage swept through all regions of our great Reich. Brimming with love and loyalty, the heart of every German rejoiced: The Führer lives! In the courtroom yesterday, we saw a sketch of the site and images of the devastation wreaked by the bomb. Amid the chaos and debris, just two metres away from the explosive device, a miracle wrought by the destiny of our Volk preserved the life of the Führer. It was as if the impact of the explosion had no power to harm him. Then, when we learned the truth, each one of us swore to marshal every last atom of our strength, to rise up, to staunchly follow our Führer in total war, to march forward to victory and thus to life.

We all know the rough details of this monstrous deed. The Führer himself informed us that very night in a radio broadcast, so that we might recognize his voice. Goebbels, in his 'Rechenschaftsbericht' [report of events], as he himself called it, gave us a more detailed account. There is no need for me to repeat all this here. On the orders of Hitler, eight of the scoundrels responsible for this monstrous act have been brought before the Volksgerichtshof today for judgement. They have all been dishonourably discharged from the army, have through their deed forfeited their honour for all time and now stand before our Volk, disgraced and branded as guilty of the most execrable crime the German nation has ever seen.

Freisler then gave his view of the level of responsibility of each of the accused for the assassination attempt:

This is therefore what we have determined in the case of all eight traitors brought before us for judgement yesterday, and of whom we have learned everything. We have found no more than what every one of the accused has admitted here in the course of this main trial. Except where I have expressly stated otherwise, there is nothing in the findings of the court that has not been confirmed by the admission of the accused themselves. And there can be no doubt: our findings reflect only the very minimum of their guilt.

141

Their guilt exceeds all bounds. Each one of them bears full responsibility for this shameful deed, and although their individual degree of culpability could be dissected on the basis of legal paragraphs and wordings, they bear an equal burden of guilt. They are guilty of treason against our free, strong German national community, its way of life and its nature, against National Socialism, guilty of the presumptuous desire to replace our inner freedom with the fetters of reactionary opposition.

The treasonous nature of these actions is evident, the paltry cowardice, the moral emasculation of the coward who in battle, loses his faith in victory instead of seizing on the certainty that victory now depends on our retaining unwavering and complete faith. The assistance which they, to a man, did not hesitate to offer our enemies, is certain . . .

No-one can have been unaware that in depriving us of our Führer, they would have dealt us a staggering blow in our existential struggle against our enemies. These men are also guilty of an act of treason against the nation in its most terrible form, which in itself exceeds all bounds of the law . . . In it can be seen the abject cowardice of the defeatist, which needs no further explanation from me . . . It is disloyalty to the Führer . . . the murder of the man who, day and night, bears the burden of care for the life of our people . . . the murder of the man we all look up to, whom we all follow on our march to liberty!

It is betrayal per se, the betrayal of the very essence of the German nation, of those who have laid down their lives in this war and in the service of our cause. It is the most consummate act of treason in our history. In the past few days, I have thought at length about our past, and in the entire history of our Volk, in the accounts of the seventy generations which preceded us, I found no case – not one – which records the execution or even the planning of a comparable deed.

The accused cannot expect that we will shrink from bringing the full force of the law to bear in their case, the shameful details of which have been fully documented, that we will allow them one iota of leeway . . . At the time when our Reich passed the law which allows execution by hanging for particularly shameful crimes, it did so under the shadow of an extremely dangerous act of terrorism in the year 1933, an act that also threatened the life of our nation. Today, we are surer of ourselves. The act which prompted the passing of that law pales in comparison with the deed which these defendants, these eight defendants, have committed. We have said all there is to say . . . There can be only one verdict: death.

We find: This is the most ignominious crime in our history. We return to our life, to battle. We have nothing more to do with these men. The Volk has purged them from its ranks and remains pure. We fight. The Wehrmacht cries: Heil Hitler! We all join in the call: Heil Hitler! We fight with our Führer, following him for the glory of Germany. We have averted the danger. We will now march forward with full strength to total victory.

This session of the Volksgerichtshof of the Greater German Reich is thus ended.

The sentence was carried out on that same day. With their hands bound behind them, the accused were led into the execution chamber of the Plötzensee prison in Berlin. One after another, in a barbarous ritual, they were hung from butchers' hooks. Hitler had ordered: 'Let them be strung up like butchered cattle!'

The death throes of the condemned men were filmed, allegedly at Hitler's personal instigation. After the war, cameraman Erich Stoll described how the recordings were made:

We were taken to the Volksgerichtshof, where we were instructed to film and photograph the proceedings as inconspicuously as possible. We set up temporary lighting and installed sound-recording cameras behind the doors, to take shots through a hole in them. Another cameraman was told to remain inside the courtroom to take close-ups and capture the general atmosphere. The then Reich Film Superintendent Hans Hinkel decided which cameraman was to take which shots. We also had to inform him exactly how much film had been used for each sequence, so that he could be sure that every inch of footage was handed over to him. The President of the Volksgerichtshof, Dr Freisler, consented enthusiastically to the recording of the proceedings, and was eager to ensure that no detail was missed.

The footage began as the defendants were brought in. Their handcuffs were removed, and they were told where to sit. Then the judges, led by the chairman and president, Dr Freisler, entered the courtroom, and the trial began. Every major defendant had to be filmed with the sound camera, while only still shots were taken of the less important ones. After the first recess, the Reich film superintendent and the President of the Volksgerichtshof inquired how the images had turned out. We were forced to inform the President that he had shouted at the defendants so loudly that it had not been possible for the technician to modulate the sound between his shouting and the quiet voices of the defendants, and that their replies were therefore almost inaudible. Unfortunately, during subsequent examinations, the President continued to bellow so loudly at the accused that the recordings were technically inadequate.

On completion, the footage – in total about 50,000m of film, edited to 15,000m by the Ministry of Propaganda – was given a public viewing, though not in the weekly Nazi newsreel, the *Wochenschau*, as Hitler had originally envisaged. Instead, it was shown to an audience comprising members of NS organizations and gauleiter.

On 20 August 1944, the aforementioned Kaltenbrunner reports emphasized the deep impression made on the general public by the way the Volksgerichtshof President conducted the proceedings:

The President's sharp, often ironical and extremely quick-witted manner was received by broad sections of the workforce with enthusiasm and satisfaction. The President's criticism of the criminal intentions of the accused was completely in accord with the indignation of the public over this base deed. The details of the preparation for the assassination attempt were discussed with particular revulsion, especially the traitors' previous plan to carry out the attempt during an exhibition.

However, Kaltenbrunner had to concede that there were also critical voices – in particular from 'the intelligentsia and legal professionals'. The 'cheap way' in which the President insulted and ridiculed the defendants was 'unbecoming to the highest German court' and reminded many of the Soviet show trials. The report of 20 August 1944 went on:

In particular, there have been objections to the President engaging in a discussion with the defendant Hoepner on whether the word 'Schweinehund' or 'ass' most aptly described him [Hoepner].

Others pointed out that some of the accused were high-ranking personages who, for their achievements and competence, were accorded the highest honours within the National Socialist state. It was considered strange that men who not so long ago had been promoted by the Führer himself and whose deeds were celebrated in the press as heroic were now regarded as foolish, abject and indecisive . . .

It was deemed inevitable that this would raise doubts regarding personnel decisions on the highest levels, as these men had remained in elevated and important positions for many years.

Kaltenbrunner's reports were addressed to Martin Bormann, but intended for Hitler, and Hitler was quite happy with the way Freisler conducted the trials. After all, had he not demanded that these men should be shown not the slightest mercy and that these traitors should be given the harshest sentence, death? Freisler had played his role as the Nazi 'Vyshinsky' to perfection, just as Hitler wanted. He was the blood judge of the hour.

This first trial, that of the conspirators of the 20 July plot, was just the beginning. Numerous generals and officers were later brought before the court, accused of collaborating with the conspirators or sympathizing with their cause. Most of them were also sentenced to death and executed.

The liquidation of resistance within the military – whose most prominent representatives had often been enthusiastic and long-standing supporters of the Hitler regime, had served in the leading ranks of the Wehrmacht and thus made the atrocities of the Nazis possible – was now followed by the suppression of political resistance. A whole series of trials against the 'civilian conspirators' began with that of Carl Goerdeler on 7 and 8 September 1944.

In Freisler's eyes, Goerdeler, a former mayor of Leipzig who had drafted numerous emergency decrees and radio speeches for the day of the assassination attempt on Hitler, was the 'head and motor' of the conspiracy. The Social Democrat trade union official Wilhelm Leuschner, the former German ambassador in Rome Ulrich von Hassell, the Berlin lawyer Josef Wirner and Dr Paul Lejeune-Jung, an industrial manager who had been a member of the Reichstag from 1924 to 1930, representing the German Nationalist People's Party, and who was in line for the office of economics minister in Goedeler's 'post-Hitler cabinet' stood accused with him.

As in the first trial, Freisler turned the courtroom into a political stage. He dominated the proceedings, delivered monologues, roared, decided who should be allowed to speak – and pronounced sentence. A report on the trial, dated 8 September 1944 and written by Reich Minister of Justice Thierack to the Personal Secretary of the Führer at Führer Headquarters, Reichsleiter Martin Bormann, deserves mention here:

In the examination of the defendants Wirmer and Goerdeler, the chairman's method of conducting the proceedings was unobjectionable and dispassionate, in that of Lejeune-Jung somewhat nervous. He interrupted Leuschner and von Hassell repeatedly, screaming at them when they attempted to reply. This created a rather negative impression, in particular in view of the fact that the President had allowed around 300 persons to be present at the trial. It will be necessary to check who exactly was issued with an entrance ticket. Such conduct before a large audience is not advisable. Politically, the direction of the proceedings was otherwise unobjectionable. Unfortunately, however, the President addressed Leuschner as 'quarter-pint' and Goerdeler as 'half-pint' and referred to the defendants as 'Würstchen' ('sausages'). That significantly impaired the seriousness of this important assembly. Repeated and lengthy diatribes by the President, delivered for their effect as propaganda, came across as repulsive in these circumstances, and this also detracted from the gravity and dignity of the court. The President exhibits a total lack of the ice-cold aloofness and restraint which must be considered a necessity in a trial of this kind . . . Heil Hitler!

All four defendants were sentenced to death for high treason, defeatism, subversion of the war effort and aiding and abetting the enemy. Lejeune-Jung, Wirmer and von Hassell were executed that same day. Leuschner was taken to a concentration camp, where he was executed twenty days later. Goerdeler was initially 'kept alive', as the Gestapo hoped to gain from him information on the organization and structure of the resistance movement. But on 2 February 1945, being of no further use to the Gestapo, he was liquidated like his fellow conspirators.

As the Allies intensified their air raids, while Germany was being reduced to ruins by a ceaseless barrage of bombs, the Volksgerichtshof, led by Freisler, continued to hand out death sentence after death sentence. On 20 October 1944, he presided over the trial of Dr Julius Leber, Dr Adolf Reichwein, Hermann Maass and Gustav Dahrendorf. The four defendants had not received the indictment until the evening before the trial, rendering any defence impossible. And anyway, the verdict of the court was a foregone conclusion. With the exception of Dahrendorf, the accused were sentenced to death. A particularly macabre detail: not only the proceedings before the Volksgerichtshof were filmed. Hitler himself had requested the filming of the barbaric executions. While the executioner and his henchmen carried out their grisly task, the film camera whirred on . . .

The numerous trials involving Socialists and trade unionists, members of the 'Kriesau Circle' and many other 'conspirators' will not be covered at length here. For details, refer to the comprehensive literature listed in the Bibliography. Here in Germany, post-war historians have devoted particular attention to the conspirators of 20 July and commended their deeds. It should be said, however, that the historiography of the resistance against the NS dictatorship has frequently been one-sided.

It is a fact that ideologically, politically and ethically, the opposition groups and circles associated with the '20 July plot' were heterogeneous. Though united in their determination to end the Hitler regime, they had very different views of the measures required to do so. Members of the 'Kriesau Circle', for example, for a long time rejected the idea of tyrannicide on religious grounds and were only won over to the idea of an assassination attempt on Hitler much later. Many – predominantly conspirators within military circles – had been closely involved with the NS regime for many years, had supported and served it – and committed crimes in the process.

The assassination attempt planned for 20 July was therefore a last, desperate attempt by a group of German generals and officers to save Germany from final defeat. One example among many: Arthur Nebe, head of the Reichskriminalpolizeiamt (Reich Criminal Investigation Department). He had joined the NSDAP in 1931 and quickly rose through the ranks: SS-Gruppenführer, Generalleutnant der Polizei. He was one of the men who interrogated Georg Elser – a carpenter from the Swabian mountains who carried out a failed assassination attempt in the Munich Bürgerbräukeller in September 1939 – in the Gestapo Headquarters in Berlin. Elser was convicted and taken to a concentration camp, where he was executed just days before the War ended.

Nebe – an ardent National Socialist – volunteered to serve in Russia in 1941. As the leader of 'Einsatzgruppe B', his mission there was to create chaos and terror behind the front. His unit functioned mainly as an execution commando. Its victims were primarily Jews who had so far escaped detection. This fanatical man did not join the group of conspirators until the year 1944. His task was to recruit officers of the Berlin Kriminalpolizei for future military actions. It is not known when exactly and for what reasons Nebe joined the resistance. He was sentenced to death on 3 March 1945 and executed by hanging one day later.

Nebe was just one of the many controversial figures within the opposition movement. The question of the motives behind the 'volte-face' of numerous conspirators in the 20 July bomb plot has remained largely unanswered to this day.

147

The resistance mythology has never allowed a differentiated perspective, far removed from glorification, and this still largely applies. To this day, '20 July' has remained synonymous with the 'other, democratic Germany', a 'moral ray of hope' under the criminal Nazi regime. Both are sweeping generalizations and therefore questionable. Moreover: measured against the vast number of German Communists, Socialists and trade unionists, radical Christians and free thinkers who, individually or in groups, without rank or title, offered resistance and were persecuted, imprisoned, murdered or driven into exile as a result, this glorification of the '20 July' conspirators is totally disproportionate. A mystification of the few that renders the many invisible. The idolization of the 'Men of 20 July' was also one of the illusions perpetrated in post-war Germany. The Federal Republic under Adenauer had no room for the sacrifices of left-wing resistors to the Nazi dictatorship.

But back to the year of terror 1944: Freisler used the '20 July' trials as a stage with the aim of deterrence. Here, in the show trials, he would deliver a final and lasting lesson to anyone who still entertained thoughts of 'treason'. Treason against the German cause – against the Endsieg. A woman who witnessed Freisler's 'performance' said later:

> Over ten hours, Roland Freisler, master of the stage and of dramatic effect, poured out an unflagging torrent of words . . . they tumbled from his lips, glittering, gleaming, powerfully eloquent and with masterful modulation, his tone now mild, understanding, fatherly, now sharply inquisitorial, cool and aloof, then suddenly striking like a thunderbolt homing in on its target. The accused are the playthings of his wit. He juggles with the fate of human beings and adds just the right twist, lighting and tone he needs to turn an insignificant detail into a trenchant act leading him inexorably to the tragic denouement he has preordained, planned and mapped out in advance.

Rarely did the proceedings depart from Freisler's script, even for a moment. When, on 9 September 1944, he pronounced verdict in the above-mentioned trial of Goerdeler and four other defendants, one of the accused, the lawyer Josef Wirmer, called out: 'If I hang, the fear will be yours, not mine!'

Freisler, foaming with rage, retorted: 'You will soon be burning in hell!'

Wirmer, a devout Catholic and aware that he was going to die, calmly replied: 'Then I will look forward to your imminent arrival, your honour'.

Freisler would be dead in less than six months.

Chapter 9

# The End

Germany, September 1944. From one day to the next, the 'Thousand-Year Reich' was crumbling ever more visibly into ruins. The Allied air raids were taking an increasingly heavy toll on the German population. The invasion was proceeding inexorably on the Western Front, while the Red Army had driven the fleeing Ostheer (Eastern Army) back to the borders of the Reich and had already reached the Vistula river.

Despite all this, the majority of Germans still hoped that the tide would turn, had confidence in the fighting power of the Wehrmacht, still saw Hitler in the aura of his earlier victories. People in the air-raid shelters and soldiers at the front said to themselves: Hasn't the Führer always been proved right before? If he says there will be retribution, then retribution will come. And in a mixture of despondency and anger, battered by the suffering they had experienced and uncomfortably aware of their own complicity, they reassured each other: after all, don't we have a new miracle weapon up our sleeves which will radically change the course of the War and allow us to get even with our enemies?

'Haltet aus! (Endure!)', the Nazi propaganda machine urged German citizens, reminding them incessantly of their 'invincible virtues': their willingness to make sacrifices, their love of the Vaterland, their courage, resolve – and obedience . . .

And just as the Nazi war propaganda intended, the failed assassination attempt of 20 July had consolidated support for the regime. Once again, the fact that Hitler had survived was presented as an act of Providence, as evidence of the Führer's unbroken will to achieve victory. And indeed, following the Führer's radio address, as people were reassured by hearing his voice again, there was a general lifting of spirits. Majority opinion and Nazi propaganda were largely congruent.

Illusions were perceived as reality: the Führer was still alive, and so was Germany. The mood was still one of optimism – if subdued – and the German people was still willing to persevere in the interest of the German cause.

Nevertheless: on the evening of 11 September, the first US troops crossed the borders of the Reich at Trier. The Westheer (Western Army) was scattered. A Führer decree of 25 September authorized the creation of the 'Volkssturm' (People's National Guard). All 'able-bodied' men from 16 to 60 years of age and who had not yet been conscripted were now called to arms – for the Allies, a sign of military weakness, an indication that the Wehrmacht was definitely on its last legs. And on 11 November, under the headline 'World affairs are no longer predictable', the *Völkischer Beobachter* even expressed first doubts, admitting to its readers that, based on reasonable analysis, Germany could no longer win the War.

Hitler's health was already in decline by this time. He suffered from fits of depression, headaches and bouts of flu, and his posture was that of an old man. The deterioration in was obvious – particularly after news of the Allied airborne landings at Arnhem on 17 September. Kept on his feet with the help of tranquillisers and stimulants, he continued to react angrily to any opposition to his decisions, which, with his customary obstinacy and doggedness, he insisted were the only possible options. Fits of rage alternated with depression. His distrust and suspicion of others became pathological.

Autumn 1944 saw the beginning not only of Hitler's agony but of the death throes of the Third Reich. At the end of November, as a further emergency measure, a corps of 'Wehrmachtshelferinnenkorps' (Wehrmacht Women's Auxiliary Corps) was created. Service was at first voluntary, but later, conscription of young women and girls from the age of eighteen to support the Wehrmacht troops was introduced. The news that the Wehrmacht was once again mounting an offensive against the Allies, the 'Ardennenoffensive' (The Battle of the Bulge), offered a last glimmer of hope for many Germans. Despite air raids at home, despite heavy casualties and deprivation, many still believed that victory was possible. And Joseph Goebbels knew how to exploit these dire circumstances for propaganda purposes. In an editorial for the weekly newspaper *Das Reich* on 10 December 1944, he had words of encouragement for the German Volksgenossen:

> We are now fighting with our backs to the wall. It goes without saying that this is extremely dangerous, but it may have advantages, too'. The coming Christmas, said Goebbels, would be 'a feast of the strong hearts.

Such exhortations to hold out now rained down on the German population almost as frequently as enemy bombs.

On 17 December 1944, in an article in the *Völkischer Beobachter* entitled 'The young soldier's belief in the Führer', war reporter Herbert Reinecker appealed once again for faith in the German virtues. 'The young soldier is loyal to the Führer', wrote Reinecker, who after the war became Germany's most successful crime novelist and was awarded the Bundesfilmpreis for the resistance film *Canaris*, 'because he is loyal to himself and to his destiny. It is unthinkable for him to question, to give up or capitulate in the face of difficulties.' Fed with such propaganda and ideologically blinded, thousands of young soldiers died a 'German' death. And in the meantime, the 'Thousand-Year Reich' continued to crumble.

The War had returned to Germany, where it had been set in motion years before. And the Volksgerichtshof did not remain unaffected. As a large proportion of the court building had been destroyed in an air raid in November 1943, the tribunal was partly evacuated to Potsdam, where trials were held in the courtrooms of the Landgericht there.

In the preceding months, the Senates had increasingly travelled the length and breadth of the Reich to administer their blood justice, quite in accordance with the wishes of Reich Minister of Justice Thierack, who, as a fanatical National Socialist, underscored the particular importance of the 'political role' of the Volksgerichtshof at that moment and advised that the toughest sentences should be handed down. In a letter to Freisler dated 18 October 1944, he requested that the 'esteemed President' should pay particular attention to the trial procedure and sentencing, as the importance of the Volksgerichtshof 'for the maintenance of the home front' had increased significantly.

'The task of the Volksgerichtshof', wrote Thierack 'is not limited to meting out well-deserved punishment to the guilty. Above and beyond this, it has an obligation to provide political leadership.'

For his busy President of the Volksgerichtshof, he went on to describe the role the court was expected to play in forceful terms:

> The people must not only recognize the judgement of the Volksgerichtshof as correct; they must also learn why a specific sentence was expedient. In some particularly important political trials, the way in which the heads of the senates conduct the proceedings often suffers due to their failure to emphasize sufficiently the particular seriousness of the deed in relation to the present situation of the Volk and the Reich . . .
>
> In conducting the proceedings, the president must make it clear why this particular offence is especially grave and why it is particularly dangerous for the Volk and for the Reich.

Everyone present at the trial must leave the courtroom not only with the inner conviction that the sentence was just, but with a knowledge of why it was just. This applies in particular measure to the so-called cases of defeatism which will now be increasingly brought before us.

Likewise, no idle talk should be allowed, for example that proceedings before a particular senate mean certain death or that the legal interpretation of the term 'public' is too broad. When such utterances occur, they can only be deflected by conducting the proceedings in a superior, calm and – if necessary – ice-cold manner. The people must always be instructed as to why, in these crucial months of the war, agitators deserve death – but not gossip-mongers, unless it is a case not merely of idle gossip, but of gossip which became dangerous because it was uttered irresponsibly.

Finally, Thierack asked Freisler to endeavour to ensure that important political cases were only presided over by judges 'who are also masters of the material involved in the political respect'. The message was clear: the 'maintenance of the home front' required an even more resolute judiciary, and as the 'front-line' tribunal, the Volksgerichtshof was expected to proceed with particular efficiency. This also meant a simplification of judicial procedures, for example with respect to the granting of pardons.

Death penalties for subversion of the war effort were not to be subject to review, even if this meant that occasionally an innocent person might be executed. In Thierack's view, the course of the war required a speedy processing of cases and the consistent enforcement of judgements. And indeed, the deterioration of the situation in the civilian and military sector went hand in hand with a rapid rise in the number of death sentences. For political and military crimes in particular, death sentences were the order of the day.

The Volksgerichtshof: the figurehead of a perverted and merciless legal system with a power that did not end with the death of its victims. In contrast to previous practice, the bodies of the executed were no longer even released to their families, but instead were cremated or handed over to university medical faculties.

And Freisler, who served this unrelentingly inhumane tribunal as its President and a judge, was its driving force. Despite the turmoil of the war, he carried on working at his customary furious pace. He continued to give lectures – though fewer in number due to the increasing disruption of transport – performed his duties as President and presided over numerous trials of its First Senate. The last schedule for the distribution of cases within the Volksgerichtshof prepared by Freisler, for the year 1945, shows that he also assigned cases that would normally have come before other senates to his own First Senate, particularly cases of treason.

Thierack was well aware of this. In November 1943, he had already written to Freisler urging him to assign more cases to the other senates. But Freisler chose to ignore this and continued to reserve all interesting cases for himself, especially after the assassination attempt on 20 July.

Germany in autumn 1944: the standing of the NSDAP, which still had over eight million members, had reached an all-time low; many Party members no longer wore their uniforms quite so proudly. They, too, could not have failed to notice that their dream of a 'Thousand-Year Reich' was crumbling to dust. They had two options for processing this sobering reality: either they marched on in step, following their old ideals, becoming more and more radical as the writing on the wall became ever clearer, or they attempted to distance themselves from the Party in order to face the post-war reality with a clean political slate or even – as was not infrequently seen – present themselves as members of the resistance against the NS dictatorship.

Freisler belonged to the group of who – despite inner doubts – still fanatically supported the Party and the Führer. On 26 October 1944, he wrote:

> In one's innermost thoughts, one has to admit that it is no longer impossible that Germany will lose the War. The V-weapons have not yielded the success which we all so eagerly expected. Even Reichsminister Goebbels shares this view, but according to his information, much more destructive weapons are being prepared, weapons whose destructive power will surpass anything the world has seen hitherto. Then we must not forget the time factor. We must hold out at all costs, because the longer we hold our positions, the sooner this unnatural alliance between the Anglo-Americans and the Soviets will break asunder. It cannot be in the interests of the Anglo-Americans, and even less in the interests of Jewish capitalists in the West, for the Russians to dominate Central Europe.
>
> Looking at developments in the last few years, I am forced to abandon my belief in a worldwide Jewish conspiracy against Germany. I now consider this a far too simple interpretation. There is an unbridgeable gap between the Jewish proletariat in Eastern Europe, from which the Jewish intelligentsia is recruited

and which does everything in its power to bring about a global Bolshevik revolution, on the one hand, and the Jews in England and America on the other, who are largely assimilated and have no interest in revolution, least of all a Bolshevik one backed by the power of Soviet Russia. The profit motive of the latter group contradicts the goals of their eastern brethren.

And Freisler continued:

But even if we should lose this war, which I fervently hope will be prevented through the genius of the Führer and providence, then we must go down with flying colours. In 1815, it was believed that the ideas of the French Revolution had been defeated. What we have seen so far and are now again seeing in France is that this is far from being the case. Those ideas have survived, and despite periods of disastrous weakness, they have become part of French life and the French national identity.

The idea of National Socialism was born in an environment of abject misery, and, contrary to all expectations, it triumphed. But one cannot change a nation from the ground up within a period of little more than a decade or transform the fabric of its society overnight. The current trials at the Volksgerichtshof have provided a clear demonstration of this. Even I was amazed at the sheer extent of the conspiracy. What I originally assumed to be the activity of just a small clique in reality drew on much larger dimensions. However, the very cowardice of the leaders of this conspiracy will have shown the German people how infinitely superior National Socialism is to goals and programmes which lack ideals and revolutionary élan.

Men whose mindset marked them as belonging to the Wilhelmine era and the Weimar system attempted to seize power over Germany, a bunch of backward-looking old men, some of whom, like that fellow Goerdeler, have had nothing better to do after their conviction than to write endless memoranda implicating numerous others in their reactionary plot. Though this might well help them to extend their own lives by a few months, they will not escape their just deserts in the end. In view of the extent of the conspiracy, which the German people has now, of course, become aware of, it is now being said that the revolution is devouring its children. Nothing could be more wrong than to view current events in this light. The revolution is not devouring its children: the National Socialist revolution is spitting out all those who were never part of it in the first place, all those who have to be eliminated before the revolution can be brought to its ultimate conclusion. These people were never part of our national community; they did not want to be part of us, they were an alien element in National Socialist Germany.

In this sense, like its predecessor in France in 1792, the Volksgerichtshof has today become the truly revolutionary tribunal which is required to purify the nation.

The nation which remains after this process will be National Socialist to the core, as so many Volksgenossen already are. Even if defeated by their enemies, they will ensure that they and their descendants, irrespective of the name and form the nation takes, will remain National Socialists, until such time as the swastika can be unfurled again over our cities and our fatherland. Whatever the future may bring, National Socialism will triumph. National Socialism, the effects of a war which was the last thing our Führer wanted and the aftermath of this war will show that they have been and will continue to be the great levellers within Germany society, sweeping away class barriers and distinctions. All Germans are now in one boat, and we all now have to pull in one direction in order to achieve victory, or, if the worst comes to the worst, to achieve recovery and with it, the ultimate and final triumph.

The words of a man blinded by an ideal? The self-exhortation of a fanatic? There can be no doubt about it: even now, in October 1944, Freisler remained a fervent National Socialist. And although he found it increasingly difficult to bring his trials to a successful conclusion, as they were frequently interrupted by Allied air raids, and though, like many of those around him, he had already sent his wife and his two sons to safety, to stay with friends in the countryside outside Berlin, it seemed that not even impending destruction could cause him to doubt or undermine his faith in National Socialism. And Freisler was by no means alone in this determination to hold on 'to the bitter end'.

On New Year's Eve 1944, in a radio broadcast, the actor Heinrich George, director of the Berlin theatres since 1943, read the 'Prussian Confession', written in 1812 by Carl von Clausewitz. Its final passage was underlaid with the sound of violins: 'I would be only too happy to find a glorious death in the noble struggle for the freedom and dignity of the fatherland!' The bells of Cologne Cathedral then rang in the New Year.

1 January 1945: The new year was only five minutes old when Hitler addressed the German people in a radio broadcast. He spoke of the reconstruction of German cities, the new order which would arise from the ruins. 'A people that has accomplished, suffered and endured so much, both at the front and in the homeland, can never perish. On the contrary: it will emerge from this furnace stronger and firmer than ever before in its history.' Hitler's unwavering conviction that Germany would be victorious may indeed have given many Volksgenossen fresh hope.

However, just twelve days later, on 12 January 1945, the German eastern front collapsed at the Vistula. The Eastern Army fled back into the Reich. The writing was on the wall, for all Heinrich Himmler's exhortations to take a hard line against 'shirkers' and his appeal to the female population to 'chase the craven cowards' back to the front 'with your dishcloths'. On 1 February 1945, the Red Army, which far outnumbered its opponents, crossed the Oder river. It could only be a matter of days before they reached Berlin. The end was nigh.

And in the meantime, the Nazi jurists of the Volksgerichtshof continued to hear cases against people accused of 'listening to enemy broadcasts', 'plundering following air raids', 'defeatism' etc. Nor was their zeal in any way abated in these final months of the war. Almost daily, the blood-red placards appeared throughout the Reich, announcing death sentences 'In the name of the Volk'. But 'Hitler's Germans' paid them little attention. Either they were still hoping for a miracle and thought it only right and fitting that 'these criminals' should be dealt with mercilessly, or they were too preoccupied with their own problems. The War left them no time for grief, compassion or shame.

In addition to hearing a never-ending stream of cases against 'nobodies', the tribunals of the People's Court were still occupied with the 'ringleaders' of the July Bomb Plot. For example, the proceedings against those members of the 'Kreisau Circle' who had not yet been brought to trial continued, and death sentences were handed down on an almost daily basis.

A further important trial had already begun on 9 January. The prisoners in the dock were Helmuth James Graf von Moltke, Eugen Gerstenmaier, Franz Sperr, Dr Franz Reisert, Fürst Fugger von Glött, Dr Theodor Haubach, Oberstleutnant Theodor Steltzer, Father Dr Josef Delp and the journalist Nikolaus Gross. They had all taken part in meetings of the 'Circle'. However, their degree of involvement varied greatly.

Moltke had been in direct contact with both Goerdeler and Stauffenberg, whereas Delp had attended just one meeting of the 'Circle' in Munich. Not that this fact was of any particular importance in Freisler's eyes. During the trial, he focussed his attention on Delp, with whom he engaged in a fierce battle of words. Freisler's anti-Catholic and anti-Jesuit prejudices had marked out Delp as a candidate for the death penalty even before the trial started. Freisler's vicious tirades against the Jesuit priest, who made no secret of his views, were clear evidence of his deep-seated hostility. Moltke was also subjected to a litany of abuse. In his defence, he stated that he had only joined the resistance movement in order to prepare for a possible enemy occupation, a statement which particularly outraged Freisler. If there was one thing he hated more than anything else, it was a coward. And in Freisler's eyes, such a feeble excuse was nothing less than cowardice. Moltke was therefore another certain candidate for the death penalty.

The verdicts were announced two days later, on 11 January 1945, while the proceedings against Haubach (a Social Democrat and a member of the Kreisau Circle since 1942), Gross (a coal miner by profession, a Christian trade union leader and also a member of the Circle) and Steltzer (a general staff officer and long-standing friend of Moltke's) were postponed to a later date.

Moltke and Delp were convicted and sentenced to death for undermining the war effort, aiding and abetting the enemy, preparation for high treason and failing to report planned crimes. Franz Sperr, a former general staff officer who had only recently had contact with the Kreisau Circle, was also sentenced to death for 'failing to report a planned crime'. Reisert, Gerstenmaier and Fürst Fugger escaped with prison sentences. Moltke and Sperr were executed on 23 January, Delp on 2 February, on the same day as Goerdeler. Haubach and Gross, who were tried together with Steltzer on 15 January, were also executed on that day. Steltzer's execution, however, was deferred due to intervention by Himmler – and he survived the War.

Day after day, as all around them, Allied bombs rained down, reducing Germany to smoking ruins, the executioners of the Volksgerichtshof continued to ply their bloody trade without respite. Were they unwilling to admit the impending defeat, or did their fanatical subservience spur them on to even greater efforts, to one last, bloody vendetta against all those they held responsible for the imminent downfall of Germany? Almost half the trials held before the Volksgerichtshof since January had ended with a death sentence. Blind zeal drove the robed henchmen to pass sentence at a frenzied pace. Right up until 3 February 1945, a Saturday.

On that day, Freisler was presiding over the proceedings against Ewald von Kleist-Schmenzin, who, although not a member of a resistance group, was an opponent of the Hitler regime and had had contact with numerous members of the resistance movement. He had been informed of Stauffenberg's plan to assassinate Hitler, and his name also featured on Goerdeler's list as a political consultant. Kleist-Schmenzin defended himself staunchly before Freisler, stating that he had fought against Hitler and National Socialism from the start, considering this a duty ordained by God.

However, it seems that Freisler seems had no interest in engaging in verbal battles on that day. He interrupted the proceedings after this statement from Kleist-Schmelzin and instead suggested bringing forward the trial against Fabian von Schlabrendorff. It has never been established why he did this. He had hardly begun when the air-raid sirens sounded and the hearing was interrupted.

3 February 1945, the day on which the American Air Force launched its heaviest bombardment of Berlin to date, in which 700 bombers, accompanied by fighter aircraft, dropped more than 3,000 tons of explosives on the city, brought death to more than 20,000 people. Victims of a cruel war that had now returned to the place where it had begun: the centre of National Socialist power. And one of the victims was Roland Freisler.

For a long time, there were three different versions of his death in circulation. The first was that reported by Fabian von Schlabrendorff himself, the last man to stand in the dock before Freisler and who was to survive the War. In a later book, he remembered the events of 3 February 1945.

The air-raid sirens went off, he said, shortly after the main hearing against him began, and everyone went down into the cellar of the court building. The President of the Court, a bundle of files in his hand, and his assessors were standing in one corner of the shelter, while he and his guards were in another. Suddenly, there was a huge detonation as a bomb struck the building. A ceiling beam cracked and fell on Freisler, killing him.

A second version of the story states that Freisler's car was hit by a bomb as he travelled from the Ministry of Justice to the Volksgerichtshof.

The third and most likely version goes as follows: Oberstabsarzt (senior staff doctor) Dr Rolf Schleicher was on his way to see Reich Minister of Justice Thierack in order to appeal for clemency in the case of his brother, Rüdiger Schleicher, an undersecretary in the Reich Air Ministry. Freisler had sentenced him to death the day before, along with Klaus Bonhoeffer, brother of Pastor Dietrich Bonhoeffer, and Friedrich Perels and Hans John. Caught in the air raid, Dr Rolf Schleicher and numerous other passengers were forced to wait for the all-clear in the tunnels of the Potsdamer Platz underground station. With him were his sister-in-law and her daughter, who had arranged to speak with Oberreichsanwalt Lautz to appeal against the death sentence. When the barrage of bombs subsided and the planes with their death-bringing cargo had departed, they emerged from the station to hear people calling for a doctor. Schleicher responded and was taken to the courtyard of the nearby Volksgerichtshof, where a 'prominent personage' had been struck by a bomb fragment as he attempted to cross the courtyard. But he was already dead. Bending down, Schleicher looked at the dead man's face. It was the very man who had sentenced his brother to death the previous day: Roland Freisler.

Schleicher refused to issue a death certificate, demanding to speak to the Minister of Justice. When he was finally admitted to see Thierack, the minister was visibly shaken by the news of Freisler's death, but promised Schleicher that he would have his brother's execution delayed, holding out the hope that an appeal for clemency might be successful when the sentence was reviewed.

However, all efforts were to be in vain. Weeks later, on the night of 22/23 April 1945, Rüdiger Schleicher and sixteen other condemned men, including Bonhoeffer, John and Perels, were shot by a firing squad of the Reich Main Security Office.

Freisler, the murderer in a blood-red robe, was dead. In a letter of condolence to his grieving widow, dated 5 February 1945, Reich justice minister Thierack wrote:

> It is with great consternation that I learned of the cruel blow which fate has dealt to you and your family. Your husband was taken from us in the midst of his ceaseless and untiring efforts and shortly before he could take on new important tasks. The extent of the loss to the German legal system has already become apparent in these few days.
>
> A man brimming with ideas, an indefatigable worker, a National Socialist deeply convinced of the greatness of the German mission, the righteousness and victory of the German cause and a loyal follower of the Führer, has been torn from our midst. While undoubtedly tragic, the fact that his death occurred at his place of work, where he had hurried despite the air-raid warning, driven by a profound sense of the responsibility entrusted to him as the President of the nation's highest political court, serves as a symbol of the culmination of a life devoted to the fight for the German cause.
>
> I write, my dear Frau Freisler, not only on behalf of the German judiciary, but also to extend my own sincerest condolences. May

the thought that your husband lives on in his sons give you the strength to comfort them.

Heil Hitler!

Your devoted servant . . .

The letter closes with Thierack's signature. The bulletin issued later the same day by the press office of the Reich Ministry of Justice, bearing instructions to editors 'to refrain from any comment on this bulletin and from the addition of further commentary by the newspapers themselves', comprised just a few lines. Under the heading 'Dr Roland Freisler fallen', it reads:

> The President of the Volksgerichtshof, NSKK Brigadeführer Dr jur. Roland Freisler, was killed during the terrorist attack on the Reich capital on 3 February. Dr Freisler, who would have celebrated his 52nd birthday this year, joined the NSDAP in 1925 and was a bearer of the Gold Party Badge. He was a member of the German Reichstag and of the Prussian state council. Dr Freisler was widely known to the German people as a tireless champion of National Socialist German law.

The funeral was just as low-key as the press bulletin. Held in the cemetery of Berlin-Dahlem, it was attended only by his family, a few colleagues from the Volksgerichtshof and a handful of Nazi functionaries. The Reich Ministry of Justice sent a representative. In this way, Thierack was demonstrating his ambivalent, at the end even negative, attitude towards Freisler.

He had always seen Freisler as a problematical, at times even unpredictable, jurist. Although Thierack respected him for his devotion to the National Socialist cause and his unconditional loyalty to the Führer, there had always been a gulf between them. Did he suspect Freisler of harbouring ambitions to become Reich Minister of Justice himself? Now Freisler was dead, and Thierack's letter of condolence to his widow was a mere formality. However, Thierack's absence at his funeral once again revealed his deep aversion to the man.

The question of Freisler's succession now arose. Dr Harry Haffner, former chief public prosecutor in Kattowitz and like his predecessor, a fervent Nazi jurist, was appointed President of the People's Court. On 14 March 1945, Goebbels wrote in his diary: 'For the present, we are not establishing courts martial in Berlin, although we have become a city close to the front. As long as the Volksgerichtshof remains in Berlin, it will, I believe, suffice.'

The jurists of the Volksgerichtshof continued to carry out their bloody task with relentless vigour under Haffner's presidency. The defendants, whose hopes had been raised after Freisler's death, still received the death sentence in the majority of cases. Freisler was dead, but his spirit lived on in the heads of his colleagues, who were no less rigorous than Hitler's dead executioner. On 15 March 1945, the Vice-President of the Volksgerichtshof, Dr Crohne, sentenced Kleist-Schmenzin to death, too. His protestations that he was an 'enemy of parliamentarianism' and that two of his sons were serving in the Wehrmacht were to no avail. On 9 April, as Allied shells rained down on Berlin, Kleist-Schmenzin was decapitated.

April 1945: Germany lay in ruins. American, Soviet and British troops occupied the German cities. The end of the War was imminent. On 20 April, Hitler's 56th birthday, Goebbels proudly announced in a speech broadcast on all remaining Reich radio stations: 'The Führer will follow his path to the end, and there awaits not the destruction of his people, but a new and happy beginning, an era in which the German nation will flourish as never before.' On the same day, Hitler – visibly a sick man – awarded the Iron Cross to members of the 'Volkssturm' in the garden of the Reich Chancellery in Berlin. One last, desperate, fake ceremony.

The Volksgerichtshof moved from Potsdam to Bayreuth, where it could continue to hand down death sentences to the bitter end. But no more trials were held. On 30 April, units of the 756th Rifle Regiment of the Red Army took the Reichstag. By evening, after last desperate skirmishes, the red Soviet flag was hoisted on the roof of the building.

Just a few hours later, Hitler committed suicide in the bunker of the Reich Chancellery with Eva Braun, whom he had married only shortly before. Hitler's valet found his master covered in blood, a pistol in his hand. Beside him lay Eva Braun, who had poisoned herself. Together with Hitler's secretary, Reichsleiter Martin Bormann, the valet wrapped the bodies in blankets and carried them up the narrow stairs of the bunker and out into the garden. There, the corpses were doused with petrol and set alight. On the evening of the same day, bodyguards buried the charred remains, together with those of two of Hitler's dogs, who had been poisoned, in a bomb crater.

One day later, Joseph Goebbels and his wife Magda committed suicide, after handing over their six children to SS doctor Helmut Kunz, reassuring them 'The doctor is going to give you an injection all children and soldiers are getting'. Kunz then administered the lethal morphine. The parents swallowed capsules of poison in the garden of the Reich Chancellery, after which soldiers poured petrol over the bodies and fired shots to ignite them. Goebbels had issued precise instructions, staging his death in the same painstaking manner in which he had staged so many events as Propaganda Minister in preceding years. The prophet was now reunited with his Messiah.

Hitler's Germany was defeated. The massacre of millions had finally come to an end. Those first days of May 1945 also marked the end of one of the darkest chapters in the history of the German judiciary – the end of the Volksgerichtshof. The bloody tribunal of terror had ceased to exist.

And Freisler, who stood for this tribunal as no other? Did he continue to exist as a diabolical legend? What manner of man was he? A psychopath? A fanatical Nazi judge? Or merely a jurist who consistently applied the laws as they were handed to him? The laws of an inhuman legal system, a murderous regime? Freisler's psychogramme is complex and full of ambiguity. Good reason to once again examine the question: who was this man?

Freisler was a fervent, even fanatical, National Socialist to the end. Even before being appointed President of the Volksgerichtshof, he fought tirelessly and relentlessly for the creation of a new National Socialist law. For him, what counted was not the crime, the deed alone, but first and foremost the political attitude of the perpetrator. In his numerous essays, he emphasized again and again that the mere intention to commit a political crime was tantamount to having actually carried it out. In this far, Freisler can be seen as the creator of a new 'Gesinnungsstrafrecht', a criminal law regulating political attitudes.

In his interpretation of the law, the judge was the focal point. He was the Führer who guided the proceedings, instructed his colleagues and the lay judges and in the end, pronounced the verdict. Freisler presided over trials in the manner of a tribunal: he was tyrannical, loud, theatrical. He ran his courtrooms as an authoritarian and with no regard for procedural rules. The sentences he meted out had only one purpose: to eradicate political opposition. His courtroom manner was arbitrary and biased. His greatest prejudice was against the Catholic clergy, while he showed slightly more leniency to Protestants. Nevertheless, not everyone brought before him was automatically lost. His second main target was the global Jewish conspiracy, though in comparison with the fanatical tirades of other prominent Nazis, his comments on this subject were more moderate.

The worst thing a defendant could do, in Freisler's eyes, was to attempt to talk his way out of a charge. In contrast, those who stood by their actions 'manfully' earned at least some measure of respect. He cannot be said to have had one consistent style in the courtroom. On one hand, he was capable of surprising the accused and his audience with unusual affability and generosity, winning them over with his ready wit, even humour, and he sometimes unexpectedly acquitted defendants or handed down lenient prison sentences. On the other hand, however, he sentenced people to death for minor offences. Freisler loved courtroom disputes, which gave him the opportunity to demonstrate his extensive general knowledge and show off his barbed rhetoric. He never shied away from verbal battles. On the contrary, they seemed to spur him on, often leading him to deliver vain, grandstanding monologues. Freisler's personality remained unpredictable, inscrutable, highly contradictory. His was not a rational nature, nor can he be said to have had a well-balanced or strong character.

However unpredictable he was psychologically, he had a keen intellect. Freisler was seen not only as a man with comprehensive knowledge and as a brilliant jurist, but also as outstandingly intelligent. But how can it be that his generally-attested intellectual capabilities deserted him as soon as the Führer, the Party and the Fatherland were involved? Historian Hansjoachim Koch called him 'a true believer', and indeed, his relationship to his idol Hitler was characterized by total and uncritical obedience.

Did Freisler really believe unconditionally in what, time and time again, ad nauseam, he set forth in his judgements as the essence of National Socialism? Did he really consider the Third Reich to be unsurpassed and without flaws? Did he really think the 'Endsieg' was an absolute certainty? These questions will not be easy to answer, and there is just cause for doubt. Freisler had access to information which was unavailable to most Germans. He could read the reports from the Gestapo, the police and the judicial bodies, which gave him insight into and allowed him to draw conclusions about the true state of affairs. Freisler travelled frequently, met with functionaries and dignitaries from the government, the Party, the armed forces, the economy, the judiciary and the administration, so that he was in a position to gain a clear picture of events and military developments even beyond the borders of the Reich. In other words, Freisler was one of the best-informed men of his time, and with his knowledge and insight, he should have been aware of the illusory nature of the regime he so idolized. The fact that he nevertheless clung so fanatically to National Socialism and considered any criticism of it as outright sacrilege worthy of punishment by death can only have had psychological reasons.

Freisler remained an unfaltering and uncompromising believer in National Socialism who refused to make any concessions, even when it became clear that the end of the Hitler regime was inevitable. He steered the Volksgerichtshof resolutely along the course for which it had been established, the eradication of all opposition, to the bitter end, no matter how dreadful that end might be. Any deviation from this course would have seemed a betrayal to him.

His fanatical stance became particularly evident again during the last trials over which he presided, especially those of the conspirators of 20 July: anyone who, like them, doubted in National Socialism and the 'Endsieg', was guilty of sabotaging the 'German cause' and 'collaboration with the enemy'. They all became victims of Freisler's insatiable thirst for revenge.

Was this a projection of Freisler's own doubts? Was he attempting to resolve his own psychological dilemma? Having to experience the downfall of National Socialism, a cause he had so fervently believed in and a vision he still clung desperately to, was he transposing feelings of guilt, dealing with the doubts he himself felt and repressed by punishing them mercilessly in others?

For many, including Thierack, Freisler's conduct, especially in the last years of the War, seemed to indicate mental abnormality. But was he mentally ill? Or was this just a convenient excuse for all the others who had shared in the guilt and subsequently tried to exonerate themselves by creating the legend of Freisler the madman?

It is a fact that the radicalization of German law and the disproportionate sentencing policy of the Volksgerichtshof did not begin with Freisler's appointment as its President. He merely interpreted the law as it had been enacted on the basis of the Enabling Acts, in accordance with the goals of the Führer and the Party, even where the law deviated from the constitution. Freisler was merely continuing a policy that had been advocated and applied by his predecessor Thierack following the outbreak of the War. As President of the First Senate, Thierack had already reserved all important cases for himself, and Freisler simply carried on where Thierack left off. When Freisler became President of the People's Court, the tide of the war was already turning against Germany. This, in particular together with the numerous Night and Fog trials and the trials of the 20 July conspirators, explains the dramatic rise in the number of death sentences, a rise which had already begun under Thierack's Presidency.

The radicalization of the legal system reflected the radicalization of the War, and Freisler was called upon to pass merciless sentences 'on the home front'. In an atmosphere which he himself had helped to create, a man like Freisler was bound to succumb to the delusion that everything that happened was lawful. In the manipulation of an unbridled system of injustice, he was a master. A master of death.

In its judgement, the Nuremberg Military Tribunal called Freisler 'the most evil, brutal and bloody judge in the entire German legal administration' and referred to him, along with Himmler, Heydrich and Thierack, as men whose 'desperate and despicable character is known to the world'.

There is no arguing with this verdict. However, post-1945, Freisler was made the scapegoat and the alibi of the German judiciary. Surviving NS jurists exploited the demonisation of Freisler in order to load their own guilt onto his back.

This allowed them to see themselves as jurists who had merely done their duty as prescribed by the law during difficult times. In this way, they could perceive themselves as innocents led astray, as victims rather than as perpetrators or active participants. Their pangs of conscience – in as far as they felt any – could be assuaged, their guilt offloaded onto others. A fanatical blood judge like Freisler was a particularly good figure onto which to project feelings of guilt.

Roland Freisler: a murderous jurist in an era rife with murder. An era in which not only Freisler, but the entire judiciary became the executioners and henchmen of a lethal regime. He was no diabolical figure, no incarnation of evil ascending from the depths of Hell. He arose from the very midst of the Reich. He was a ruthless German of his age – and the Germans had made him possible

# Chapter 10

# No 'Stunde Null'

L ate summer 1945: the nation that had so enthusiastically cheered the National Socialists now seemed to have been struck dumb. But did the Germans, who were both victims and perpetrators and had brought so much suffering upon other nations, feel anything akin to shame? Or were they merely embarrassingly aware of being on the losing side? Were they able to comprehend what had taken place, what they had been complicit in and allowed to happen? 'Stunde Null', – Zero Hour – was also to be the hour of a necessary 'cleansing' of German society.

With this aim, the heads of government of three of the Allied powers met in Potsdam and signed a decree which stated that:

> All members of the National Socialist Party who have been more than nominal participants in its activities . . . shall be removed from public and semi-public office. Such persons shall be replaced by persons who, by their political and moral qualities, are deemed capable of assisting in the development of genuine democratic institutions in Germany.

An entire nation now faced a process of political and moral cleansing by the Allied powers. And what the Allies called 'denazification' was designed as a prerequisite for the collective rehabilitation of the German people. The Potsdam Agreement also aimed to regulate procedure for the removal of former NSDAP members, as the tracking-down and detention of former Nazis which had already begun in the occupied zones had taken widely differing courses.

Local 'anti-fascist committees' prevented former Nazi functionaries going into hiding, and there had even been occasional acts of revenge. This, however, was not in the interests of the 'Allied Control Council', which wanted a coordinated approach to denazification across Germany. In January 1946, a further Directive containing a precise definition and categorization of which persons were to be removed from which offices and positions was issued. Yet another Directive, in October 1946, laid down joint guidelines, applicable in Germany as a whole, for the punishment of war criminals and of National Socialists who had aided and abetted the Nazi regime.

A difficult task. Who was a perpetrator, and who merely a 'Mitläufer' (hanger-on)? And didn't everyone have an excuse, an explanation for their actions? To allow the principles set out in the Potsdam Agreement to be put into practice, 'war criminals and potentially dangerous persons' were first divided into five categories 'to provide for the implementation of sanctions': Major Offenders – Offenders (activists, militarists and profiteers) – Lesser Offenders – Hangers-On – and Exonerated Persons (those who were able to prove themselves not guilty before a denazification tribunal called a 'Spruchkammer').

An entire nation on trial. The Allied powers now set about a 'cleansing' of the disillusioned Hitler Germans within their occupation zones. The cleansing of a people which, although it saw itself as defeated, did not necessarily consider itself guilty.

The Americans began with great zeal. They distributed a six-page questionnaire to be filled out by Germans. It required the respondent to give clear answers to 131 questions – including details ranging from weight to income and assets, military service, travel abroad, previous convictions and religious affiliation. There were penalties for incomplete answers and omissions. The key section of the questionnaire, comprising questions 41 to 95, demanded truthful answers to questions on membership of National Socialist organizations. Judges, public prosecutors and lawyers were also required to fill in a supplementary form on which the first question concerned membership of the Volksgerichtshof. Other questions covered contact with the Gestapo, the nature and extent of participation in trials and details of the respondent's previous legal career.

By the beginning of December 1945, more than 13 million such questionnaires had been submitted to the authorities in the American zone. The cleansing was restricted to a verification of the information, where possible, in order to separate the tainted Nazi wheat from the untainted chaff. The worst Nazis fell under the category designated for 'immediate arrest'. Others lost their jobs, while harmless hangers-on were allowed to retain their positions and remained in office.

In the French and British zones, denazification efforts concentrated primarily on removing the Nazi elite from their posts. As the top priority was to ensure the maintenance of essential supplies and a functioning administration, the cleansing was pursued with less vigour. The focus here was on pragmatic rather than legal solutions. In the British Zone, for example, the classification of Germans either as 'politically not acceptable' or 'politically acceptable' was supplemented by an intermediate classification, 'acceptable with a change of office'. This helped to overcome many staffing bottlenecks.

On the whole, the denazification procedures brought a multitude of problems with them. On the one hand, the removal of all incriminated persons caused serious personnel shortages, and not only at the higher levels; on the other hand, for example, the internment camps in which, by the spring of 1946, far in excess of 100,000 Germans subject to 'automatic arrest' were detained, were not conducive to the Western Powers' aim of re-educating the Germans in democracy.

Denazification efforts were carried out most consistently in the Soviet Zone, where the aim was a radical purging of former Nazis and their replacement with a new elite as part of an 'anti-fascist, democratic' revolution. However, from 1947 onwards, the focus here also shifted towards rehabilitation, particularly in the case of mere NSDAP followers. The judicial system was to deal extensively with the crimes of the activists – but were there enough politically-untainted judges?

As early as September 1945, the Soviet military administration had ordered the establishment of a democratic judicial system in which there was to be no place for former NS jurists. Almost 90 per cent of legal personnel were fired as a result. In order to quickly fill the vacuum this created, laymen received crash courses in the administration of justice in so-called 'Volksrichterschulen' (schools for the training of people's judges).

A policy introduced by the British military administration and which stated that up to 50 per cent of judges and public prosecutors in the British Zone could be former NSDAP members took a far more pragmatic line. This clause, which became known as the 'piggyback procedure' at the time, had the advantage that for every 'clean' judge installed in office, one judge with a tainted record, who had been a member of the Party, could also be appointed.

On the whole, however, interest in denazification, particularly on the part of the Allies, had already perceptibly waned by the end of 1947. The purge from the outside, also referred to as 'the Nuremberg of the man on the street' in reference to the Nuremberg War Trials of the leading Nazis, had failed. Responsibility was soon turned over to the newly-founded federal states and the denazification committees they created specifically for this purpose. With dubious success.

Many Germans were still of the opinion that on the whole, National Socialism had not in itself been a bad thing; it had just been badly applied.

And these Germans were now responsible for organizing their own denazification.

But ultimately, all efforts to separate the decent Germans from the bad Nazis and the decent Nazis from the bad Germans failed. There was hardly anyone willing to give incriminating evidence. On the other hand, there was no shortage of persons willing to provide others with affidavits of innocence. The Germans felt that they had been punished enough by losing the War. There was no room for feelings of guilt, for a desire to atone or for shame.

The prevailing view was that the 'real culprits' should be punished, but that innocent believers in the Nazi cause should merely be dismissed 'in Gnaden' (without loss of honour). The real culprits were the high-profile Party functionaries, the Nazi criminals, the concentration-camp butchers, not the Party cell and block leaders, its treasurers and Unterführer, who had, after all, only wanted 'the best for Germany and the German people'. And the Nazis' accomplices in leading positions, too – the officers, the business managers, the bureaucrats, the professors and the jurists – all fell through the holes in the loosely-woven net of the denazification process.

Those who took upon themselves the mammoth task of self-cleansing – the representatives of the newly-established political parties – were untainted, but overwhelmed by its magnitude, and those who were already once again employing their legal expertise for the 'German cause' in the denazification tribunals and boards of appeal were above all united by a common desire to finally draw a line under their National Socialist past.

Unsurprisingly, many judges, masters of adaptability and opportunism who were now entrusted with the business of 'wrapping up' the past, took a positivist view of the task of 'cleansing' assigned to them and saw it primarily as an opportunity to salvage their own careers – and those of their fellow jurists.

They did their level best to ensure that no colleague was left without a job. Persons who had been issued with a certificate of exoneration were considered as no longer compromised. Persons who had meted out draconian punishments and handed down death sentences under Hitler were not necessarily National Socialists. After all, had they not merely been enforcing valid law? And surely no-one could condemn them as criminals for adhering to the law? In the years that followed, this argumentation would acquire the power of a legal conviction whenever the role of the Nazi judiciary came under scrutiny – which was seldom enough the case.

Many former Nazi jurists argued that they had merely been doing their duty and had in fact saved Germany from even worse misery. This stock defence had already been used, and with some success, in the Nuremberg Judges' Trial.

On 17 February 1947, in the third of twelve trials against major war criminals before US military courts, sixteen German jurists and lawyers stood charged with war crimes, crimes against humanity and membership of criminal organizations. For the prosecution, these men were 'the embodiment of what passed for justice in the Third Reich' and represented the entire German legal system under the Nazis. The leading perpetrators, of course, could no longer be held to account: Reich Minister of Justice Gürtner had died in 1941, his successor Thierack committed suicide in a British internment camp in 1946, and the President of the Reichsgericht, Bumke, had also committed suicide when the US Army entered Leipzig in 1945.

Sixteen prominent representatives of the German legal system against whom adequate evidence had been gathered were now indicted. For the Reich Ministry of Justice, former undersecretary and provisional Reich Minister of Justice Dr Franz Schlegelberger, the highest-ranking defendant, and the two undersecretaries Curt Rothenberger and Ernst Klemm, public prosecutor Joël and three other ministry officials. One mistrial was declared due to illness, and one defendant committed suicide before the trial began. Also indicted were the former Oberreichsanwalt at the Volksgerichtshof, Ernst Lautz, and senior public prosecutor Paul Barnickel, three chief justices from the special courts in Nuremberg and Stuttgart, Günther Nebelung, President of the Fourth Senate of the Volksgerichtshof, and a lay judge, also from the Volksgerichtshof.

In this trial, all defendants stood charged as representatives of the entire system. The purpose of the Judges' Trial was not to prove individual deeds – although these were examined in detail – but to show that to the end, the German judiciary had been part of and complicit in the National Socialist reign of terror. The main charges were 'judicial murder and other atrocities, which they committed by destroying law and justice in Germany and then utilizing the emptied forms of legal process for persecution, enslavement and extermination on a major scale', as the prosecution put it.

The evidence heard in the trial was just as devastating for the German judiciary as for the individual defendants. While some were indeed fanatical National Socialists like Freisler or Thierack, others were typical conservative representatives of the German legal system, a fact which only served to underscore how closely it was intertwined with the brown-shirted terror regime. They were revealed as the very type of compliant jurists without whom the Nazi regime could not have survived.

Altogether, the testimony of 138 witnesses was heard and more than 2,000 motions to take evidence were submitted. The proceedings lasted ten months, during which the tribunal examined in detail the misdeeds of the judicial system, the 'Night and Fog Decrees', the Criminal Law Decree for Poles and Jews, the cooperation between the courts and the SS and Gestapo. The prosecution finally concluded:

> The defendants are charged with crimes of such immensity that mere specific instances of criminality appear insignificant by comparison. The charge, in brief, is that of conscious participation in a nationwide, government-organized system of cruelty and injustice, in violation of the laws of war and of humanity, and perpetrated in the name of law by the authority of the Ministry of Justice and through the instrumentality of the courts. The dagger of the assassin was concealed beneath the robe of the jurist.

Schlegelberger, whom the tribunal referred to as a 'tragic figure', based his defence on the claim that he had remained at his post only in order to prevent worse misery, an argument also used by the other defendants in the Judges' Trial and which was to be proffered by many other Nazi perpetrators in the years that followed. The court pronounced judgement on 3 and 4 December 1947: Schlegelberger, Klemm and two other defendants were sentenced to lifelong imprisonment, the others received prison terms of between five and ten years. Mild sentences for desk-murderers and henchmen in blood-red robes – nor were they enforced with rigour. Almost all of those convicted were granted early release from prison. Schlegenberger himself was released in 1951.

Although the Nuremberg Judges' Trial was one of the few attempts, perhaps even the most earnest, to shed light on and condemn the justice system in the Third Reich, the prosecution of the acts of injustice committed by the NS judiciary had failed. And even more than that: the Trial had no purifying effect on German jurists. On the contrary: many dismissed the Nuremberg Trials as evidence of 'victor's justice and a thirst for retribution' at work and were in solidarity with their colleagues. After all, had they not all simply been doing their duty?

The majority thought like their colleague, former navy judge and later Minister President of the state of Baden-Wuerttemberg Hans Karl Filbinger, who in later years defended himself with the same argument used by all former Nazi jurists: 'What was lawful then cannot be unlawful today'.

In such an atmosphere, jurists were hardly likely to develop any pangs of conscience about their complicity in the crimes of the Nazi regime. They placed the responsibility squarely on the shoulders of the political leadership. As early as 1947, in a speech at the convention of German jurists, criminal law professor Eberhard Schmidt – one of the leading teachers of law in post-war Germany – had already phrased the appropriate rationalisation:

> It was not the judicial system, but the legislature which departed from the path of the law. And neither the world of jurisprudence nor the judicial system can be held accountable for the consequences today. The blame must be laid solely at the door of a legislature which had lost all foundation in law.

This argument was not a new one. Judges under the Weimar Republic had claimed to be servants not of the Republic, but of the 'state', and in the same way, the former judges of the Third Reich no longer saw themselves as accomplices of the Nazis, claiming that they had only served the state. It is an undisputed fact that the majority of judges were members of the Nazi Party or of the National Socialist Association of German Legal Professionals. But denazification was no longer a priority, and there was no longer any stigma associated with having been a 'nominal' Party member.

Did they really have any other option? In the end, hadn't they all wanted no more than to be allowed to pursue their careers within the judicial system? Hadn't they merely been fulfilling their duty as judges, as public prosecutors, as magistrates? A judge who claimed to have been acting solely for the good of the state was above reproach. Or, to put it in other words: even the most fervent supporter of the Nazis might have had noble intentions.

Even Nazi jurists who had played a particularly prominent role in Hitler's Germany had no cause to fear for their careers in the post-war years. Thousands of politically-compromised judges were not only spared but reinstated, and were soon once again dispensing justice as presidents of the Landesgerichte and Oberlandesgerichte or in positions in the ministries of justice. This was a generation of judges with little interest in coming to terms with Germany's recent history, which was hardly surprising, as many judges had served the Nazi terror regime and should by rights have first undergone a denazification process. But it was a case of 'honour among thieves': you don't pick out my eyes, and I won't pick out yours.

The dilemma of the early days of the Weimar Republic now repeated itself: it was deemed impossible to establish a functioning administration and justice system in post-war Germany without drawing on the expertise of those who had formerly served the Nazi regime. There was no determined effort to break with the past and engage in a political fresh start.

Even a man like Thomas Dehler, who had been expelled from the civil service by the Nazis for his Jewish connections and was now liberal Justice Minister in Adenauer's cabinet, in a speech at the opening ceremony for Germany's new supreme court, the Bundesgerichtshof, on 8 October 1950, spoke of the 'outstanding achievements of the Reichsgericht' and expressed a hope that 'the spirit of this court will also permeate the work of the Bundesgerichtshof'. In the same vein, his undersecretary Dr Georg Petersen wrote in the commemorative publication that it was the goal of the Federal government 'to appoint to the Bundesgerichtshof former members of the Reichsgericht who are familiar with its tradition'.

Both institutional and staffing continuity had thus been ensured. Jurists who had been willing accomplices of the Nazi regime were now employed by the Ministry of Justice in Bonn. They included Dr Josef Schafheutle, who in 1933 had been responsible for special political criminal law in the Reichsjustizministerium and thus one of Freisler's most industrious collaborators, or Dr Ernst Kanter, a former judge at the Reichskriegsgericht who became a military judge in occupied Denmark and was involved in handing down death sentences there. Kanter's Nazi past by no means hindered his post-war career: in 1958, he was appointed President of the Third Criminal Senate of the Bundesgerichtshof.

Then again, why should things have been any different in the Ministry of Justice? Almost two-thirds of those employed by the Auswärtige Amt (Federal Foreign Office), for example, were former National Socialists and were now responsible for German foreign policy.

Adenauer appeased critics with the argument that 'You can't build a foreign office if you don't at least have people in senior positions who understand something about earlier history'. For example, men like his chief aide Dr Hans Globke, who had been involved in drafting the Law for the Protection of German Blood and German Honour and the Law for the Protection of the Hereditary Health of the German People, passed in 1935, and was the author of an interpretation of the Nuremberg race laws. As an expert on 'racial defilement', he had also attended the Wannsee Conference in 1945, at which the 'Endlösung', the final solution to the Jewish Question, was discussed. This prominent role under the Nazis was now followed by a meteoric career in post-war Germany.

A vast number of former Nazi supporters continued their dubious careers in the Federal Republic under Adenauer. For example, Dr Friedrich Karl Vialon, who, in the Reich Commissariat for the Eastern Territories, had been responsible for the confiscation of Jewish property and handing the Jews over for forced labour. He later became an undersecretary, first in the Federal Ministry of Finance and then in the Federal Chancellery. Or Dr Heinz-Paul Baldus, who had conscientiously 'carried out his duties' in the legal department of the Führer's Chancellery. He, too, became a prominent judge in post-war Germany: president of a senate at the Bundesgerichtshof.

Yet another man with a tainted past who succeeded in becoming one of the highest-ranking jurists in the Federal Republic was Wolfgang Fränkel. As a ruthless Nazi jurist in the Third Reich, he had been instrumental in ensuring that harsher punishments were meted out to Jewish, Polish, Czech and French defendants. This did no damage to his post-war career: in 1962, he was appointed Chief Federal Prosecutor. Fränkel did not hesitate to accept the office, despite the fact that his active involvement in the Nazi legal system must have cast doubt on his political and moral credibility.

But then again, why should he? In interviews with the press following his appointment, he painted himself as a staunch opponent of dictatorship in any form. And there was little protest. Although the East German authorities had compiled a dossier containing irrefutable documentary evidence of his National Socialist past, when it came to raking through the ashes of the past, the Federal Republic was reluctant to accept assistance from East German courts. The Cold War thus offered an ideal smoke screen into which the perpetrators of the past could vanish.

And when it came to 'Vergangenheitsbewältigung' (coming to terms with the past), after the 'Waldheim Trials' in 1950, the justice system of the German Democratic Republic (GDR) was hardly a suitable role model for democratically-minded jurists in West Germany. In these summary hearings, quite in the style of Nazi justice, numerous death sentences were handed down to former National Socialists. Defendants were denied fundamental rights. They had no legal counsel, and no evidence was examined. Witnesses for the defence were not heard. The public were excluded from all but a few show trials. Most of the accused had been hangers-on rather than fervent Nazis, a fact which did not interest the new East German public prosecutors and judges. The most frequent charges were 'crimes against humanity' and 'fundamental support' of the Hitler regime. The majority of the defendants received prison sentences of ten years or more, and twenty-four were executed on the night of 3/4 November 1950.

But the 'Waldheim Trials' were not the only example showing how the 'Sozialistische Einheitspartei Deutschlands' (SED) used the East German judicial system as an instrument of its apparatus of power. Proceedings in the courtrooms of the newly-established Socialist 'workers' and farmers' state' – and not only in the case of political crimes – were frequently Stalinist show trials incompatible with the rule of law. The accused had few rights, there were no independent lawyers, public prosecutors abused the courtroom as an ideological tribune, judges handed down sentences dictated in advance by the SED and the Staatssicherheit (East German Ministry for State Security). This was not an independent judiciary.

'Criminal justice should be a political act', stated Hilde Benjamin, ruthless judge in many East German show trials. Together with Dr Ernst Melzheimer, first state prosecutor of the GDR (who had already rendered obedient service as a Kammergerichtsrat under the Nazis), she was one of the most fanatical defenders of SED dogma. Like her predecessors in the Volksgerichtshof years before, she subjected defendants to tirades of abuse or shouted them down. Her propensity for handing down death sentences marked her out for bigger and better things: she was East Germany's Minister of Justice until 1967. In other words, the judicial system in the GDR was neither suitable as a role model nor as a partner for the West German courts. A stroke of luck for the many Nazi criminals whose files were now held under lock and key in East Germany and who could therefore gaily devote themselves to their post-war careers without fear of prosecution.

German careers in the legal system, in politics, business, science or the civil service – the pages of this book would not suffice to list the names of all the Nazi criminals and accomplices who were quickly reinstated in key positions under the Adenauer government. There was very little protest against this process of 're-nazification'. On the contrary: the majority of Germans were eager to forget the Third Reich, as were their elected political representatives. Not only Adenauer in the 1950s, but also later West German politicians frequently trotted out pithy statements calling on their compatriots to 'draw a line under this endless rehashing of the past', for example Bavarian Minister President Franz-Josef Strauss, who early on had stated that the process of trying to come to terms with the past was a 'long-term project of penance' and that the Germans were 'a normal nation which had had the ill fortune to have bad politicians at its head'. Hitler as an unfortunate glitch in history?

Strauss and many others appealed to the Germans to 'step out from under Hitler's shadow'. They were vociferous in their portrayal of 'Germans as victims' and in their demand for mutual and general reconciliation, as if there had been not both perpetrators and victims, but only victims. The Germans as a collectively betrayed people?

The historical misrepresentation of the Germans as 'Hitler's victims', the Third Reich as the work of a band of thugs, was a strange but extremely convenient version of affairs, and it was one which was not only put forward by conservative politicians in self-justification.

Soon, even former members of the SS were once again able to hold their heads high in German society, former concentration-camp guards could exonerate themselves on the basis of having acted under 'superior orders' and the new German national anthem became 'We had no knowledge of what was going on'. People were still attempting to play down the monstrous nature of the NS regime: the rubble of the War had only just been cleared aside, but already many, possibly even the majority of Germans were thinking 'It wasn't all bad . . .'.

In the few, usually long drawn-out, trials of former Nazis, for example the proceedings against former personnel of the concentration camps of Majdanek and Auschwitz, where hundreds of thousands had been murdered, judicial authorities and courts showed little interest in the prosecution and punishment of the guilty. These major post-war trials in particular often turned into a farce as examples of criminal proceedings. It was extremely difficult to produce proof that the defendants had been guilty of specific murders – a mandatory prerequisite for a conviction. The witnesses were dead, and the perpetrators argued again and again that they had only been following orders. The presiding judges often showed particular leniency towards Nazi criminals, especially when it came to sentencing. Often, years passed before a verdict could be announced. A macabre saying did the rounds among prosecutors: 'The average sentence works out at about ten minutes per victim.'

But it was not only concentration-camp personnel who could count on lenient treatment. The dubious '131 Law', passed with a large majority by the German parliament in 1951 and referred to by the German supreme court as 'socially necessary', guaranteed former National Socialists reinstatement by the Federal Republic, or at least the right to claim generous retirement benefits. As a result, 'men of expertise and experience' who had formerly served the Nazi regime soon found their way back into key positions in business and industry, at universities, in the German army or the judicial system. And while the '131 Law' was applied with vigour from the start, there was no great hurry to recompense the victims. It was not until five years later that a Bundesentschädigungsgesetz (German Restitution Law) was passed, subjecting all claimants to an embarrassing procedure.

Due to a lack of implementing provisions, the victims of the Nazi regime were only entitled to receive compensation if they could prove that they had not committed any crime, had never aided and abetted a tyrannical regime, never violated United Nations or international law – and had never been a member of any National Socialist organization. The reinstated and generously-remunerated former Nazis, on the other hand, had to furnish no such proof. Those falling under the '131 Law' had to be provided for, independent of their financial circumstances. Those caught in the net of the denazification process had no reason to fear the loss of their privileges as civil servants. Appointments and promotions between 1933 and 1945 were also taken into account, albeit with restrictions. These restrictions, however, did not apply to the signing of death sentences, but merely to cases where civil service regulations had been violated.

In this way, an entire generation of jurists took early retirement with generous benefits, perpetrators in robes who saw themselves as free from guilt and as having successfully 'come to terms with' their National Socialist – and often personal – past history. 'The demise of the rule of law has been not so much confronted as gilded over', as Rolf Lamprecht sarcastically put it in the magazine *Der Spiegel*.

'We have to get the machinery running again', Adenauer had said. And indeed, it was running. In his book *The Second Guilt, or the Burden of Being German*, publicist Ralph Giordano impressively described the comprehensive, collective repression of the Nazi past as the socio-psychological foundation for reconstruction in the Federal Republic under Adenauer. For former Nazi party members and hangers-on, the historically-distorting formula 'We were the victims of Hitler' had its practical value, and not only in the era of the denazification tribunals. Almost all Germans – with the exception of a very small minority – saw themselves as victims. No-one was willing to admit to having been actively involved, having aided the Nazis, having stood by or looked the other way. In his powerful psychological analysis *Die verklemmte Nation – Zur Seelenlage der Deutschen*, Heleno Saña writes: 'They refused to admit even to themselves with what alacrity they had followed the Nazis; not only at the start, but also later, when there could no longer be any doubt where Hitler and his supporters were heading.'

The year 1945 marked the beginning of an era in which in public life, Germany could not deny the atrocities that had been committed under the Nazi regime. In their private lives, however, most Germans found the constant reminders of the Third Reich almost insulting. Adenauer reinforced them in this defensive stance. And so the great 'act of reinstatement of the perpetrators' (Giordano) was able to proceed without notable protest.

This was particularly true of and within the judicial system. After the War, all over the Federal Republic, almost without exception, judges and public prosecutors who had held office up to 1945 took up where they left off. Was there no alternative to this staffing continuity?

In the FRG, in contrast to the GDR, it had been decided that everyone should be involved in the social and political reconstruction. Including the perpetrators of the Third Reich. Including the jurists. The darkest chapter of German history thus ended with 'comprehensive social rehabilitation', as Jörg Friedrich put it.

This also answers the question of why the process of bringing Nazi criminals to justice got off to such a slow start and was pursued with such obvious disinterest in the years that followed. Little effort was made to track down and prosecute the innumerable Nazi war criminals, even less so if the perpetrator in question was a fellow judge. The legal system did not instigate investigations; it merely reacted on the basis of allegations brought to its attention. And it was now far too busy prosecuting thieves and con-men in the new Germany of the 'economic miracle' to bother about the Nazi judges or concentration-camp murderers of Hitler Germany. For the post-war German legal system, it seemed that the past was just that: over and done with. Hand in hand, politicians and jurists were engaged in a highly questionable 'clearing-up exercise'. In their soapbox speeches, of course, they distanced themselves from the National Socialists, and there were indeed a few symbolic gestures such as the scandalously lengthy Auschwitz trials, but it cannot be maintained that any serious effort to prosecute the crimes of the Nazi past was ever made.

The statistics illustrate this: between 1945 and 1965, public prosecutors in the Federal Republic instituted proceedings against a total of 61,716 persons suspected of involvement in Nazi war crimes. A mere 10 per cent – 6,115 – ended with convictions, and the perpetrators were frequently granted early release after serving only a few years in prison.

Moreover, not a single former member of the Volksgerichtshof can be found among these convicted war criminals. The role of this terror tribunal as a Nazi institution had not been examined at the Nuremberg War Trials and even now, when it was left to the Germans to cast light on one of the darkest chapters in the history of its judiciary and bring the remaining blood judges to justice, the necessary steps were not taken.

The only case which offered an opportunity to escape from the shadow of the past was that of former Kammergerichtsrat Hans Joachim Rehse, the most incriminated Volksgerichtshof judge – after Freisler. Investigation of Rehse, a former associate judge in Freisler's First Senate, where he served on the bench from 1941 to 1945, began in 1962. The Munich public prosecutor's office had already investigated him, but declined to prosecute with the common justification that it could not be proven that the accused had had the wilful intent to kill.

Two days later, Dr Robert M. W. Kempner, former Chief Prosecutor in the Nuremberg War Trials, filed criminal charges with the public prosecutor's office in Berlin against Rehse and all those involved in the persecution of the members of the 20 July conspiracy. A ruthless jurist, Rehse was responsible for handing down at least 231 death sentences at the Volksgerichtshof. Now, on 20 January 1967, the public prosecutor brought charges against him before the Berlin regional court based on seven of these cases. Rehse was indicted on three counts of murder and four of attempted murder, committed by him through independent actions and 'for base motives' in 1943 and 1944 by voting for the death sentence as an associate judge of the Volksgerichtshof in seven trials, three of which sentences had been demonstrably carried out.

On 3 July 1967, the Berlin regional court found the former blood judge guilty of being an accomplice to murder in three cases and an accomplice to attempted murder in a further four and sentenced him to a total of five years' imprisonment. Although in the opinion of the court, the actual perpetrator of the Volksgerichtshof murders was Freisler, who exerted a 'dominant influence' on the First Senate, assessor Rehse had failed to express criticism of the judgements and had deferred to Freisler's authority. The court found that as 'a fully qualified jurist who could be expected to have a sense of what constituted fair sentencing policy', Rehse 'should have recognized the illegal nature of his actions'. Both the public prosecutor's office and Rehse himself subsequently lodged an appeal against the court's ruling.

On 30 April 1968, the Fifth Criminal Division of the Bundesgerichtshof overturned the judgement in a statement comprising only two pages and referred the case back to the lower court for retrial. The Bundesgerichtshof ruling essentially turned on the question of whether Rehse was to be considered as a perpetrator or an accomplice. This time, in contrast to the usual practice in other NS trials, Rehse had been charged not with being an accomplice in but with being an accessory to legal murder. And in the opinion of the judges of the Bundesgerichtshof, this meant that 'the accused can only be convicted if he can be proved to have voted for the death penalty for nefarious reasons'.

The ruling further stated that the Berlin regional court had wrongly concluded that the key issue was Freisler's motives and whether Rehse had been aware of them but nevertheless failed to protest.

On 6 December 1968, the former blood judge Rehse was acquitted in a retrial before a different chamber of the Berlin regional court, presided over by Kammergerichtsrat Oske. Even more macabre than the exoneration of this grisly caricature of a servant of justice were the concluding statements of the young Kammergerichtsrat, who instead of citing, with regret, the ruling of the Federal Court of Justice, as might have been expected, staunchly and assertively stated that this was a test case in which it was important to finally underscore that the actions of the courts in the Third Reich were fully concordant with the 'exceptional circumstances' of that time. Oske stated that 'in no case was it ascertained that any one of the seven judges of the Volksgerichtshof deliberately perverted justice'. One of those judges was Freisler, and Rehse was his assessor. In his concluding statements, Oske said: 'Every state, even a totalitarian state, has the right to assert itself. It cannot be reproached for having resorted to unusual and dissuasive measures in a time of crisis.'

These death sentences handed down for telling an anti-Nazi joke, for making a careless comment about the Führer, these barbaric sentences for violation of the Law for the Protection of German Blood or showing compassion for a humiliated Polish 'foreign labourer' – were all these merciless judgements to be discounted as nothing more than an expression of 'the right of the state to assert itself?'

This was the acquittal not only of one man, but of the entire Volksgerichtshof and the entire legal system of the Third Reich. Rehse left the courtroom vindicated. The court had confirmed that as a Nazi jurist, he had not been guilty of any crime, but had simply been doing his duty. The public prosecutor lodged an appeal, but former blood judge Rehse died before the case was re-examined, and the court's ruling stood unchallenged.

Robert M. W. Kempner, however, was not prepared to accept this general absolution for the Volksgerichtshof. On 18 March 1979, he filed a further action with the Berlin public prosecutor's office against 'all persons suspected of participation in trials at the Nazi Volksgerichtshof after 20 July 1944 or, where applicable, before that date'. However, this case, too, was soon dropped on the grounds of the previous rulings. Kempner refused to give up and found an ally in the then Berlin senator of justice, Gerhard Meyer. In October 1979, the public prosecutor's office resumed its investigations before the regional court. Would it be possible to bring at least some of the 570 members of the Volksgerichtshof, the 67 judges and public prosecutors who were still living, before a court?

Meyer supported Kempner because he, too, was convinced that the assessment of the Volksgerichtshof as a 'regular' court of law had nothing to do with the historical truth. Once again, post-war jurists engaged in a legal battle: the Federal Court of Justice had ruled that a judge could only be convicted of murder if it was simultaneously proved that he had perverted justice.

This was a virtually impossible task. The former Nazi jurists maintained that they had acted in accordance with the valid law at the time, refusing to accept the notion that the regime, the legislature and the laws it passed were criminal. Did this mean that it would never be possible to render the Nazi jurists accountable for the consequences of their actions as long as they could credibly claim to have been subjectively convinced of the legality of the judicial system they served? Did this mean that a Nazi judge could not have committed a crime as long as he was convinced that he was simply following the will of the state as legislator? Did these legal positivist arguments excuse all perversions of justice under the Nazis? Could judges who had sentenced people to death for telling political jokes really get off scot-free?

They could and they did. On 26 October 1986, following seven years of investigation – during which time almost half of the defendants died of old age – the Berlin prosecutor's office finally closed the books on the matter.

Meyer's successor, West Berlin justice senator Rupert Scholz, announced that there would be no further action taken against members of the Volksgerichtshof. In his personal opinion, this was 'unsatisfactory and extremely regrettable for anyone who believes in justice'. Euphemistic and mollifying words for what publicist Walter Boehlich referred to at the time as 'a catastrophe and an unbelievable travesty of justice'.

Yet again, the Volksgerichtshof, the figurehead of a system of injustice, had once again escaped being placed in the dock, although the Berlin prosecutor's office had been hard at work, putting together 113 ring binders full of sentencing documents, 59 containing personnel files, 85 ring binders with background material and 150 volumes of material generated by the investigations. When the Berlin prosecutors put away their files – which, in the words of the *Frankfurter Allgemeine Zeitung*, represented 'a painful but welcome final act of closure', it could not be said that they had not done their best. The irreparable failings and errors committed by the judicial system in the years immediately following the war were to blame. German judges had been far too preoccupied with sentencing low-ranking members of the Communist Party to deal with their Nazi colleagues. Things would have taken a completely different course if a court had come to a conclusion in those years which the German parliament had also taken years to reach.

On 25 January 1985, in an unusual show of unity, the Bundestag declared that 'the institution known as the "Volksgerichtshof" had not been a court as defined by rule of law, but rather an instrument of terror for the implementation of arbitrary National Socialist rule'.

This declaration had been prompted over two years before. In the closing credits to the film *The White Rose*, which told the story of a student resistance cell in Munich, it stated that the Bundesgerichtshof had still not annulled the judgements brought against the members of the White Rose group. This was vehemently denied by Gerd Pfeiffer, then President of the Bundesgerichtshof, who pointed out that the sentences had indeed been annulled: partly under the law in the occupied zones, partly by legislation of the German Länder which had become federal law in 1949, and partly as a result of retrials in individual cases. The film credits were subsequently revised and supplemented. But the debate was far from over.

The SPD (Social Democratic) parliamentary group in the Bundestag called on the federal legislature to repudiate the sentences pronounced by the Volksgerichtshof. The Federal Ministry of Justice – at the time led by the Social Democrats – replied that it was not possible to nullify judgements handed down by a legal system that no longer existed. The ministry also stated that it was necessary to take a more differentiated view, in particular when it came to the early years of the Volkgerichtshof, pointing out that untainted witnesses confirmed that some senates had indeed given defendants the benefit of the doubt. However, the Social Democrats in the German parliament refused to back down and demanded that the Bundestag at least should distance itself from the Volksgerichtshof.

And they succeeded. In accordance with a guideline from the legal committee, the members of the federal parliament – from Christian Democrats to Greens – agreed that the decisions of the tribunal had no 'Rechtswirkung' (legal effect). The term 'Rechtswirkung' had been the subject of lively debate. Firstly because, as the legal committee argued, the decisions of the Volksgerichtshof no longer had any legal effect; secondly, because the Bundestag, as a parliament, was not competent to adjudicate in the matter; and thirdly, because the Volksgerichtshof had in some, albeit few, cases, pronounced verdicts of not guilty, which would now, by the same token, also be 'legally invalid'. This was why Minister of Justice Hans Engelhardt was particularly prominent in opposing the annulment of sentences passed by the Volksgerichtshof and the special courts. A grotesque argumentation, but one which convinced the legal committee. And so it was agreed that none of the sentences would be repealed, but that the German parliament would dissociate itself from the sentencing policy and declare that the sentences had no 'legal effect'. The politicians were prepared to distance themselves symbolically from the perversion of justice under the Nazis, but not to pass any clarifying law.

And anyway, the Bundestag resolution had no effect on criminal prosecution in Germany – as the acquittal of Rehse and other trials had already shown. The mills of justice ground even more slowly than those of God, and Nazi jurists were seldom caught up in them.

The crimes of Rehse and other blood judges, these murderers in robes, went unpunished because to punish them would have meant having to take action against a large number of judges of the special courts and courts martial as well. It would have triggered an avalanche. Jörg Friedrich, radio journalist and author, wrote: 'Judge Rehse of the People's Court could not have committed murder, for this would have meant that the judicial system of West Germany had been established by murderers in their hundreds.' However, that indeed was the shameful truth.

Apparently, no-one was bothered by the fact that seriously-tainted former Volksgerichtshof judges were back on the bench in the Federal Republic and frequently held prominent positions.

For example, Dr Paul Reimers, judge at the Volksgerichtshof, involved in handing down 124 death sentences, and Otto Rahmeyer, prosecutor at the Volksgerichtshof, with shared responsibility for at least 78 death sentences. After the War, these two executioners became regional court judges in Ravensburg, where they served in the German legal system until 1963.

Other former Nazi jurists who resumed their careers in post-War Germany were; Dr Gerhard Lehnhardt, prosecutor at the Volksgerichtshof, with shared responsibility for at least forty-seven death sentences and higher regional court judge in Neustadt an der Weinstrasse until 1960; Dr Helmut Jaeger, senior public prosecutor at the Volksgerichtshof, with shared responsibility for at least four death sentences and a judge at the Munich higher regional court until 1966; Dr Kurt Naucke, senior public prosecutor at the Volksgerichtshof, with shared responsibility for at least nineteen death sentences and later a senior public prosecutor in Hanover; Walter Roemer, senior public prosecutor and administrator at the Volksgerichtshof, with shared responsibility for at least twenty-five death sentences, including those against Alexander Schmorell and Professor Kurt Huber from the White Rose resistance group. Roemer also supervised executions at the Munich Stadelheim prison. On 11 August 1944, he reported: 'Convict Willibrand Bradl – calculated from the moment the prisoner left his cell, the execution took one minute and thirteen seconds. Signed ppa. Roemer, Senior Public Prosecutor.' This executioner with a stopwatch promptly resumed his career after the War: as a director and head of department in the West German Ministry of Justice.

Neither was the career of Johannes Lorenz – regional court director at the Volksgerichtshof and with shared responsibility for at least three death sentences – in any way hindered by his tainted past: he served as a supreme court judge in West Berlin until 1979.

Edmund Stark, a Volksgerichtshof prosecutor who shared responsibility for at least fifty death sentences, found employment in the idyllic city of Ravensburg, as did his colleagues Reimers and Rahmeyer, and worked as a regional court director until 1968. Dr Paul Emmerich, who was a regional court judge in Berlin and under the senior Reich prosecutor at the Volksgerichtshof and also supervised executions, rose to the position of regional court director in Saarbrücken before retiring with a generous pension. These were not isolated cases. The judicial system of the Federal Republic of Germany failed to confront the legacy of its Nazi past.

Acquittals for former Nazi jurists were not the exception, but the rule. Injustice was routinely legitimized, inhumane sentences were declared 'valid under rule of law' or as 'just about acceptable'. Three cases – three among many – will serve as examples here:

In the proceedings against the former judge of a special court in Kassel who had sentenced a man to death for 'racial defilement', the Kassel regional court found on 28 March 1952 that it was 'necessary to take into consideration the special circumstances of war', which created 'an atmosphere of sensitivity towards law-breakers of any kind'. The court ruled that no 'error of law' had been committed at the time. At a hearing in 1950, the judge, the chairman of the special court, again defended his actions: 'I stand by the sentence I handed down at the time.' And the court agreed with him, stating that 'the application of the blood-protection law was without a doubt the correct procedure at the time', and that the special court judges had in no way 'departed from the German tradition of an immaculate judiciary'. Such loyalty to tradition deserved to be rewarded. The verdict: acquittal.

On 23 April 1960, the regional court in Ansbach re-examined events which had taken place near the Franconian village of Brettheim in the last stages of the war, just a few hours before the arrival of the American troops. In a militarily hopeless situation, the mayor and the local Nazi Party leader had refused to sign a death sentence as judges in a summary court martial. Their refusal cost them their lives; they, too, were executed immediately. The regional court in Ansbach found that the two men had acted contrary to their duty, because 'in aiding and abetting the previous perpetrators, they had attempted to cripple and subvert the will of the village population and thus that of the German people to defend itself'. In other words, in the eyes of the post-war jurists, the execution of the two men was not legally objectionable.

Equally, the regional court in Berlin found little fault with the trial of the conspirators of the 20 July conspiracy before the Volksgerichtshof tribunal. Although the death sentences had already been decided on before the proceedings began, in 1971, the Berlin judges saw no evidence 'that the executed members of the resistance movement, disregarding the fact that only minimal procedural requirements were observed and that they were therefore sentenced to death in a sham trial, were murdered'. Three examples – three among thousands.

More than 16,000 death sentences were handed down by the criminal courts in Nazi Germany, and more than two-thirds of these defendants were executed. The military courts passed more than 30,000 death sentences. A comparison with other periods in the history of the German judiciary system reveals how significant these figures are: in the period between 1907 and 1932, a total of 1,547 death sentences were passed in Germany: 377 of the convicted were executed.

Prior to 1933, only three offences carried the death penalty. In 1944, a death sentence could be imposed for more than forty crimes. And fanatical judges had no scruples about sending the accused to their deaths: between 1941 and 1945 alone, German criminal courts handed down approximately 15,000 death sentences, in most cases in trials held before the special tribunals and the Volksgerichtshof. However, these judges had nothing to fear after the War. On the contrary: in almost all legal proceedings against members of the Nazi judiciary, the defendants could rely on receiving particularly sensitive and understanding treatment from their colleagues. Virtually no sentence was arbitrary or barbaric enough that it was not legitimized by 'the law applicable at the time'.

Hampered investigations, generous understanding, lenient sentences, numerous acquittals – all characteristic of the legal system in post-war Germany when it came to the activities of jurists in the Third Reich. The mantra of 'no awareness of having been guilty of wrongdoing' became a 'get-out-of-jail-free card' for the former Nazi legal professionals. The strong *esprit de corps* among jurists ensured them the support of their fellow judges. And the majority of the German population was in agreement with this lax treatment. The West German legal system was therefore acting in accordance with the prevailing sentiments of the people. That judges were not called to account under criminal law for their crimes was just one element in the overall process of collective denial.

And today – seventy years after the end of the Nazi regime? Even now, those who were involved at the time, accomplices and hangers-on, still attempt to gloss over, misrepresent and play down the role of the judiciary in the Third Reich. They still insist on the distinction between the upright, conservative jurists (who after all, were only doing their duty and frequently prevented even worse things from happening) and the Nazis in judge's robes (the group which alone was responsible for the criminal side of the system of justice in the National Socialist era). A foolish distinction, used since the 'Stunde Null' as a justification for the uncomfortable fact that it was in the main precisely those conservative jurists who, with their 'blind positivism' were responsible for creating the preconditions in which legal culture could be eradicated and perverted by the Nazis in the first place.

It is a fact that of the thousands of jurists working within the legal system under the Nazis, only a minority were sworn National Socialists. The vast majority, however, secured and guaranteed the power of the Hitler dictatorship. Yet despite the fact that the jurists were compliant in implementing the political dictates of the National Socialist regime, Hitler was far from satisfied with the legal system.

His attitude to law and the judiciary was always characterized by a strong aversion, resulting from his fear that laws and the courts would restrict his scope of action. But instead of opposing him, the jurists became the accomplices of the Hitler regime. Laws and ordinances were abrogated or enacted as the Nazis saw fit, but no matter how legally incapacitating and abusive they were, the majority of jurists followed the Führer and the Party – to the bitter end.

After the War, no-one wanted to carry the inherited burden of injustice – and indeed, almost no-one was forced to carry it. As the Bremen jurist Ingo Müller very aptly put it, the jurists' collusion with the Nazis 'dwindled to a mere misdemeanour if it was rooted not in National Socialist, but in German nationalist sentiment'. In this way, legends were born, 'semi'-resistance fighters created – and a tainted judiciary got off scot free. An entire professional group was granted absolution under the effects of historical amnesia.

It is true that in recent years, a large number of enlightening books and articles have been published, knowledgeable and critical works on the dubious role of the judiciary under the Third Reich. In the 1970s, numerous attempts were made to establish a new, democratic legal culture, to re-establish the link with Germany's buried legal tradition. And today's generation of judges is constitutionally anchored and more critical of the authority of the state.

The time for punishment of the compromised individuals has passed. The majority of the Nazi perpetrators in judge's robes are no longer among the living, and to haul the last survivors before a court could not make good the failings and failure of the post-War legal system.

What remains is our moral obligation to ensure that the Nazi system of injustice – and with it, the names of Gürtner, Thierack, Frank, Rothenberger, Freisler and others like them – is not forgotten, to point out how the system made such men possible and where it ultimately led.

To draw a cloak of oblivion over the past would be to deny the victims the respect they deserve.

Appendix I

# The Life of Roland Freisler

| | |
|---|---|
| 30 December 1893 | Born in Celle. |
| 1903 | Attends grammar school in Celle. |
| 1908 | Attends grammar school in Kassel. |
| | Begins law studies in Jena. |
| 4 August 1914 | Volunteers for military service in the First World War. |
| 18 October 1914 | Taken prisoner of war by the Russians. |
| 1917 | Appointed a commissar of the POW camp. |
| 23 July 1920 | Returns to Kassel. |
| 1921 | Completes his law studies, becomes a Doctor of Law, graduating 'summa cum laude'. |
| 2 October 1923 | Second state examination in law in Berlin. |
| 13 February 1924 | Establishes a law practice in Kassel. |
| 1924 | Admitted to the bar at the Reichsgericht. |
| | Elected a city councillor for the Völkisch-Sozialer Block in Kassel. |
| | Member of the Prussian Landtag. |
| 1925 | Becomes a member of the NSDAP in February, membership number 9679. |
| | Defends numerous Party comrades in criminal proceedings. |
| 23 March 1928 | Marries Marion Russegger. |
| 1932 | Member of the Reichstag. |
| February 1933 | Appointed Department Head in the Prussian Ministry of Justice. |
| 1 June 1933 | Undersecretary in the Prussian Ministry of Justice. |
| 1 April 1934 | Undersecretary in the Reich Ministry of Justice. |
| 1 November 1937 | Birth of son Harald. |
| 12 October 1939 | Birth of son Roland. |

| | |
|---|---|
| 20 January 1942 | Attends the Wannsee Conference, where the 'final solution to the Jewish question' was discussed. |
| 20 August 1942 | President of the Volksgerichtshof. Presiding judge of its First Senate. |
| 3 February 1945 | Killed during an air raid on Berlin. |

Appendix II

# The Volksgerichtshof Judges and Lawyers

For the victims of the Volksgerichtshof there is no day of remembrance. No memorial site exists in Germany. In fact, they have become victims a second time – victims of a collective forgetting.

The Volksgerichtshof lawyers and judges, on the other hand, were the beneficiaries of the 'great peace with the perpetrators' (Giordano). None of them has ever been legally convicted, and many returned to their judge's chair after the war. Many of the survivors received, and may still receive, healthy pensions. Their judgments did not hurt them – many of the perpetrators of yesterday had successful careers after 1945.

Who knows the names of the Volksgerichtshof judges and prosecutors? The following list identifies them, their function at the Volksgerichtshof, and – where possible – their post-war career. Lawyers who were both judges and prosecutors are named in the list of judges. In previously-published lists of names, there are variations in names and service descriptions. Even the list of names printed here is not complete due to incomplete files and archives.

The severity of the guilt of the named is different. All, however, were executors and assistants of an inhumane, fanatical judiciary. The publication of their names takes place in memory of their victims and as a reminder against repression and oblivion.

## Glossary (translation of German terms)

| | |
|---|---|
| Amtsgerichtsrat | Municipal Court Judge |
| Ermittlungsrichter | Examining Magistrate |
| Hilfsrichter | Assistant Judge |
| Kammergerichtsrat | Judge |

| | |
|---|---|
| Landgerichtsdirektor | District Court Director |
| Landgerichtsrat | Magistrate |
| Oberlandgerichtsrat | High Court Judge |
| Obermatsrichter | Chief Judge |
| Oberreichsanwalt | Senior Attorney |
| Oberstaatsanwalt | Attorney General |
| Präsident | President |
| Rechtsanwalt | Lawyer |
| Reichsanwalt | Prosecutor |
| Senatspräsident | Senate President |
| Staatsanwält | Prosecutor |
| Verwaltungsgerichts-Direktor | Administrative Court Director |
| Vizepräsident | Vice-President |
| Volksgerichtsrat | Peoples' Judge |

## Professional Judges at the Volksgerichtshof

| Name | Role | Position After 1945 |
|---|---|---|
| Albrecht, Dr. Kurt | Senatspräsident | |
| Arndt, Hans-Dietrich | Ermittlungsrichter | Senatspräsident OLG Koblenz |
| Bach, Dr. Bernhard | Landgerichtsrat | |
| Brem, Walter | Ermittlungsrichter | Landgerichtsdirektor in Nürnberg-Fürth |
| Bruner, Wilhelm | Senatspräsident | |
| Carmine, Dr. Erich | Ermittlungsrichter | Amtsgerichtsrat in Nürnberg |
| Cecka, Herbert | | |
| Crohne, Dr. Wilhelm | Vizepräsident | |
| Dahl, Dr. Otto | | |
| Dengler, Dr. Heinrich Anton | Landgerichtsrat | |
| Diescher, Georg Ernst | Volksgerichtsrat | |
| Diester, Dr. Hans | | |
| Duve, Hans | Volksgerichtsrat | |
| Engert, Dr. Karl | Vizepräsident | |
| Falckenberg, Dr. Robert | Landgerichtsdirektor | |
| Fikeis, Dr. Franz | Oberlandgerichtsrat | |
| Freisler, Dr. Roland | Präsident | |

| Name | Role | Position After 1945 |
|---|---|---|
| Fricke, Dr. Andreas | Ermittlungsrichter | Landgerichtsrat in Braunschweig |
| Granzow, Hermann | Volksgerichtsrat | |
| Greulich, Dr. Hermann | Volksgerichtsrat | |
| Großpietsch, Dr. Max | Oberlandesgerichtsrat | |
| Haffner, Dr. Harry | Präsident (1945) | |
| Hammel, Erich | | Landgerichtsdirektor in Duisburg |
| Hartmann, Walter | Senatspräsident | |
| Haumann, Paul | Oberlandgerichtsrat | Rechtsanwalt in Hamm |
| Heider, Hermann | Landgerichtsdirektor | Rechtsanwalt in Hamburg |
| Hellrung, Paul | Ermittlungsrichter | Landgerichtsrat in Konstanz |
| Hörner, | Volksgerichtsrat | |
| Illner, Dr. Josef | Volksgerichtsrat | |
| Indra, Dr. Rudolf | Ermittlungsrichter | Landgerichtsdirektor in Giessen |
| Jank, Dr. Richard Ludwig | | |
| Jasching, Bruno | | |
| Jenne, Ernst | Volksgerichtsrat | |
| Jezek, Dr. | Amtsgerichtsrat | |
| Klein, Dr. Peter | Landgerichtsdirektor | |
| Köhler, Dr. Alfred | Senatspräsident | |
| Köhler, Dr. Emil | Kammergerichtsrat | |
| Köhler, Dr. Johannes | Volksgerichtsrat | |
| Ladewig, Dr. Karl | Landgerichtsrat | |
| Lämmle, Paul | Volksgerichtsrat | |
| Leberl, Dr. Alfred | Ermittlungsrichter | Landgerichtsdirektor in Heilbronn |
| Lob, Dr. | Landgerichtsrat | |
| Lochmann, Dr. | Landgerichtsdirektor | |
| Löhmann, Dr. Günther | Volksgerichtsrat | |
| Lorenz, Dr. Adam | Landgerichtsdirektor | Amtsgerichtsrat in Düsseldorf |
| Lorenz, Dr. Johannes | Landgerichtsdirektor | Kammergerichtsrat in West Berlin |

| Name | Role | Position After 1945 |
|---|---|---|
| Luger, Ludwig | Landgerichtsrat | Landgerichtsrat in Mannheim |
| Makart, Dr. Bruno O. Paul | Kammergerichtsrat | Verwaltungsgerichts-Direktor in Cologne |
| Merten, Dr. Johannes | Volksgerichtsrat | |
| Merten, Dr. Kurt | Volksgerichtsrat | |
| Mittendorf, Gerhard | Landgerichtsdirektor | |
| Mörner, Johannes | Volksgerichtsrat | |
| Müller, Hans | | |
| Müller, Karl | Volksgerichtsrat | Amtsgerichtsrat in Bad Kreuznach |
| Münstermann, Dr. Wolfgang | Landgerichtsdirektor | Rechtsanwalt in Celle |
| Nebelung, Günther | Senatspräsident | Rechtsanwalt in Seesen/Harz |
| Nötzold, Herbert | Landgerichtsrat | |
| Ochs, Dr. Albrecht | Ermittlungsrichter | |
| Pfeifer, Dr. Waldemar | | |
| Preußner, Heinrich | Landgerichtsdirektor | |
| Raszat, Dr. Wilhelm | Landgerichtsdirektor | |
| Rehn, Dr. Fritz vorl. | Präsident | |
| Rehse, Hans-Joachim | Kammergerichtsrat | Hilfsrichter in Schleswig |
| Reimers, Dr. Paul | Kammergerichtsrat | Landgerichtsrat in Ravensburg |
| Rinke, | Landgerichtsrat | |
| Ruepprecht, Hans Ulrich | Ermittlungsrichter | Oberlandesgerichtsrat in Stuttgart |
| Schaad, Dr. Friedrich | | |
| Schauwecker, Erich | Senatsvorsitzender | |
| Schenck zu Schweinsberg | | |
| Schiller, Dr. Franz | Amtsgerichtsrat | |
| Schlemann, Dr. Erich | Landgerichtsdirektor | |
| Schlüter, Dr. Hans | Amtsgerichtsrat | |
| Schneidenbach, Dr. Hans | Landgerichtsdirektor | |
| Schreitmüller, Dr. Adolf | Landgerichtsrat | Landgerichtsdirektor in Stuttgart |
| Schulze-Weckert, Dr. Gerhard | Landgerichtsdirektor | |
| Schwingenschlögl, Michael | | Landgerichtsrat in Kempten |

| Name | Role | Position After 1945 |
|---|---|---|
| Springmann, Dr. Eduard | Senatspräsident | |
| Stäckel, Dr. Arthur | Kammergerichtsrat | |
| Stier, Martin | Landgerichtsdirektor | |
| Storbeck, Dr. August | Landgerichtsdirektor | |
| Strödter, Gustav | Ermittlungsrichter | Amtsgerichtsdirektor in Wetzlar |
| Taeniges, Dr. Reinhard | Volksgerichtsrat | |
| Thierack, Dr. Georg | Volksgerichtshof-Präsident 1936–42 | |
| Waller, Marno | | Rechtsanwalt in Hamburg |
| Weber, Dr. Kurt | Ermittlungsrichter | |
| Weber, Otto | Ermittlungsrichter | Amtsgerichtsrat in Ahrensburg |
| Wettengel, Dr. Alfred | Ermittlungsrichter | Amtsgerichtsrat in Heilbronn |
| Wilbert, Dr. Paul | Landgerichtsrat | |
| Wildberger, Dr. Ernst | Volksgerichtsrat | Rechtsanwalt in Fulda |
| Wolff, Friedrich | | |
| Zieger, Dr. Albrecht | Volksgerichtsrat | Rechtsanwalt in Hamburg |
| Zippel, Dr. Georg | Volksgerichtsrat | Rechtsanwalt in Bonn |
| Zmeck, Dr. Alfred | Landgerichtsrat | |

## Prosecutors at the Volksgerichtshof

| Name | Role | Position After 1945 |
|---|---|---|
| Adam, Otto | Staatsanwalt | Arbeitsgerichtsrat in Bonn |
| Alter, Dr. Bruno | Staatsanwalt | |
| Bach, Dr. Gerhard | Staatsanwalt | Amtsgerichtsrat in Wuppertal |
| Bandel, Dr. Robert | Staatsanwalt | |
| Barnickel, Dr. Paul | Reichsanwalt | Rechtsanwalt in Munich |
| Baxmann, Dr. Karl | Staatsanwalt | |
| Becker, Herbert | | |
| Bellwinkel, Karl-Hermann | Staatsanwalt | Erster Staatsanwalt in Bielefeld |

| Name | Role | Position After 1945 |
|------|------|---------------------|
| Benz, Dr. Ottomar | Landgerichtsdirektor | |
| Beselin, Dr. Werner | Amtsgerichtsrat | Rechtsanwalt in Hamburg |
| Bischoff, Adolf | 1. Staatsanwalt | |
| Bogenrieder, Dr. Alfons | Staatsanwalt | Justice Minister in Baden-Württemberg |
| Bose, Bernhard | Staatsanwalt | Amtsgerichtsrat in Recklinghausen |
| Brenner, Dr. Peter | Landgerichtsdirektor | Landgerichtsrat in Hagen |
| Bringmann, Walter | | Erster Staatsanwalt in Kiel |
| Bruchhaus, Dr. Karl | Staatsanwalt | Staatsanwalt in Wuppertal |
| Brunner, Dr. Arthur | | |
| Busch, Dr. Werner | Staatsanwalt | |
| Busch, Dr. Wolfgang | 1. Staatsanwalt | |
| Christian, Ernst-Georg | Staatsanwalt | |
| Dede, Christian | Staatsanwalt | Landgerichtsdirektor in Hannover |
| Dettmann, Dr. Gustav | | |
| Dölz, Bruno | Amtsgerichtsrat | |
| Dörner, Karl Emil | | Amtsgerichtsrat in Ravensburg |
| Domann, Karl-Heinz | 1. Staatsanwalt | Staatsanwalt in West Berlin |
| Dose, Dr. Hans Rudolf | | |
| Drullmann, Dr. Ernst | 1. Staatsanwalt | |
| Eichler, Hermann | Oberstaatsanwalt | |
| Eisert, Dr. Georg | Oberstaatsanwalt | Landgerichtsdirektor in Würzburg |
| Emmerich, Dr. Paul | Landgerichtsrat | Landgerichtsdirektor in Saarbrücken |
| Figge, Karl | 1. Staatsanwalt | |
| Folger, Wolfgang | Reichsanwalt | |
| Folwill, Josef | | |
| Franzki, Dr. Paul | Reichsanwalt | |
| Friedrich, Ernst | 1. Staatsanwalt | |

| Name | Role | Position After 1945 |
|---|---|---|
| Frischbier, Dr. Eduard | Staatsanwalt | Erster Staatsanwalt in Heilbronn |
| Gauster, Dr. | | |
| Geipel, Dr. Siegfried | | |
| Geißler, Erich | Landgerichtsrat | |
| Görisch, Dr. Gerhard | 1. Staatsanwalt | |
| Götzmann, Karl | | |
| Grendel, Wilhelm | | Oberlandesgerichtsrat in Celle |
| Guntz, Dr. Eduard | | Oberlandesgerichtsrat in Munich |
| Gustorf, Dr. Wilhelm | | Landgerichtsdirektor in Wuppertal |
| Hager, Dr. Willmar | Landgerichtsrat | Rechtsanwalt in Usingen/Taunus |
| Harzmann, Willy | 1. Staatsanwalt | |
| Hegner, Wilhelm | | Amtsgerichtsrat in Salzkotten |
| Heintel, Karl | | |
| Hellmann, Dr. Walter | Staatsanwalt | |
| Hennig, Herbert | 1. Staatsanwalt | |
| Herrnreiter, Dr. Ferdinand | | Landgerichtsdirektor in Augsburg |
| Heugel, Dr. Heinz | 1. Staatsanwalt | |
| Höbel | 1. Staatsanwalt | |
| Hoffmann, Bernhard | Staatsanwalt | |
| Hoffmann, Engelbert | | Erster Staatsanwalt in Münster/Westfalen |
| Hoffmeister, Willi | | |
| Hoffschulte, Paul | | |
| Höher, Dr. Konrad | | Staatsanwalt in Cologne |
| Huhnstock, Wilhelm | Oberstaatsanwalt | |
| Jaager, Kurt | | Staatsanwalt in Flensburg |
| Jacobi-Wermke, Dr. Rudolf | | |
| Jaeger, Dr. Helmut | 1. Staatsanwalt | Oberlandesgerichtsrat in Munich |
| Janssen, Dr. Gerhard | Landgerichtsrat | |

THE VOLKSGERICHTSHOF JUDGES AND LAWYERS

| Name | Role | Position After 1945 |
| --- | --- | --- |
| Joetze, Hans Werner | | Landgerichtsrat in Amberg |
| Jorns, Paul | Oberreichsanwalt | |
| Kaven, Dr. Kurt | | |
| Klitzke, Wilhelm | Staatsanwalt | |
| Kluger, Dr. Carl Josef | | Amtsgerichtsrat in West Berlin |
| Klüver, Dr. Heinrich | Landgerichtsrat | |
| Koalick, Erich | | Rechtsanwalt in Hamburg |
| Köhler, Karl-Heinz | Staatsanwalt | |
| Kömhoff, Dr. Franz | | Oberstaatsanwalt in Hagen |
| Köppen, Einhart | | |
| Kraemer, Dr. Leo | | Erster Staatsanwalt in Cologne |
| Kranast, Helmuth | | |
| Krebs, Adolf | Amtsgerichtsrat | |
| Krefft, Hans Georg | | |
| Krumbholtz, Gustav A. | Oberstaatsanwalt | |
| Kühne, Dr. Hans | | |
| Kurth, Hans Heinrich | | |
| Ladewig, Dr. Erich | Landgerichtsrat | |
| Lautz, Ernst | Oberreichsanwalt | |
| Lay, Hans-Werner | | Oberlandesgerichtsrat in Karlsruhe |
| Lell, Heinz-Günther | | Oberstaatsanwalt in West Berlin |
| Lenhardt, Gerhard | | Oberlandesgerichtsrat in Neustadt/Weinstraße |
| Liebau, Dr. Johannes | | Oberamtsrichter in Seesen/Harz |
| Lincke, Dr. Hans | | |
| Maaß, Dr. Gustav | 1. Staatsanwalt | |
| Maaß, Dr. Walter | 1. Staatsanwalt | |
| Meenen, Günther van | | Landgerichtsdirektor in Duisburg |
| Mier, Dr. Bodo | | Rechtsanwalt in Bremen |

| Name | Role | Position After 1945 |
|---|---|---|
| Menzel, Dr. Hans-Heinrich | | Landgerichtsdirektor in Marbug/Lahn |
| Metten, Dr. Alfred | | Oberstaatsanwalt in Essen |
| Möller, Dr. Herbert | | |
| Münich, Dr. Alfred | | Senatspräsident am Oberlandesgericht |
| München Naucke, Dr. Kurt | | Staatsanwalt in Hannover |
| Nellessen, Dr. Wilhelm | | Oberstaatsanwalt in Aachen |
| Neuber, Dr. Kurt | | Oberstaatsanwalt in Osnabrück |
| Nöbel, Rudolf | 1. Staatsanwalt | |
| Obermayer, Dr. Werner | | Rechtsanwalt in Mosbach |
| Öhlckers, Dr. Sophus | | |
| Öhmke, Dr. Fritz | | |
| Öing, Josef | | Amtsgerichtsrat in Gelsenkirchen |
| Ölze, Heinz | 1. Staatsanwalt | |
| Opalka, Franz | | |
| Orzechowski, Dr. Wolfgang | | Oberstaatsanwalt in Köln |
| Ostertag, Ernst | | |
| Pamp, Dr. Alfred | | Oberstaatsanwalt in Hagen |
| Parey, Friedrich | Oberreichsanwalt | |
| Parrisius, Felix | Reichsanwalt | |
| Peich, Arthur | Oberstaatsanwalt | |
| Picke, Paul | | Senatspräsident am Oberlandesgericht Sa |
| Pilz, Dr. Bruno | Amtsgerichtsrat | |
| Prietzschk, Hans Robert | Kammergerichtsrat | |
| Ranke, Werner | 1. Staatsanwalt | |
| Rathmeyer, Otto | | Amtsgerichtsrat Landgerichtsrat in Landshut |
| Reichelt, Dr. Erich | | Erster Staatsanwalt in Koblenz |

| Name | Role | Position After 1945 |
|---|---|---|
| Renz, Dr. Leopold | Landgerichtsdirektor | |
| Ricken, Dr. Hans | | Amtsgerichtsrat in Nürnberg |
| Rommel, Paul | Landgerichtsrat | |
| Rothaug, Dr. Oswald | Reichsanwalt | |
| Sauermann, Dr. Karl | | Oberlandesgerichtsrat in München |
| Schaub, Richard | | |
| Scherf, Hellmuth | Staatsanwalt | Staatsanwalt in Düsseldorf |
| Schlüter, Dr. Franz | | Senatspräsident am Bundespatentamt München |
| Schmidt, Dr. Friedrich | | Amtsgerichtsrat in Hannover |
| Schoch, Dr. Hermann | | |
| Scholz, Dr. Helmut | | |
| Scholz, Dr. Robert | Landgerichtsrat | |
| Schreiber, Karl | | |
| Schürmann, Siegbert | | |
| Schwabe, Dr. Walter | | |
| Seib, Dr. Walter | | Rechtsanwalt in Viernheim |
| Seidler, Dr. Oskar | | |
| Shok, Dr. Herbert | | Oberstaatsanwalt in Hamburg |
| Simander, Dr. Walter | | |
| Sommer, Dr. Karl | | |
| Spahr, Karl | Oberstaatsanwalt | Landgerichtsrat in Stuttgart |
| Spelthahn, Kurt | | |
| Stark, Edmund | Amtsgerichtsrat | District Court Director in Ravensburg and chairman of the examination board for conscientious objectors |
| Steinke, Max | Staatsanwalt | Obermatsrichter in Singen |

| Name | Role | Position After 1945 |
|---|---|---|
| Stettner, Dr. Emil | | |
| Stier, Martin | Staatsanwalt | |
| Suhr, Edmund | | Oberstaatsanwalt in Hamburg |
| Teicher, Hans | | Landgerichtsrat in Landshut |
| Thomsen, Willy | | |
| Treppens, Herbert | Amtsgerichtsrat | Landessozialgerichtsrat in Celle |
| Volk, Hans | 1. Staatsanwalt | |
| Vollmar, Franz | Staatsanwalt | |
| Voß, Dr. Adolf | 1. Staatsanwalt | |
| Wagner, Harald von | Staatsanwalt | Staatsanwalt in Lüneburg |
| Wagner, Dr. Richard | | |
| Wedel, Wolfgang | | |
| Wegener, Heinrich | Amtsgerichtsrat | |
| Wegner, Friedrich | Amtsgerichtsrat | |
| Weisbrod, Dr. Rudolf | Oberstaatsanwalt | |
| Welp, Karl | Landgerichtsrat | |
| Welz, Dr. Arthur | | |
| Weyersberg, Albert | Reichsanwalt | |
| Wilhelm, Hermann Georg | Oberstaatsanwalt | |
| Wilherling, Dr. Joachim | Oberlandesgerichtsrat | |
| Wilkenhöner, Johannes | | Amtsgerichtsdirektor in Minden |
| Winkels, Fritz | | |
| Wittmann, Heinz | 1. Staatsanwalt | |
| Wrede, Dr. Christian | 1. Staatsanwalt | |
| Zeschau, Gustav von | | Landgerichtsrat in Ulm |

As well as the Volksgerichtshof there was the work undertaken by the Reich Ministry of Justice in Austria. In the Oberlandesgerichtssprengel of Vienna, Graz and Innsbruck, there were about thirty judges (as a rule upper and regional court councillors) who undertook Nazi judicial work. In addition, there were more than 150 honorary Volksgerichtshof judges (SA and SS brigade and group leaders, NSKK Obergruppenfuhrer, Generalmajore der Polizei, Generalarbeitsführer, Generalmajore from the Wehrmacht, Kreisleiter, Oberbereichsleiter, HJ-Obergebietsführer and others).

# List of Sources and Annotations

In writing this, I have made use of a wide variety of archived material, essays and books. I have used no footnotes or annotations within the text. The sources on which I have drawn can be found below, arranged by individual chapter. This may not be the traditional academic approach, but I willingly accept criticism on this point in the interest of greater readability and a more reader-friendly work. A list of the literature used and quoted from can be found in the Appendix.

In particular, I would like to draw attention to two outstanding publications: *Der Volksgerichtshof im nationalsozialistischen Staat*, a comprehensive work by Walter Wagner, published by Oldenbourg Verlag, Munich 2011 and the extremely detailed *Volksgerichtshof – Politische Justiz im 3. Reich* by Hansjoachim Koch, Universitas Verlag, Munich 1988. I strongly recommend these two works to anyone interested in a more detailed account of the formation, structure and jurisdiction of the Volksgerichtshof and in its political and historical background.

## Prologue: A Death Sentence – or: The Second Career of Roland Freisler

The interview with Margot Diestel took place on 23 February 1991 in her house in Steinhorst. The book quoted from, *Gerettetes Leben – Erinnerung an eine Jugend in Deutschland*, was published in 1988 under her maiden name, Margot von Schade. The judgement of the Volksgerichtshof against Margot von Schade is documented in detail in this book, beginning on page xviii.

The *Süddeutsche Zeitung* published a report on the Freisler Sühneverfahren on 30 January 1958. The author is in possession of a copy of the ruling of the Berlin Spruchkammer of 29 January 1958 with the case number Sprkn 7/56.

The pension award to Freisler's widow received widespread press coverage, including articles in: *Süddeutsche Zeitung* from 13 to 19 February 1985; *Der Spiegel*, 18 February 1985; *Frankfurter Rundschau*, 13 and 18 February 1985.

## Chapter 1: The Ceremony

The speech delivered by Minister of Justice Gürtner and the commentary by Freiherr du Prel, published in the Nazi Party newspaper the *Völkischer Beobachter* on 15/16 July 1934, are documented in Jahntz and Kähne, 1986, p. 49.

The *Deutsche Allgemeine Zeitung* of 13 July 1934 is quoted in Jahntz and Kähne, ibid., p. 5.

For the quote from Reich Minister of Justice Gürtner on reactions in the foreign press, see Wieland, 1989, p. 14.

On Hitler's reaction to the Reichgericht's judgement against the Reichstag arsonists, see Picker, 1951, p. 241, quoted in Wagner, 2011, p. 17.

The commentary from editor-in-chief Wilhelm Weiss in the *Völkischer Beobachter* of 19 November 1935 is quoted from Koch, 1988, p. 87.

For the description of Hitler's 45th birthday in the *Düsseldorfer Nachrichten* of 20 April 1934, see Pollmann, 1991, p. 79.

## Chapter 2: The Lawyer from Kassel

A description of the occurrences surrounding the theatre performance in Kassel can be found in: Tucholsky, 1989, Vol. 4, p. 540. Also Koch, op. cit., pp. 62–5.

The description of Freisler as undersecretary is based on Buschheit, 1968, p. 25.

For the quote on the decline of the Weimar Republic, see Koch, op. cit. p. 72.

The excerpts from Hitler's speech on 14 December 1930 in Munich are quoted from Hofer, 1957, p. 28.

The letter from Prussian Minister of Justice Kerrl to Freisler dated 31 May 1933 and Freisler's letter to the President of the Landgericht in Kassel dated 19 June 1933 are quoted from Freisler's personnel file, stored in the Federal Archive in Koblenz under inventory number R 22, a copy of which was furnished to the author.

The details of the telephone conversation between Freisler and Dr Kirchstein and Freisler's meeting with Dr Anz following the occurrences in Kassel are based on the description by Buschheit, op. cit., p.24.

The report by Karl Linz on his speech of 7 April 1933 is quoted in excerpts from Senfft, 1988, p. 158.

## Chapter 3: One Volk, One Reich, One Führer – and One Judiciary

Karl Linz, chairman of the Deutscher Richterbund, is quoted in excerpts from Müller, op. cit., p. 44.

The declaration of the Deutscher Richterbund of 19 March 1933 was published in the *Deutsche Richterzeitung*, 1933, from page 122, and is quoted here in excerpts from the exhibition catalogue *Im Namen des Volkes*, published by the Federal Ministry of Justice, 1989, p. 90.

Further quotes from the same publication: declaration of the Preussischer Richterverein of 20 March 1933, resolution of the members of the Reichsgericht of 23 March 1933 and excerpts from Hitler's government declaration of 23 March 1933.

On judges in the Weimar Republic, see primarily Heinrich Hannover and Elisabeth Hannover-Drück, *Politische Justiz von 1918 bis 1933*, 1966.

See also Angermund, *Deutsche Richterschaft*, 1990, pp. 19ff and Heinrich Senfft, *Richter und andere Bürger*, 1988, pp. 12ff.

The declaration of loyalty by Richterbund chairman Linz can be read in full in *Deutsche Richterzeitung*, 1933, pp. 155f, here quoted in excerpts from Müller, op. cit., p. 45.

For the report of Linz' audience with Hitler, cf. *Deutsche Richterzeitung*, 1933, pp. 155f.

Frank's oath of loyalty at the end of his speech in Leipzig is quoted from: Hans Wrobel, 'Der Deutsche Richterbund im Jahre 1933', in: Redaktion Kritische Justiz (eds.), *Der Unrechtsstaat II*, 1984, p. 93.

The membership figures of the BNSDJ are quoted from Angermund, op. cit., p. 57.

Hermann Göring's speech is documented in excerpts in *Im Namen des Volkes*, op. cit., p. 110.

The isolated quotes from Carl Schmitt were taken from Müller, op. cit., p. 20. The longer passage is quoted from Walther Hofer, 1965, p. 102 and p. 105.

The comments by Otto Koellreutter and the statement from the faculty assistant at Breslau are quoted in excerpts from Hillermeier, op. cit., pp. 26–8 and p. 110.

On the debate on the Rechtsstaat and the role of jurisprudence, cf. Müller, op. cit., p. 79f. On the cleansing of the legal profession, see p. 67 of the same work.

## Chapter 4: Undersecretary and Publicist

The memorandum of the Prussian Ministry of Justice was published in Berlin in 1993 under the title *Nationalsozialistisches Strafrecht*.

The quote from President of the Hamburg Oberlandesgericht Rothenberger can be found in Buschheit, op. cit., p 99.

Freisler's essay with the title 'Nationalsozialismus und aufbauende Kritik' was published in the journal *Deutsche Justiz*, February 1934, pp. 223ff.

Gauland's critical remarks are quoted in excerpts from Buschheit, op. cit., pp. 81f.

Freisler's response was published in the April 1934 edition of the journal *Deutsche Justiz*, p.471ff.

Freisler's article on the Volksgerichtshof appeared in the journal *Akademie für Deutsches Recht*, March 1935, p. 90, and is quoted from Buschheit, op. cit., p. 33.

Freisler's comments on the 'Röhm Putsch' were published in the April 1934 edition of the journal *Deutsche Justiz* under the title 'Des Führers Tat und unsere Pflicht', Edition B, No. 27, p. 850.

On the legal proceedings in Kassel in connection with the so-called Röhm paper, see the description in Buschheit, op. cit., pp. 44f.

Freisler's comments on *Die Aufgaben der Reichsjustiz, entwickelt aus der biologischen Rechtsauffassung* were published in the journal *Deutsche Justiz*, 1935, p. 468ff.

His remarks on racial hygiene can be found, among other publications, in his essays 'Schutz von Rasse und Erbgut im werdenden deutschen Strafrecht', published in the journal of the *Akademie des Deutschen Rechts*, 1936, pp. 142ff and 'Zur Reichstagung der deutschen Ärzte des öffentlichen Gesundheitsdienstes', which appeared in the journal *Deutsche Justiz* 1939, p. 946ff,

With reference to Freisler's definition of the state of law, compare his essay 'Der Rechtsstaat' in *Deutsche Justiz* 1937, pp. 151ff.

His comments on the unity of the Führer and his followers can be found in *Deutsche Juristenzeitung*, 1934, p. 167ff, under the title 'Rechtspflege und Verwaltung, Justizverwaltung und Richtertum'.

The *Deutsche Verwaltungsblätter* are quoted in accordance with the documentation of the exhibition *Im Namen des Volkes*, op. cit., p. 108. For Freisler's vision of a 'Germanic law', see his essay 'Einiges vom werdenden deutschen Blutbanngericht' in *Deutsche Juristenzeitung*, 1935, pp. 625ff. His essay 'Aktive Rechtspflege!' appeared in *Deutsche Justiz*, 1934, pp. 625ff. Freisler's comments on the training of jurists can be found in the essay

'Deutsche Rechtswahrerausbildung', published in *Deutsche Justiz*, 1941, pp. 833ff and in the article entitled 'Eignung zum Beruf des deutschen Rechtswahrers' in *Deutsche Justiz*, 1941, pp. 645ff. The article 'Deutscher Osten' appeared in *Deutsche Justiz*, 1941, p. 737. His remarks on the new measures for wireless owners can be found in the article 'Zur Verordnung über ausserordentliche Rundfunkmassnahmen', also published in *Deutsche Justiz*, 1940, pp. 105ff.

For the quote from Freisler on the unity of Party and state in the personnel policy of the judiciary, cf. Buschheit, op. cit., p. 75. For Freisler's guiding principles, see his essay 'Richter, Recht und Gesetz' in *Deutsche Justiz*, 1934, pp. 134f.

## Chapter 5: Against Traitors and Parasites

Thierack's letter to Freisler dated 9 September 1942 is quoted in excerpts from the documentation of the Federal Archive in Koblenz, Archive No. E 43 II/1518. Thierack's assessment of judges can be found in Hillermeier, op. cit., p. 34.

On legal, geographical and personnel development, cf. Wagner, op. cit., pp. 59ff. The comments are based on detailed facts presented by Wagner.

The list of laws, offences and sentences is based on Koch, op. cit., pp. 219ff, as are Frank's comments, which are quoted in excerpts. Ibid., pp. 198ff.

The excerpts from Frank's diary were taken from: W. Präg and W. Jacobmeyer, *Das Diensttagebuch des deutschen Generalgouverneurs in Polen 1939-1945*, 1975, pp. 446ff.

The public statements of SS Gruppenführer Ohlendorf are quoted in excerpts from Koch, op. cit., p. 206, as are Hitler's remarks, ibid., p. 188.

Passages from Hitler's speech before the Reichstag on 26 April 1942 were published in Ilse Staff's documentation *Justiz im Dritten Reich*, 1978, pp. 95ff, as was the quoted Judge's Letter No. 1, p. 67.

Goebbel's speech before the Volksgerichtshof is reproduced based on Document NG-417 of the Archiv für Zeitgeschichte, Munich.

Hitler's decree granting special powers to the Reich Minister of Justice is quoted from Koch, op. cit., p. 196.

## Chapter 6: The Political Soldier

Freisler's letter to Hitler dated 15 October 1942 is archived under NG-176 at the Archiv für Zeitgeschichte, Munich.

Thierack's letter is quoted in excerpts from Koch, op. cit., p. 215, as is Freisler's letter to Thierack dated 9 September 1942, ibid., p. 217 (§5 KSSVO), see also Jahntz and Kähne, op. cit., pp. 119ff.

For a detailed account of the student resistance group The White Rose and the arrest of Hans and Sophie Scholl, see Gerd van Roon, *Widerstand im Dritten Reich*, 1987, pp. 47ff.

Further details of the proceedings against Professor Huber from Munich and others can be found in Buschheit, op. cit., p. 117.

On the death sentence for Elfriede Scholz, sister of the author Erich Maria Remarque, for undermining the war effort, see the detailed documentation *Mitteilungen der Erich-Maria-Remarque-Gesellschaft*, Issue 4, Osnabrück, 1988.

The verdict against Fritz Gröbe and the letters from Thierack and Freisler are quoted in excerpts from Jahntz and Kähne, op. cit., pp. 121ff.

Freisler's letters dated 2 October 1943 and 4 February 1944 are quoted in excerpts from Koch, op. cit., pp. 296ff.

Freisler's comments on the function of the Volksgerichtshof of 1 December 1944 appeared in his publication *Der deutsche Volksgerichtshof in Rednerdienst der Reichsgemeinschaft Partei und Wehrmachtschulung*, No. 24/25, here quoted from Hillermeier, op. cit., pp. 37ff.

The so-called 'Mordregister' of the Federal Archive in Koblenz is the register (bills of indictment and judgements) of all death sentences carried out in Nazi prisons, including those handed down by the Volksgerichtshof. The main part of the register is formed by files from the Document Centre in Berlin, where further files from around 15,000 trials and 2,000 sentences are still held. Further files were located in the documentation from the so-called Lawyer's Trial before the American military tribunal in Nuremberg. The inventory also included verdicts and bills of indictment in connection with accusations against judges still in office which came to the Federal Ministry of Justice from the former German Democratic Republic and are stored in the former Central State Archive in Potsdam.

In addition, the 'Mordregister' of the Federal Archive contains copies from the Institut für Zeitgeschichte in Munich, the Wiener Library in London, the Dokumentationsarchiv des österreichischen Widerstandes in Vienna, files from the Staatspolizeileitstelle Düsseldorf in the Hauptstaatsarchiv Düsseldorf. There are plans to archive all files from the Third Reich in the inventory of the Federal Archive in Potsdam in future.

## Chapter 7: In the Name of the Volk

The quoted and documented death sentences pronounced by the Volksgerichtshof were taken from the following sources/archives:

Death sentence against Emma Höltershoff – Archiv des Studienkreises zur Erforschung und Vermittlung des deutschen Widerstandes von 1933-1945 e.V., Frankfurt/Main, (AdS), AN/3426.

Death sentence against Johanna Schmidt – ibid., AN/971.

Death sentence against Dietrich Tembergen – Federal Archive Koblenz, R 60 II/69.

Death sentence against Bernhard Firsching – Federal Archive Koblenz, R 60 II/77-1.

Death sentence against Ehrengard Frank-Schultz – Federal Archive Koblenz, R 60 II/74.

Death sentence against Wilhelm Alich – Jahntz and Kähne, op. cit., p. 56.

Death sentence against Georg Jurkowski – ibid., p. 66.

Death sentence against Max Josef Weber – ibid., p. 60.

Freisler's remarks during the trial against Metzger are quoted from Hillermeier, op. cit., p. 66.

The bill of costs for the criminal proceedings against Max Josef Metzger can be found in the AdS, AN/351.

On the sentence against Fritz Bahner, cf. Jahntz and Kähne, op. cit., p. 70.

Death sentence against Walter Arndt – ibid., p. 83

Death sentence against Josef Müller – ibid., p. 87

## Chapter 8: The 20 July Plot

A wide variety of works on the 20 July Bomb Plot is available – on the extent of the conspiracy, its organization, development, motives, the assassination attempt itself and the subsequent trials before the Volksgerichtshof. See the Bibliography.

The description of the attempt on Hitler's life in the 'Wolfsschanze' is based on the account of Otto John, *Falsch und zu spät – Der 20. Juli 1944*, 1984, p. 11ff.

The timeline of the events of 20 July 1944 is based on the documentation *Chronik 1944*, 1988, p. 116f.

Hitler's radio address of 21 July 1944 is quoted from Hillermeier, op. cit., p. 95.

The SD reports on the 'effects of the attempt on the Führer's life on the mood of the nation' can be found in the two volume work *Opposition gegen Hitler und der Staatsstreich vom 20. Juli 1944*, Volume 1, edited by Hans-Adolf Jacobsen, 1989. These two volumes, with an introduction by the editor, document the confidential reports of the former Reich Main Security Office. These reports, named 'Kaltenbrunner Reports' after the head of the office, were sent to Hitler and Bormann as 'Geheime Reichssache' and covered the assassination attempt of 20 July in detail. The reports were based on the transcripts of Gestapo interrogations and gave Hitler, who still considered the plot to be the work of a small clique of conspirators, a comprehensive overview of opposition groups within Germany, their motives and the mood of the German people. They also offer insight into the thought patterns of the Nazi leadership and document the Nazi regime's all-embracing surveillance and its extensive network of informers.

Hitler's announcement that the conspirators of 20 July would be liquidated 'without mercy' is quoted from Hillermeier, op. cit., p. 96.

Hitler's comments comparing Freisler to Stalin's chief public prosecutor and chief prosecutor during the Moscow show trials, A. J. Vyshinsky, are taken from W. Scheid's account of conversations with Hitler in *Echo der Woche*, 9 September 1949 and quoted here in excerpts from Buschheit, op. cit., p. 127.

A notable work on the life and career of Andrei J. Vyshinsky, who succeeded Molotov as Foreign Minister in 1949 and died in 1954 – of natural causes, an unusual occurrence in the Stalin era – is available in a German translation by Arkady Vaksberg: *Gnadenlos – Andrei Wyschinski – Der Handlanger Stalins*, 1991.

The indictment against Oberreichsanwalt Lautz in the first 20 July trial and Freisler's remarks are quoted from Buschheit, op. cit., p. 141.

Freisler's reaction to Witzleben's 'German salute' is quoted from Koch, op. cit., p. 336.

The comprehensive shorthand transcript of the trials of 7 and 8 August 1944 before the Volksgerichtshof was prepared by the Reichstag stenographer on the order of the Volksgerichtshof. It was published for the first time after the war in 1951, in the book *Der 20. Juli* by Eigen Badde and Peter Lützsches.

On the film material on the 20 July trial, see the 20 July 1978 edition of the *Hamburger Abendblatt*, the 21 July 1978 edition of *Die Zeit* and the *Süddeutsche Zeitung*, 21 July 1979. A film documentary titled *Geheime Reichssache* had its première on the occasion of the 29th Berlin International Film Festival and was shown on 20 July of the same year on German TV channel ZDF. Film material on the 20 July trials can also be found in the Federal Archive in Koblenz.

For the quote from cameraman Erich Stoll, see Buschheit, op. cit., p. 270.

Kaltenbrunner is quoted in excerpts from SD reports on 20 July trials No. 57536/44. See also the SD reports, Jacobsen, 1989, op. cit., Vol. 1 and Vol. 2.

In his verdict on Carl Goedeler, Wilhelm Leuschner, Josef Wirmer, Ulrich von Hassell and Paul Lejeune-Jung, Freisler stated 'These five men and the other traitors of the officer's conspiracy already brought to justice have betrayed the sacrifice of our fallen soldiers, our people, the Führer and the Reich in a manner unparalleled in our history . . . This utmost betrayal renders them outcasts from our people . . . The punishment for this betrayal can only be death': see Archiv des Studienkreises zur Erforschung und Vermittlung der Geschichte des deutschen Widerstands 1933-1945 e.V., Frankfurt/Main, AN 306.

The female witness to Freisler's performance in court was in the audience at the trial of Elisabeth von Thadden and others on 1 July 1944. Her description appeared in *Elisabeth von Thadden – Ein Schicksal unserer Zeit* by Irmgard von der Lühe, 1966, and is quoted here from Wagner, op. cit., p. 837.

The dialogue between the condemned Josef Wirmer and Freisler in the trial held on 8 September 1944 was recorded on film. The film material is held by the Federal Archive in Koblenz. The dialogue was quoted here from a film review in the *Hamburger Abendblatt*, 20 July 1978.

## Chapter 9: The End

Goebbels' leading article in the weekly newspaper *Das Reich*, 10 December 1944 is quoted from Hans-Jürgen Eitner's excellent work Hitlers Deutsche, 1991, pp. 498f, as are Reinecker's comments, ibid., p.498.

For Thierack's letter to Freisler dated 18 October 1944, see Wagner, op. cit., pp. 885f.

Freisler's comments in a letter dated 26 October 1944 are quoted from Koch, op. cit., pp. 500ff.

The radio broadcast of Clausewitz' 'Prussian Confession' read by the actor Heinrich George on New Year's Eve 1944 is quoted from Eitner, op. cit., p. 501, as are Hitler's New Year address and Himmler's call for a hard line against shirkers.

For the varying reports of Freisler's death, see Buschheit, op. cit., pp. 274f and *Der Spiegel*, No. 39, 23 September 1968, p. 52.

Thierack's letter of condolence to Freisler's widow dated 5 February 1945 and the Reich Ministry of Justice press statement on Freisler's death can be found in the Federal Archive in Koblenz, inventory number R 22. Copies of these documents were furnished to the author.

For the extracts from Goebbels' diary, see his *Tagebücher 1945, Die letzten Eintragungen*, Hamburg 1977, p. 115.

Goebbels' radio speech on the occasion of Hitler's 56th birthday on 20 April 1945 is quoted from *Der Spiegel*, No. 29, 13 July 1992, p. 109.

The verdict of the Nuremberg Military Tribunal on Freisler is quoted from Wagner, op. cit., p. 843.

## Chapter 10: No 'Stunde Null'

With reference to the denazification procedure, see Wolfgang Benz, *Zwischen Hitler und Adenauer*, Frankfurt am Main 1991, pp. 109ff and Jörg Friedrich's extremely knowledgeable work *Die kalte Amnestie*, Frankfurt am Main 1988, in particular pp. 132f and pp. 357f.

The sections on the Nuremberg Lawyers' Trial are based on Müller, op. cit., pp. 270ff and Diestelkamp, op. cit., pp. 131ff. For the quotes from the prosecution, see Müller, pp. 272 and 273.

For the so-called Waldheim Trials, see the essay by Falco Werketin, 'Scheinjustiz in der DDR – Aus den Regieheften der "Waldheimer Prozesse"' in *Kritische Justiz*, issue 3, 1991, pp. 330ff and *Der Spiegel*, issue 37, 1992, pp. 93ff.

The influence exerted on the judiciary of East Germany by the state and the Staatssicherheit was documented by journalist Günther Klein in his film *Der, wer kämpft für das Recht, der hat immer recht*, first broadcast on the German TV channel ZDF on 25 November 1992.

The excerpt from Eberhard Schmidt's speech at the Deutsche Juristentag in 1947 is quoted from Senfft, op. cit., p. 172. For the statements from Dehler and Petersen at the opening ceremony of the West German federal supreme court, ibid., p. 173, and the quote from Adenauer, ibid., p. 174.

The exemplary careers of Vialon, Baldus, Schafheutle, Kanter and others like them are described, for example, by Bernd Engelmann in his *Deutschland-Report*, Göttingen, 1991. The career continuity of former Nazi perpetrators was also the focus of my book *Gnadenlos deutsch*, Göttingen, 1992.

The statistics and quotes in connection with the investigation of former Volksgerichtshof associate justice Hans-Joachim Rehse are based on Müller, op. cit., pp. 281ff and Gerhard Meyer in, *Für immer ehrlos*, in Hillermeier, op. cit., pp. 115f. A detailed documentation of the investigations against former Volksgerichtshof jurists can be found in Jahntz and Kähne, op. cit., and in the essays of Gerd Denzel, 'Die Ermittlungsverfahren gegen Richter und Staatsanwälte am Volksgerichtshof seit 1979', in *Kritische Justiz*, issue 1/1991, pp. 31ff and –with particular reference to the role of the Bundesgerichtshof – Günther Frankenberg and Franz J. Müller, 'Juristische Vergangenheitsbewältigung – Der Volksgerichtshof vorm BGH', in Redaktion Kritische Justiz (eds.), *Der Unrechts-Staat II*, op. cit., pp. 225ff.

On the failure to prosecute former Volksgerichtshof jurists, see also Walter Boehlich, 'Ein Ende ohne Schrecken', in *Konkret*, issue 12/1968, from which the quote from justice senator Rupert Scholz was taken, also the *Frankfurter Allgemeine Zeitung*, 23 October 1985 and *Der Spiegel*, 27 October 1986, where the quote from Rolf Lamprecht can be found.

The recommendation of the legal committee of the Deutsche Bundestag on the subject of the invalidity of the rulings of the institutions of the Nazi regime of injustice known as the 'Volksgerichtshof' and the 'special courts' was published in Bundestag Document 10/2368, 10th legislative period.

See also the parliamentary question raised by member of the Bundestag Christian Ströbele from the party Die Grünen, documented in the *Frankfurter Rundschau* on 3 and 4 April 1986 under the title 'Nicht einmal die Zahl der gefällten Urteile ist bekannt'.

The statistics on the death sentences pronounced by civil courts and the military courts were taken from Gerhard Fieberg's *Justiz im nationalsozialistischen Deutschland*, Cologne, 1984, p. 54. In an extremely detailed study, private researcher Fritz Wüllner has impressively refuted the manipulated statistics and misrepresentations in the argumentation presented in accounts of NS military history.

In his work *Die NS-Militärjustiz und das Elend der Geschichtsschreibung*, Baden-Baden, 1991, Wüller also uses a wide variety of documentary evidence to correct the number of death sentences (more than 50,000 rather than the 'played-down' figure of 10,000).

For the quote from Ingo Müller, see op. cit., pp. 295ff.

# Bibliography

Angermund, Ralph, *Deutsche Richterschaft 1919–1945*, Frankfurt am Main 1990.

Badde, Eugen, and Lützsches, Peter, *Der 20. Juli*, Düsseldorf 1951.

Benz, Wolfgang, *Zwischen Hitler und Adenauer, Studien zur deutschen Nachkriegsgesellschaft*, Frankfurt am Main 1991.

Boberach, Heinz (ed.), *Richterbriefe – Dokumente zur Beeinflussung der deutschen Rechtsprechung 1942–1944*, Boppard a. Rhein 1975.

Boss, Sonja, *Unverdienter Ruhestand. Die personalpolitische Bereinigung belasteter NS-Juristen in der westdeutschen Justiz*, Berlin 2009.

Braun, Konstanze, *Dr Otto Georg Thierack (1889–1946)*, Frankfurt am Main 2005.

Broszat, Martin, and Möller, Horst, *Das Dritte Reich – Herrschaftsstruktur und Geschichte*, Munich 1983.

Bundesminister der Justiz (ed.), *Im Namen des Deutschen Volkes*, Cologne 1989.

Buschheit, Gert, *Richter in roter Robe*, Munich 1968.

Diestelkamp, Bernhard, and Stolleis, Michael, *Justizalltag im Dritten Reich*, Frankfurt am Main 1988.

Eitner, Hans-Jürgen, *Hitlers Deutsche – Das Ende eines Tabus*, Gernsbach 1991.

Engelmann, Bernt, *Deutschland-Report*, Göttingen 1991.

Fieberg, Gerhard, *Justiz im nationalsozialistischen Deutschland*, Cologne 1984.

Fischer, Fritz, *Hitler war kein Betriebsunfall*, Munich 1992.

Flade, Stephan, and Narr, Wolf-Dieter, *Die deutschen Vergangenheiten und wir*, Sensbachtal 1992.

Frei, Norbert, *Hitlers Eliten nach 1945*, Munich 2003.

Friedrich, Jörg, *Freispruch für die Nazi-Justiz*, Hamburg 1983.

_____, *Die kalte Amnestie – NS-Täter in der Bundesrepublik*, Frankfurt am Main 1984.

Fuchs, Jürgen, . . . *und wann kommt der Hammer?*, Berlin 1990.

Giordano, Ralph, *Die zweite Schuld oder Von der Last ein Deutscher zu sein*, Hamburg 1987.

Goebbels, Joseph, *Tagebücher 1945. Die letzten Aufzeichnungen*, Hamburg 1977.

Graml, Hermann (ed.), *Widerstand im Dritten Reich – Probleme, Ereignisse, Gestalten*, Frankfurt am Main 1984.

Güstrow, Dietrich, *Tödlicher Alltag – Strafverteidiger im Dritten Reich*, Berlin 1981.

Habermas, Jürgen, *Vergangenheit als Zukunft*, Zürich 1990.

Hannover, Heinrich, and Hannover-Drück, Elisabeth, *Politische Justiz 1918–1933*, Hamburg 1977.

Harenberg, Bodo (ed.), *Chronik, Tag für Tag in Wort und Bild, 1939 bis 1945*, Dortmund 1988.

Hillenbrand, Klaus, *Berufswunsch Henker. Warum Männer im Nationalsozialismus Scharfrichter werden wollten*, Frankfurt am Main 2013.

Hillermeier, Heinz (ed.), *Im Namen des Deutschen Volkes – Todesurteile des Volksgerichtshofs*, Darmstadt und Neuwied 1980.

Hofer, Walther, *Der Nationalsozialismus, Dokumente 1933–1945*, Frankfurt am Main 1957.

Hoffmann, Peter, *Claus Schenk Graf von Stauffenberg und seine Brüder*, Stuttgart 1992.

Jacobsen, Hans-Adolf, *Opposition gegen Hitler und der Staatsstreich vom 20. Juli 1944*, 2 vols, Stuttgart 1989.

Jahntz, Bernd, and Kähne, Volker, *Der Volksgerichtshof – Darstellung der Ermittlungen der Staatsanwaltschaft beim Landgericht Berlin gegen ehemalige Richter und Staatsanwälte am Volksgerichtshof*, Berlin 1986.

John, Otto, *'Falsch und zu spät' – Der 20. Juli 1944*, Munich, Berlin 1984.

Klönne, Arno, *Rechts-Nachfolge, Risiken des deutschen Wesens nach 1945*, Cologne 1990.

Knesebeck, Rosemarie von dem, *In Sachen Filbinger gegen Hochhuth*, Reinbek 1980.

Koch, Hansjoachim W., *Volksgerichtshof – Politische Justiz im Dritten Reich*, Munich 1988.

Lühe, Irmgard von der, *Elisabeth von Thadden – Ein Schicksal unserer Zeit*, Düsseldorf and Cologne 1966.

Mauz, Gerhard, *Die Justiz vor Gericht*, Munich 1990.

Meding, Dorothee von, *Mit dem Mut des Herzens – Die Frauen des 20. Juli*, Berlin 1991.

Moltke, Freya von, *Die Kreisauerin*, Göttingen 1992.

Müller, Ingo, *Furchtbare Juristen*, Munich 1987.

Müller, Klaus-Jürgen (ed.), *Der deutsche Widerstand 1933–1945*, Paderborn 1986.

Niedhart, Gottfried/Riesenberger, Dieter (ed.), *Deutsche Nachkriegszeiten 1918–1945*, Munich 1992.

Ortner, Helmut, *Gnadenlos deutsch –Aktuelle Reportagen aus dem Dritten Reich*, Göttingen 1994.

_____, *Der einsame Attentäter – Georg Elser, der Mann, der Hitler töten Wollte*, Frankfurt am Main 2010.

Pirker, H., *Hitlers Tischgespräche im Führerhauptquartier 1941–1942*, Bonn 1981.

Präg, W./Jacobsen, W., *Das Diensttagebuch des deutschen Generalgouverneurs in Polen 1939–1945*, Stuttgart 1975.

Rätsch, Birgit, *Hinter Gittern, Schriftsteller und Journalisten vor dem Volksgerichtshof 1934–1945*, Bonn and Berlin 1992.

Ramm, Arnim, *Der 20. Juli vor dem Volksgerichtshof*, Berlin 2007.

Redaktion Kritische Justiz (ed.), *Der Unrechts-Staat – Recht und Justiz im Nationalsozialismus*, 2 vols, Baden-Baden 1983 and 1984.

Richter, Isabel, *Hochverratsprozesse als Herrschaftspraxis im Nationalsozialismus. Männer und Frauen vor dem Volksgerichtshof 1934–1939*, Münster 2001.

Roon, Gerd van, *Widerstand im Dritten Reich*, Munich 1987.

Rottleuthner, Hubert, *Karrieren und Kontinuitäten deutscher Justizjuristen vor und nach 1945*, Berlin 2010.

Rüthers, Bernd, *Entartetes Recht*, Munich 1988.

Saña, Heleno, *Die verklemmte Nation, Zur Seelenlage der Deutschen*, Munich 1992.

Schad, Martha, *Frauen gegen Hitler, Vergessene Widerstandskämpferinnen im Nationalsozialismus*, Munich 2010.

Schade, Margot von, *Gerettetes Leben – Erinnerung an eine Jugend in Deutschland*, Munich 1988.

Senfft, Heinrich, *Richter und andere Bürger*, Nördlingen 1988.

Staff, Ilse (ed.), *Justiz im Dritten Reich*, Frankfurt am Main 1978.

Steffahn, Harald, *Die weisse Rose*, Reinbek 1992.

Sternburg, Wilhelm von (ed.), *Für eine zivilisierte Republik*, Frankfurt am Main 1992.

Tucholsky, Kurt, *Gesammelte Werke*, Vol. 4, *1925–1926*, Reinbek 1989.

Ule, Carl Hermann, *Beiträge zur Rechtswirklichkeit im Dritten Reich*, Berlin 1987.

Wachsmann, Nikolaus, and Schmidt, Klaus-Dieter, *Gefangen unter Hitler. Justizterror und Strafvollzug im NS-Staat*, Berlin 2006.

Wagner, Walter, *Der Volksgerichtshof im nationalsozialistischen Staat*, Munich 2011.

Waksberg, Arkadi, *Gnadenlos, Andrei Wyschinski – der Handlanger Stalins*, Bergisch Gladbach 1990.

Waltenbacher, Walter, *Zentrale Hinrichtungsstätten. Der Vollzug der Todesstrafe in Deutschland von 1937-1945, Scharfrichter im Dritten Reich*, Berlin 2008.

Wassermann, Rudolf, *Auch die Justiz kann aus der Geschichte nicht aussteigen*, Baden-Baden 1990.

Wieland, Günther, *Das war der Volksgerichtshof*, Pfaffenweiler 1989.

Wüllenweber, Hans, *Sondergerichte im Dritten Reich – Vergessene Verbrechen der Justiz*, Frankfurt am Main 1990.

Wüllner, Fritz, *Die NS-Militärjustiz und das Elend der Geschichtsschreibung. Ein grundlegender Forschungsbericht*, Baden-Baden 1991.

Zur Mühlen, Bengt von (ed.), *Der vergessene Verschwörer. General Fritz Lindemann und der 20. Juli 1944*, Munich 2014.

# Index of Names

All family relations are to Roland Friesler.